FAT WEDNESDAY

To John —
with Thanks

jL

FAT WEDNESDAY

Wittgenstein on Aspects

JOHN VERDI

PAUL DRY BOOKS

Philadelphia 2010

First Paul Dry Books Edition, 2010
Philadelphia, Pennsylvania
www.pauldrybooks.com

Printed in the United States of America

Library of Congress Cataloging-in-Publication Data
Verdi, John.
    Fat Wednesday: Wittgenstein on aspects / John Verdi.
       p. cm.
    Includes bibliographical references and index.
    ISBN 978-1-58988-054-2 (alk. paper)
      1. Wittgenstein, Ludwig, 1889–1951. I. Title.
      B3376.W563T73855 2010
      192—dc22
                                              2010003568

To Eleanor, Antonia, and Luca

CONTENTS

PREFACE   *ix*

CHAPTER ONE
The Aspects Family   *1*

A. The Duck-Rabbit   *1*
B. The Necker Cube   *7*
C. Faces, Faces, Faces   *10*
D. Illusions   *13*
E. "Puzzle-Pictures"   *18*

CHAPTER TWO
Aspects and Words   *23*

A. Introspection and Experiment   *28*
B. How We Do Things with Words   *42*
C. How We See Things with Words   *66*
Conclusion   *105*

CHAPTER THREE
Aspect Blindness   *109*

A. Imagination   *109*
B. Aspect Blindness   *116*
C. Fat Wednesday   *136*

CHAPTER FOUR
Aspects and Art   *157*

A. Experience   *157*
B. Seeing a Painting   *161*
C. Musical Aspects   *187*

D. Emergent Meaning and Wine   *195*
E. Talk About Paintings   *203*

CHAPTER FIVE
Ethics and Aesthetics Are One   *229*

A. Science   *231*
B. From a Religious Point of View   *240*

BIBLIOGRAPHY   *261*
NOTES   *269*
ACKNOWLEDGMENTS   *289*
INDEX   *293*

PREFACE

Ludwig Wittgenstein (1889–1951) believed that a serious philosophical work could be written consisting almost entirely of jokes, especially jokes that turn on grammar. One mines their humor from the depths of language, and from those same depths we extract philosophical problems and their solutions. He never wrote such a book, but he had in mind the sorts of jokes Lewis Carroll makes in *Alice's Adventures in Wonderland*:

> "Then you should say what you mean," the March Hare went on.
> "I do," Alice hastily replied; "at least—at least I mean what I say—that's the same thing, you know."
> "Not the same thing a bit!" said the Hatter. "Why, you might just as well say that 'I see what I eat' is the same thing as 'I eat what I see'!"

Wittgenstein says that we can be led into trouble in our thinking, especially in philosophy, if we are not always on the lookout for how analogous forms of sentences can disguise important differences in their meanings. We find this passage from Carroll funny because we realize, if only dimly at first, that the words "meaning" and "saying" behave differently from "eating" and "seeing," even though all four are active, transitive verbs. That is, their "surface grammars" may be the same while their "depth grammars" differ. I've included some jokes in this book; I only hope that you notice them.

Wittgenstein also believed that a serious philosophical work could be written that consisted of nothing but questions. His *Philosophical Investigations* contains 784 questions, of which only 110 are answered—and 70 of those answers are meant to be wrong! The questions, including those with wrong answers, challenge readers to think for themselves, which Wittgenstein believed was the only way we can come to see how language misleads us when it is not left alone to do its ordinary work. Wittgenstein's style is dialectical, in the Socratic sense. He articulates no theories, but rather raises questions "over a wide field of thought, criss-crossing in every direction." He thereby offers his readers something like sketches that he makes while journeying. No wonder he can be so difficult to understand.

In *Fat Wednesday*, I explore two related concepts: aspect-seeing and experiencing the meaning of a word. Wittgenstein developed a sustained interest in them only late in life, though remarks he makes throughout his writing indicate that he considered them important from a much earlier time. He could only just begin to pursue their importance and the extent to which they might illuminate psychology, aesthetics, and religious belief. In a modest way, I have tried to continue this inquiry. I think *Fat Wednesday* can also serve to introduce a reader who is not familiar with Wittgenstein to the breadth and depth of his understanding of how language works. I have learned much from other books and articles about aspect-seeing. I do not point out where they and I see things differently, in large measure because this book is primarily for lay readers, not professional philosophers. I have acknowledged in the course of the book those whose ideas have most obviously furthered my own, but I have also avoided the critical dissection of those with whom I disagree.

The first chapter, "The Aspects Family," introduces the phenomena of aspects. It begins innocently enough with the ambiguous figure of the duck-rabbit, which can be seen as either a duck or a rabbit. Then the Necker cube seems to flip from pointing up to pointing down as I look at it. Both figures display their aspects as I look at them. In a related way, when I suddenly notice something that had been right in front of my eyes, or recognize an old friend whom I haven't seen for years, I am seeing aspects. When I come to see a painting differently because someone points out to me a feature of it to which I had not been paying attention, I am seeing a new aspect of the painting. I am most struck in all these cases by my awareness that *something* has changed about what I see, yet *nothing* has changed in what I see. My book tries to get at the root of this paradoxical experience.

The second chapter, "Aspects and Words," explores the possibility that our seeing of aspects depends on our ability to speak a language. Seeing and saying are joined in aspect-seeing. To appreciate why this is so, we must first understand what Wittgenstein says about how language works in ordinary life. I tackle this in the section titled "How We Do Things with Words." This may be the most difficult part of the book. Don't skip it, because most of what follows won't make much sense without it. Wittgenstein urges us to think of the meaning of a word or a sentence as its use and to think of words and sentences as tools with which we can do things. Their primary purpose may not be to describe or name, though they can have this use, too. For example, the exclamation "my foot hurts" might be a way to call attention to myself, or to express how I feel, or to justify my behavior, and not necessarily to describe something that is going on in my foot. I contend that our ability to use words enables us to see aspects. In the following section of chapter two, I explain this connection between seeing and saying, and how it arises from Wittgenstein's conception of the workings of ordinary language.

The remaining three chapters of the book take this understanding of the relation between language and perception and try to develop some of its implications. Chapter three, "Aspect Blindness," considers several ways in which a person might not be able to see aspects and how this disability might manifest itself in behavior and speech. I suggest that several common disabilities, such as perceptual deficiencies that follow some brain injuries and those detected in certain forms of autism, might be grouped together under the heading of *aspect blindness*, and also suggest that they are essentially *language* disabilities. An inability or diminished ability to use words manifests itself as a failure to see or recognize things in the world. I also suggest new ways to diagnose these problems and perhaps treat them.

The place of aspect-seeing in our experiences of visual art and music occupies chapter four, in which I extend Wittgenstein's views beyond his explicit remarks, but in ways I think he would approve. A representational painting is essentially ambiguous: it is both paint on canvas and a representation of people and objects. We are not fooled by the painting; we see that it is both paint and picture. We take an interest in it *because* we take an interest in aspects. Further, descriptions of works of art, such as those by a good critic, often require the use of words in other than their usual meanings. Wittgenstein relates "experiencing the meaning of a word" to what he calls "secondary meaning." The meaning of a word is its use, and so we don't usually experience *meaning* because we don't experience *use*. Wittgenstein points out, however, that we do experience a word's losing its meaning—when, for example a word is repeated many times in succession. These kinds of experiences suggest to Wittgenstein that, because some form of meaning seems to be lost on such occasions, perhaps the word usually possesses a meaning which can remain with it. That meaning is not the word's ordinary use-meaning, but it is somehow connected with it. I call this secondary meaning "emergent meaning" because it emerges from primary or use-meaning.

I suggest that this secondary or emergent meaning plays a crucial role in art criticism and, therefore, in how we can come to see works of art in new ways. Emergent meanings lead us beyond the ordinary use of a word to a realm we cannot easily describe or explain. The "fat" in "fat Wednesday" is an example. If I ask which of the two days, Tuesday or Wednesday, is fat and which is lean, most people (though not all) will be able to give an answer. More important than which answer they choose is the fact that the question *makes sense* to them, even though they cannot say why it does. Any explanation that one might offer for an answer seems incomplete and inconsequential. Emergent meaning is something like an aspect emerging from a picture. We cannot say where it comes from or why we suddenly see the picture differently, but we do. In a similar way, we cannot explain why the question, "What color is the vowel *e*?" makes sense (if you agree that it does). Critics often use words with emergent meanings to help us to move beyond a merely ordinary experience of a painting or piece of music, and thereby perhaps to reawaken our wonder at the ordinary.

In chapter five, I suggest that aspect-seeing and emergent meaning serve important roles in science and religion as well as in art. In science, discoveries are often the reconfiguration of existing data in new ways. And might not miracles be a form of aspect-seeing? Of course, the hard problems of science and religion won't be solved in any simple way. I suggest, however, that an appreciation for the roles played in our lives by aspect-seeing and emergent meaning, tempered with what I call "active tolerance," might help us keep talking together. And who knows to where that might lead?

CHAPTER ONE

The Aspects Family

"Seeing the figure *as . . .*" has something occult, something ungrasp-
able about it. One would like to say: "Something has altered, and
nothing has altered."—But don't try to explain it! Better look
at the rest of seeing as something occult too. (*RPP I,* 196)

A. The Duck-Rabbit

This is a duck.   This is a rabbit.   This is the duck-rabbit.

Figure 1   Figure 2   Figure 3

We can see the duck-rabbit either as a duck or as a rabbit. When
we see it as one or the other, we are seeing one or the other of its
aspects. To a large degree, but not entirely, we can control which way
we see the duck-rabbit. That is, someone else can reasonably ask us
to *try* to see it as a duck, say, by thinking of ducks while we look at
it, or by saying the word "duck" to ourselves as we look, or just by—
trying. If you'd never before seen a duck, or a picture of a duck, or
didn't know what the noun "duck" meant, it wouldn't make much
sense to say that you were really *trying* to see the picture as a duck,
no matter how many times you might say the word "duck" to yourself, or use any other tactic. Trying to do something, such as seeing the duck-rabbit as a duck, presupposes knowledge both of what
ducks look like and what the word "duck" means. In like manner,
trying to move a pawn in a chess game to your opponent's last row
requires that you know both what a pawn looks like and how it is
used in the game.

If you were to come upon the duck-rabbit in a field of rabbits,
or its picture in a field of unambiguous picture rabbits, you would

1

likely not even notice its "duck aspect." Noticing "the duck in it"—
as if someone had asked, you to "pick out the duck in this picture"—would be next to impossible, even though the figure of the
duck-rabbit would be exactly the same in both cases. One might even
be asked to pick out the one that's different. Would the duck-rabbit
always be chosen?

It should seem remarkable that we can see the figure of the duck-
rabbit as either a duck or a rabbit without any cues, hints, or signals
from the background. We seem able to focus our attention on the
picture in a certain way and *see* it *as* one or the other animal. Do we
know what we do when we attend in this way? Do we supply a background of ducks or rabbits in thought or imagination? Do we focus
on the eye, with that of the duck looking left and that of the rabbit looking right? If so, how do we make the eye look in one direction or the other? That seems to be as slippery a problem as how we
see the duck or the rabbit itself. The looking eye cannot be detached
from the head, and it looks in a direction because we see it as the
eye of an animal. We might say things to ourselves, or conjure up
images of lakes or forests. Perhaps another person would have success in helping us. He could read us a story that began, "Once upon a
time there was a rabbit," and this picture could illustrate the opening
of the story. Here the story supplies a background of words.

When we see the duck-rabbit first as a duck and then as a rabbit, we experience a *change in aspect*. The same picture—for we don't
think the picture itself has changed—is seen now as a duck, now as a
rabbit. It is possible that I never experience this change, but instead
always see the picture *only* as one or the other animal. When I see
only the duck, it is not obvious that I should then say that I see only
one aspect of the picture; all I see is a picture of a duck. In that case,
I might more easily see the rabbit if there were something else in the
picture that could serve as an object for a rabbit's eye, such as a car-
rot. This ploy draws on my knowledge of what rabbits eat, what and
where an eye is, and the sense I have that a gaze has direction away
from the eye. I might even notice some sort of expression in the rabbit's eye, which might change if the object of its gaze changed to, say,
a snarling dog.

The duck-rabbit (fig. 4) first appeared in 1892 in *Fliegende Blät-
ter* ("Flying Leaves"), a German humor magazine (Oct. 23, 147). The

text under the image poses a question and offers an answer: Which animals resemble one another most? Duck and rabbit. The duck-rabbit appeared in *Harper's Weekly* with the same look, but with English text (Nov. 19, 1892, 1114). We might consider the picture and inscription to be a sort of joke. Would it ever have occurred to us to think of a duck and a rabbit as so very similar? Even

Figure 4. The original duck-rabbit.

here, ears replace beak, the suggestion of a nose replaces the back of the head, fur replaces feathers, a mammal replaces a bird. How different might two things be? I've couched the question in terms of animals, when perhaps it is the pictures of these animals that are alike, as the picture of a saucer might be mistaken for a flying saucer, while a real saucer would never be mistaken for a real flying saucer. In reality, we would not say that rabbits and ducks look alike. Nor is a duck or rabbit itself ambiguous. But pictures of them can be ambiguous, and these pictures can therefore look alike.

Leaving jokes aside for now, I recognize that the duck-rabbit portrait poses a serious question: What is it for two things—in this case animals, or rather pictures of animals—to resemble one another?[1] If, as in this case, the very same picture can represent both duck and rabbit, isn't there a way in which their resemblance is of a high order, almost like that of identical twins, who can also be represented by the same picture? They inhabit the same picture space. Nevertheless I'm left uneasy by this way of putting it. We sense that a duck and a rabbit are not alike in the most important ways and that we would not mistake one for the other in real life. After all, it's pictures we're talking about. Yet the question has been asked: How can the same picture represent different things?

The duck-rabbit began to attain legitimacy and appear as more than a trivial oddity when the American psychologist Joseph Jastrow wrote about it in 1900 in *Fact and Fable in Psychology* (pp. 292–5). Jastrow used the duck-rabbit to argue that a perception is a product of more than mere incoming stimulus. It also involves mental activity—the mind as well as the eye sees.[2] We might even say that the mind informs the eye and is present in it (and perhaps elsewhere).[3] Jastrow writes:

> [T]here is a . . . class of illustrations in which a single outward impression changes its character according as it is viewed as representing one thing or another . . . [A]s we shift the attention from one portion of the view to another, or as we view it with a different mental conception of what the figure represents, it assumes a different aspect, and to our mental eye becomes quite a different thing. (p. 282 f.)

Jastrow anchors the ambiguity of ambiguous figures squarely in what he calls our "tendency to view lines as the symbols of things" (p. 286). The ambiguity of a figure such as the duck-rabbit depends on its being a symbol or representation, or more broadly, something that points away from itself, and has meaning. This seems right in a very general sense and implies that seeing aspects is not a purely optical phenomenon. "Sense-impressions are simply the symbols or signs of things or ideas, and the thing or the idea is more important than the sign. Accordingly, we are accustomed to interpret lines, whenever we can, as the representations of objects" (p. 285 f.). Figure 5 shows two more examples of what Jastrow means by symbolic lines. The first picture in figure 5 can be seen as a half-opened book either from the outside or the inside, showing either the cover or the pages. The top part of the second picture looks flat when the entire figure is seen as an arrow. Cover up the arrowhead and shaft, however, and the picture becomes ambiguous. Jastrow suggests that these kinds of drawings illustrate the principle that "when the objective features are ambiguous, we see one thing or another according to the impression that is in the mind's eye. What the objective factors lack the subjective ones supply" (p. 294).[4]

Jastrow, however, does not try to explain exactly what the mind's eye is or what relation it has to the body's eye. What does it mean to "view lines as symbols of things"? What place does this activity occupy in the family of concepts related to perception? What connection might this

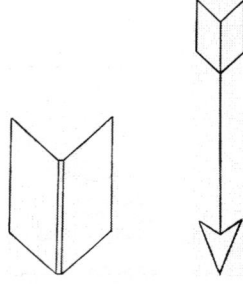

Figure 5. Book and arrow.

sort of viewing have to language, our most pervasive and complex symbolic system? What does it mean to view a figure "with a different mental conception of what the figure represents"? These questions interest Wittgenstein, who read Jastrow and seems to have learned about the duck-rabbit from his book (*PI*, p. 194). Jastrow, however, leaves muddied just what Wittgenstein wants clarified. He maps a bit of the terrain of the *phenomena* of aspect-seeing and proposes a rudimentary theory to explain it. Wittgenstein's interest centers on exploring the place of the *concept* of aspects in the world of seeing, speaking, thinking, and imagining. Put another way, Wittgenstein takes an interest in the phenomena of aspects to the degree that they help us get clear about the concepts of seeing and aspect-seeing. Unless we understand the concepts, we don't know what the phenomena mean. That is why in the arena of seeing, conceptual (linguistic) questions ground causal questions, not the other way around.

Since the birth of the first duck-rabbit, other forms have been invented (or discovered).[5] Consider the "bird-antelope" in figure 6 (Hanson 1958, 13 f.). When seen in figure 7, as one of many in a field of birds, the bird-antelope loses its antelope aspect and fully portrays its birdness. Against

Figure 6. The bird-antelope.

a similar background of antelopes, the bird disappears (fig. 8). All three drawings of the bird-antelope are exactly the same. If I laid one on top of the other, we would see at once that they are congruent. Yet are they the same? One is a bird, one an antelope, and one a bird-antelope. Perhaps I should simply say that they are the same, but what we see is not the same. Do we not see what is there? Does the mind's eye see *something else*?

Figure 7. Birds.

Figure 8. Antelopes.

The duck-rabbit and the bird-antelope are called *ambiguous* figures or pictures. The etymology of "ambiguous" (from Latin) suggests that the word can mean something like "going about hither and thither," "taking on different forms." Ambiguous figures pull us along with them in different directions. The word can also mean "uncertain or doubtful," "obscure," and even, by extension, "untrustworthy." ("You can't water this plant too much.") Proteus, the prophetic old man of the sea in classical Western mythology, is given the epithet *"ambiguus"* by the Roman poet Ovid.[6] Proteus could foretell events. If he could be caught and asked a question, he would tell the truth. In order to avoid capture, however, he would assume all sorts of shapes. In the *Odyssey*, Menelaus says: "[W]e rushed upon him, flung our arms around him—he'd lost nothing, / The old rascal, none of his cunning quick techniques! / First he shifted into a great bearded lion/ and then a serpent—a panther—a ramping wild boar— / a torrent of water—a tree with soaring branchtops— / but we held on for dear life, braving it out" (Bk. IV, 510–15, Fagles trans.). The duck-rabbit and the bird-antelope can be called "Protean figures," though they can assume only two forms, not the many of the god. Do they, however, outtrick Proteus himself since, it seems, they cannot be captured, pinned down, and forced to assume their *true* shapes? The duck-rabbit is not *really* a duck that sometimes takes on rabbit form, nor is it a rabbit that sometimes takes on duck form. Its essence lies in its ambiguity, in its pulling in more than one direction. I feel that I, too, am being led around when confronted by a picture that won't tell me once and for all what it portrays—as if it can't or won't make up its own mind, is shifty, maybe even untrustworthy. I can't believe my own eyes, but I must. The ambiguity of the duck-rabbit cannot be resolved.

The duck-rabbit is not indefinite or vague, because it is either clearly a duck or clearly a rabbit. It is not like a picture of a landscape in fog or a face seen behind a veil. "Ambiguous" implies multiple meanings, any one of which might be clear and precise, especially in the right context. Experimental psychologists call ambiguous figures like the duck-rabbit "bistable" or "multistable."[7] No, if I consider the duck-rabbit seriously, the correctness of its name strikes me, hyphen and all: It is both duck and rabbit. I can't see its two aspects simultaneously and cannot synthesize them visually, but they form a verbal unity.

B. The Necker Cube

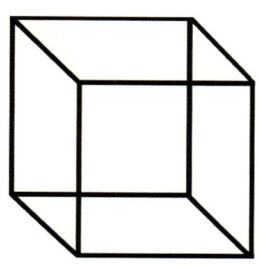

Figure 9 shows another ambiguous form, another member of the aspects family. Look at it for a while. Do you notice a change in the cube while you are looking? If so, how would you describe the change? Most people see the cube jump without actually traversing the intervening space. That is, while you are looking at it, quite suddenly and without warning—aha!—its front side goes from pointing down and to

Figure 9. The Necker cube.

the right, to pointing up and to the left (or vice versa). If you blink your eyes a few times, you might be able to make the cube jump. Of course the cube is not actually jumping, because we don't see a smear as it passes from one aspect to the other. The leap is a quantum one: first here, then there, with nothing in between.

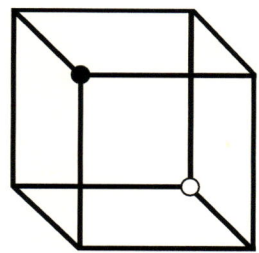

If you're still having trouble seeing this change of aspect, figure 10 might help. Here, the two ways of seeing the cube (or the two ways the cube appears, or the two aspects under which the cube can be described) are emphasized by dots.

First imagine the black dot as closer to you than the white dot. Then reverse this relationship and try to see the white dot as closer. What do you do when you try

Figure 10. The Necker cube with dots.

to see the one or the other? Most of us, though not all, know what it means to make this attempt to imagine the dot closer. If, however, I tried to explain what we were doing to someone who was having trouble seeing the cube change aspects, what would I tell her? If the outside of the cube were painted one color (say blue) and the inside another (say red), and I imagine I can see both inside and outside simultaneously, I might say that when I see one aspect (call it the "black-dot-closer aspect"), the leftmost rectangle will be blue. In the "white-dot-closer aspect," it will be red. The rectangle (actually a rhombus) shifts from inside to outside. This tells me that I can paint outside blue and inside red only for an unchanging aspect. Once the aspect changes, some of the sides that were inside will now be outside, and vice versa. Would any sides retain their original color? That is, would any side that was "inside" remain "inside," or any "outside" side remain "outside"? And what is a "side" anyway? The flat, two-dimensional figure consists entirely of triangles and trapezoids, with one small square in the center. The solid, three-dimensional figure consists entirely of squares. (The rhombuses are squares viewed from an angle.) I find it difficult to see this figure as flat. I struggle to keep it from popping out of the page. When the painted Necker cube flips, it exposes what was inside and hides what was outside. This or some similar coaching might help someone who could not see the two aspects, but it is unlikely to be a description of what *we* do when we notice the change, or bring the change about voluntarily. Even after receiving instruction, some people will not see the cube jump between aspects. They may see both aspects, when the backgrounds are different, but they might never see the change from one aspect to the other. They might not even notice that the figure was the same in the two contexts. Other people can manage to see only crisscrossed lines in a plane. If you can see both aspects, how long can you hold one of them? Is one easier for you to maintain?[8]

The Necker cube is named for a Swiss mineralogist who in 1832 reported observations he'd made of a crystal, a drawing of which presented "an optical phenomenon" he thought worthy of relating.[9] Figure 11 recreates his original drawing of the crystal. We can see that it is properly a rhomboid, not a cube, but at some point in its history it was replaced by a cube, which became known as the Necker cube. Struck by the "sudden and involuntary change in the apparent situation of the drawn crystal," Necker wonders if the orientation reversal he sees is "optical" or "mental."[10] He concludes that it is optical, because he experiences a "special feeling in the eyes" that resembles the sensation of shifting from binocular to monocular seeing. He goes on to explain that when one tries to see corner A clearly,

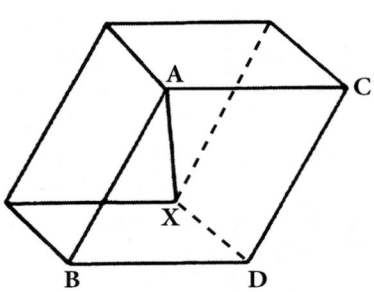

Figure 11. The original Necker cube.

it naturally appears closer, and the rest of the figure falls into place. The change in orientation falls under his control when he concentrates on either corner A or corner B.

Necker does not experience the change in aspect while viewing the crystal itself. His discovery depends on his viewing a drawing. It is important, however, that the drawing is of a crystal in which both inside and outside can be seen simultaneously and so can be accurately represented by an open line figure. Neither the crystal itself nor its orientation in space is ambiguous. Were we to view the crystal resting on a table, we would see it only one way. If we saw the crystal attached to a wall with one face flat against the wall, we would see it the other way. In Jastrow's words, the crystal itself is not taken for a symbol, as the drawn lines are. The crystal does not have two meanings, because it does not have any meaning at all. This is not to say that the cube or rhomboid could not serve a symbolic function in some other context. In that context we could wonder about its ambiguity and about whether a physical object could also display aspects, as a drawing of it does. The drawing represents the crystal and can be seen in more than one way if the context allows. What should be puzzling, however, is the context in which we look at the Necker cube. When it flips, what context has changed? Were we to draw the cube as resting on a table, or draw it as being pressed up against a wall, we would notice only one of its aspects in each instance. The context would ensure that I did not see the other, as would also be true of the duck-rabbit in a field of picture ducks or rabbits. When I look at the drawing of the Necker cube alone, there is no obvious sense in which context or background changes when the figure flips.

Figure 12 is related to the Necker cube. Here we see only the outsides of the stacked cubes, so they aren't properly Necker cubes. How many cubes do you count? The correct answer is six or seven, depending on which aspect you see while you count: six if you see the black squares on the tops of the cubes, seven if

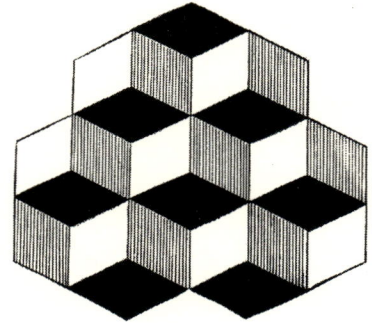

Figure 12. How many cubes?

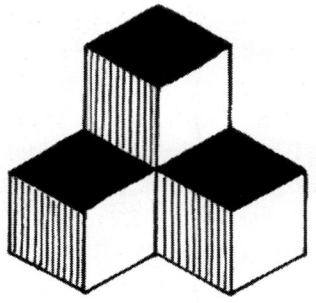 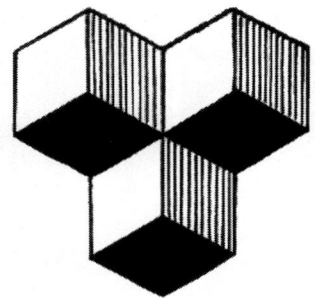

Figure 13. Two ways of seeing the cubes.

you see them on the bottoms. If you can see only six or only seven, you might get help from the two drawings in figure 13. The individual cubes do not change aspects, but the entire set of cubes shifts simultaneously. We might call this an ambiguous collection.

Both the Necker cube and the duck-rabbit are representations. Jastrow said that we have a tendency to view lines as symbols, that is, as pointers to something other than themselves. As representations, the duck-rabbit and the Necker cube exhibit this characteristic of lines. As ambiguous figures, however, they go overboard, because each one stands for two different things. They are both representations and ambiguous. Perhaps all representations can be seen in more than one way. Perhaps ambiguity lies at the heart of representation itself.

C. Faces, Faces, Faces

The paradoxical quality of the duck-rabbit and the Necker cube rests in our recognition that, after the change of aspect, nothing has changed in one sense of "what I see," and yet "what I see" is different: "The expression of a change of aspect is the expression of a *new* perception and at the same time of the perception's being unchanged" (*PI*, p. 196). In what does this difference consist? If I asked you to draw what you saw in both instances, and you were to represent both by exact copies—and wouldn't these be good representations?—no change would be shown because the copies would be congruent. If I see the duck-rabbit as a duck, I could point to other pictures of ducks, or to real ducks, and say that in addition to the copy I drew for you, I am also seeing something like *that*. If I trace the Necker cube and hand you the drawing and tell you that this is what I see, I will still have failed to express in any more complete way that I see two aspects in the one drawing. It seems that the best way for me to let you know what I see is to tell you. It is as if the unchanging drawing is not sufficient to reveal the full character of my visual experience and that a description is needed to bring out its dual nature. The description might also serve to get you to see the two aspects. This connection between what we see and what we say is important.

Consider now what happens when I contemplate a face and then suddenly notice its resemblance to another. Perhaps I see that the daughter looks like her mother or grandmother, or that this middle-aged man in front of me is the grade-school friend I haven't seen for so many years. I see the mother in the daughter; I see the boy in the fifty-something. This is not an uncommon experience. It can strike us suddenly and may cause a slight intake of breath along with that feeling of "aha!" Does the face now look different to me? I'll probably say yes, because now I see something I hadn't seen before. What exactly have I suddenly seen? I see the resemblance of this face to another. I don't infer it or reason through to it. I don't draw the conclusion that this girl looks like her mother because of the shape of her face, the color of her eyes, or any collection of her individual traits. I am struck by a similarity I did not before notice, though I know that the face in front of me has not changed. The resemblance asserts itself, and now I cannot help but see it, whereas before I did not see it at all. I am not merely imagining it, because I *see* it. I think others might see it, too, or be brought to see it. My imagination, whatever that is, must also be playing a part, because nothing out there has changed when I suddenly recognize a resemblance. My imagination seems to add an awareness of a resemblance to what my eyes see.

When I recognize a face or notice the similarity between two faces, I am not looking at a picture or a representation. One face does not represent the other or stand as a symbol for it. It simply looks like the other face. These examples are different, therefore, from the duck-rabbit and the Necker cube, both of which are ambiguous drawings that can be seen as one thing or another. It seems right to say that I have noticed something that I had before not seen, even though it was there right in front of me. I failed to see it not because it was disguised or camouflaged or masked in any ordinary sense. When I see the resemblance between the faces, no disguise is shed, no camouflage removed, no mask taken off. The new aspect dawns on me unexpectedly. It is not itself a property of the face, like a hooked nose or blue eyes. And yet I see what I see *in* the face or faces.

The concept of aspect-seeing is what Wittgenstein calls a "family resemblance" concept. In explaining what family resemblance means, he uses the example of games. Do all "games" necessarily have something in common, some essential property or description, by virtue of which we call them games? "Don't say: 'There *must* be something in common, or they would not be called "games,"'—but look and see whether there is anything common to all.—For if you look at them, you will not see something that is common to *all*, but similarities, relationships, and a whole series of them at that" (*PI*, sec. 66).[11] What we call "aspects" are similarly related. They share a "family resemblance,"

> for the various resemblances between members of a family: build, features, color of eyes, gait, temperament, etc., etc., overlap and crisscross in the same way. . . . [W]e extend our concept . . . as in spinning a thread we twist fiber on fiber. And the strength of the thread does not reside in the fact that some one fiber runs through the whole length, but in the overlapping of many fibers. (*PI*, sec. 69)

All this is by way of warning that we should not assume that everything we call "seeing an aspect," or "seeing *x* as *y*," will share essential characteristics by virtue of which it can be called such. There will be characteristic ways of describing both the change of aspect (as in the duck-rabbit and Necker cube) and the dawning of an aspect (as in noticing the resemblance between two faces, or between the present face and the absent one). In the case of the duck-rabbit, I might be inclined to say: Now it's a duck. With the Necker cube: Now it's pointing up. When I suddenly recognize my old friend, there will be other kinds of responses. His newly recognized aspect probably will not change once it has dawned, but it is unlikely that I will always pay it the sort of attention I do when it first strikes me. The dawn does not last long, but it marks the transition from night to day.

You may be worried that a concept that cannot be given distinct boundaries, that cannot be defined, might not be useful, or might even be dangerous to clear thinking. Wittgenstein cautions us against assuming that a workable concept must be clear and distinct. Rather, we ought to look at the concepts we have. If we do, we'll see that many of those we use every day cannot be demarcated with clarity, nor would we want them to be so. They serve their purposes just as they are, fuzzy, messy, and knit together in surprising ways. In speaking of the concept of games, Wittgenstein says:

> Is it senseless to say: "Stand roughly there"? Suppose that I were standing with someone in a city square and said that. As I say it I do not draw any kind of boundary, but perhaps point with my hand—as if I were indicating a particular *spot*. And this is just how one might explain to someone what a game is. One gives examples and intends them to be taken in a particular way. . . . [H]e is now to *employ* those examples in a particular way. (*PI*, sec. 71)

As we go along, we'll continue to see how aspects form a family. Now, let's turn to a class of phenomena that lies outside the family of aspects—what we usually call "illusions."

D. Illusions

An illusion appears to be what it isn't, or to manifest properties it does not actually have. We're all familiar with many examples of optical illusions, those of color, motion, or contour. We may be less familiar with auditory and tactile illusions.[12] A famous tactile illusion from antiquity is found in Aristotle's *On Dreams* (1984, ch. 2). If we touch a small ball with crossed fingertips, we feel two balls instead of one. Aspects can be confused with illusions, sometimes even by psychologists.[13] I'll look at only a few accounts that have been given—just enough to be sure I've made clear why aspects are *not* illusions. Illusions can get our heads to spin. The study of illusions can reveal a great deal about the workings of the senses and the brain. Illusions, however, can be exposed for what they are, even if we can't keep ourselves from falling under their spell. In this way and others they differ from aspects.

Distortion Illusions

In the Müller-Lyer pattern, two equal lines appear to have strikingly different lengths when set between pairs of oppositely oriented "arrowheads" (fig. 14). Which vertical line is longer? My initial, uncontemplative answer is that the left line must be longer. I suspect, however, that were I to measure the two lines with a ruler, I would discover that their true relationship was not their apparent one. To decide which appears longer, I need only my eyes. Yet even after I have learned through measurement that the two lines are the same length, the illusion persists. Knowledge of the truth does not make its way into my eyes. One possible explanation is that I see the lines as three-dimensional, such as the outgoing and ingoing corners of a room. Another possible explanation is that the line with arrows pointing inward may appear longer simply because the arrows themselves extend past the line.

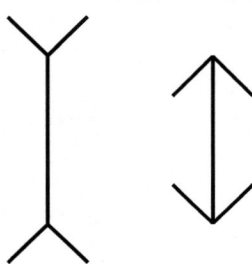

Figure 14. The Müller-Lyer Illusion.

Figure 15 shows two other forms of length illusions. Figure 15(a) (from Jastrow) shows two congruent curved figures, the lower of which appears bigger than the upper. In 15(b), the Ponzo figure, the two horizontal lines are the same length, which can easily be verified by measuring them.

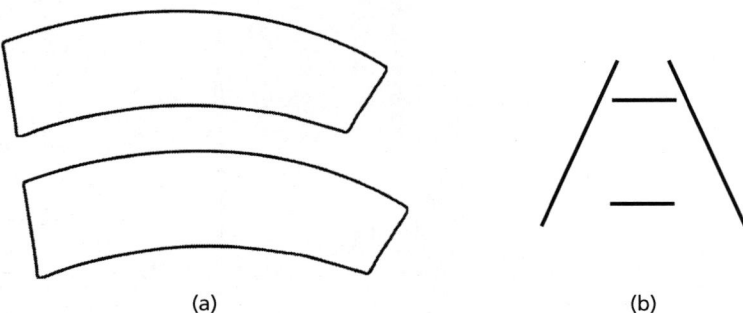

(a)   (b)

Figure 15. (a) From Jastrow; (b) The Ponzo Illusion.

Boundary or Contour Illusions

In the following figures, you see something that in a very real sense does not exist. In Kanizsa's triangle (fig. 16),[14] everyone sees a bright, white equilateral triangle in the foreground (in Petry and Meyer 1987, 40–49). It partially covers the black-outlined triangle under it, while those black disks with congruent wedges missing seem to be biting into the vertices of the foreground figure, like PacMen. The contours of the white triangle seem to be a creation of the mind. Psychologists say the brightness of the nonexistent triangle is a result of "brightness contrast"

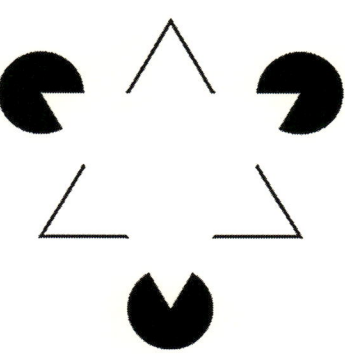

Figure 16. Kanizsa's Triangle.

caused by the triangle's partially covering the black disks. This is a remarkable figure: even though the white triangle does not exist, it possesses several very specific properties.

Figure 17 is similar. It is the nonexistent version of the Necker cube. Although the Necker cube is not actually present, whatever is "there" still manifests the double-aspect property of a true Necker cube. The cubic frame is seen in front of the eight disks despite the fact that there is no cubic frame at all. Specifically, the bars of the frame are seen between the disks even though these regions are physically uniform. Psychologists say the appearance of these illusory bars is the outcome of "visual processing" in which possible shapes are "recovered" from fragmented images. Sometimes you may see a cube behind a dark wall through eight circular "windows." In this case, the frame is clearly visible but the illusory bars are not. Paradoxically, the brain makes us see a thing as if it exists as long as there is no evidence for its nonexistence. (Similar "completion" phenomena exist in audition as well.) Gestalt psychologists, like Wolfgang Köhler, have argued that we see, hear, and feel "integrated wholes" (*Gestalten*) rather than a combination of separate parts (Köhler 1947, Chs. 5 and 6). The perception of the cube in figure 17 might be the mind's way of integrating what is presented to the eyes, thus allow-

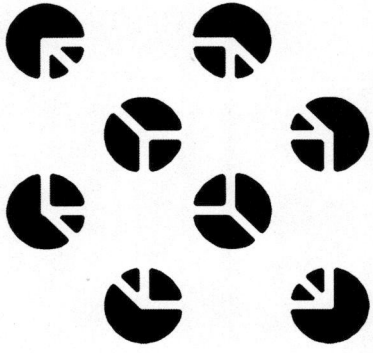

Figure 17. The nonexistent Necker cube.

ing us to "see" what isn't there, yet to see what provides us with a pattern of unity. The organization finds its focus in the cube and in a way brings the cube into existence, at least as an organizational element. What does not exist (the cube) serves to organize what does exist (the lines and circular figures), much as the memory of a dead general might serve to rally his troops.

Brightness Illusions

Look carefully at Hermann's grid in figure 18 and describe what you see. Most people see dark shadows flickering at the intersections of the white lines.

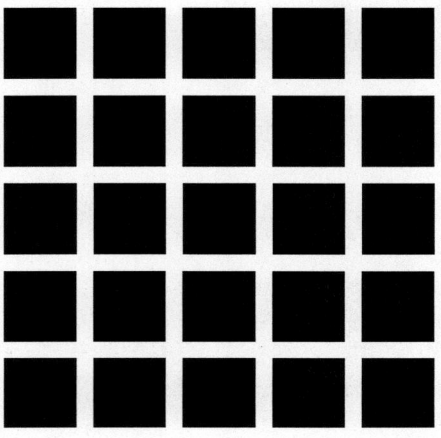

Figure 18. Hermann's grid.

Psychologists and neurophysiologists tell us that this illusion is caused by "lateral inhibition of the retina." The response of a visual neuron "looking" at the intersections is more suppressed by the surrounding white regions than that of the other neurons. As a result the regions at the intersections appear darker than other white regions. The illusion is more pronounced in your peripheral field of vision; at the center of your gaze you may not see the illusion at all. Because the spatial area to which visual neurons respond is very small in the center of your visual field, lateral inhibition takes place in too small an area to cause the illusion. Even armed with this knowledge, we cannot stop the illusion. It is out of our control, a consequence of the equipment of our visual system. Still, we can know that it is an illusion, even as we look at the grid. We can know that there are no flickering dark spots at the intersections of the white lines, even though our eyes are clearly telling us a different story. Why do we not trust our eyes? What makes us certain there are no shadows on the paper? What's your answer?

Many optical illusions are understood when we learn something about how the eyes and brain work. (In the case of auditory and tactile illusions, we need to learn about how the ears and sense of touch work.) An optical illusion is a kind of trick that can be of value in understanding how we see, in a causal, physiological sense. Once we come to know why we see flickering dark spots in the Hermann grid or a white triangle in Kanizsa's triangle, or why the two equal lines in the Müller-Lyer illusion appear unequal, we can rest easy. We are comfortable in knowing that the engineering of our sense organs and brain, often so useful in helping us come to know the world and act in it, has limits. Illusions are indicators that we have run up against some of these limits. Rather than continuing to deceive us, they reveal truths about how we perceive. They also provide entertainment, as in motion pictures, where individual still pictures merge to produce the illusion of motion. But illusions raise questions that are limited. Their answers tend not to arouse our wonder about what seeing really is. As we will explore more fully in chapter two, the experience and concept of aspect-seeing is of interest precisely because it is not explicated through physiology. That is not because we don't yet know enough about the eyes and brain, but because aspects cannot be made any clearer through such an approach. This is why it is important to sort through the rather mixed bag of illusions and keep aspects to one side. Unlike Proteus, who has a true form but assumes others—a real master of illusion—the Necker cube does not have a *real* orientation. Its identity consists in its ambiguity. Likewise, behind the duck-rabbit there is no true image that is obscured or that distracts us by its double form. Its ambiguity is its essence.

E. "Puzzle-Pictures"

In 1961 and 1962, a television game show called *Camouflage* aired on ABC. At the start of each show an announcer would describe the object of the game as simply being "to find something that is right

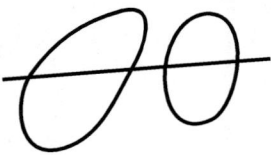

Figure 19. Camouflage "4".

before your very eyes." The contestant who first answered some factual question correctly was then given a chance to find an object in a complex line drawing on a large board. Figure 19 is a simpler example from Wittgenstein (*RPP II*, 41). The object to find is the number four.

For the early part of the game, the contestants had no guidance other than the name of the object for which they were looking. After each round of questions, some of the lines were removed from the picture for the person who answered the question correctly. Then, after a contestant had scored a threshold number of points, he or she (the majority were women) would be shown a drawing of the camouflaged or hidden figure. This almost always gave that player the winning advantage, because while a hairpin might not have many shapes or orientations, a dragon certainly could. There were some players who could see the object immediately, without the removal of any lines. These were the great champions—at least so I thought as a 10-year-old who watched the show religiously on my lunch break every weekday. There was also always someone in the audience who right away let out the kind of sound that let others know he'd seen it, an "aha!" moment on national television.

It's true that the object was in a sense already seen from the moment the screen became visible. The slice of bread or teapot or dog was right there, not obscured or obliterated or scrambled. This can be small comfort. The game show resembles Michelangelo's account of creating his *Pieta*. The figures of the serene Mary and the dead Jesus were right there in the piece of marble the artist found at the quarry in Carrara. All he had to do was remove the parts that didn't belong. "Some have eyes / That see not; but in every block of marble / I see a statue—see it distinctly / As if it stood before me shaped and perfect / In attitude and action. I have only / To hew away the stone walls that imprison / The lovely apparition, and reveal it / To other eyes as mine already see it."[15] Perhaps Michelangelo's genius lay first and foremost in his seeing.

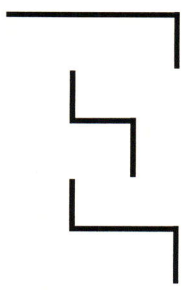

Figure 20 will be clear to many readers almost from the first glance. Those, however, who do not notice a change in aspect right away will be helped by some words.

Speech can encourage someone to experience a change in aspect that she otherwise might notice only later, or not at all. Spoken words can affect what we see, which suggests that there is a connection between seeing and language. Expressed in this general way, the hypothesis is not novel. Wittgenstein tries to show, however,

Figure 20. What is it?

that language does not just influence how we think about or interpret or categorize what we see. Rather, language participates in our seeing as an essential component of many of our visual experiences, especially those of changes of aspect. This idea is rooted in how we learn to speak as children and how we teach children to speak. We'll examine how in chapter two. By the way, figure 20 is the capital letter "E."

The "puzzle-picture" of figure 21 seems to most people to lack any unity. It looks like an assemblage of black and white patches that do not portray anything. Is there any depth in it? Can you say with

Figure 21. Puzzle-picture.

Figure 22. Puzzle-picture rotated.

certainty whether the white or black seems the closer? How would you begin to make sense of this image if you hadn't been told that you would eventually see something in it?

Now let's turn it 180 degrees (fig. 22). Some of you will see something you did not see before. Most (but not all) of the rest of you will be helped by this brief description. The picture is of a man, shown full face and shoulder: "The upper margin of the picture cuts the brow, thus the top of the head is not shown. The point of the jaw, clean shaven and brightly illuminated, is just above the geometric center of the picture. A white mantle or serape covers the right shoulder. The upper sleeve is exposed as the rather large black area at the lower left. The hair and beard are after the manner of a late medieval representation of Christ."[16]

Do you see the hidden man now? Some people never see, but for those who do, dark marks have become human eyes, and blobs of black and white have become an expressive human face. I find that now I cannot *not* see the figure of the man. The picture never returns to its previous chaotic state for me, even when I come upon it unexpectedly. I could trace an outline around the figure for those who cannot see it, but even that might only allow the viewer to know that he ought to be seeing a man there. I can help him to figure it out, but he still may not see the expressive face, the posture, the penetrating eyes in a fully natural way.

The picture acquires *meaning* when we see the human shape in it. Before it was meaningless, not a representation at all. But how does this transition from meaninglessness to meaning happen?

> I suddenly see the solution of a puzzle-picture. Before, there were branches there; now there is a human shape. My visual impression

has changed and now I recognize that it has not only shape and color but also a quite particular "organization."—My visual impression has changed;—what was it like before and what is it like now? (*PI*, p. 196)

Perhaps if I drew what I saw before my revelation and after, I would draw a different picture. But nothing has changed in the puzzle-picture, so by all rights, my second drawing should be identical to my first. If I did draw identical pictures, however, I would not be drawing "what I see," which has changed. We're at an impasse.

CHAPTER TWO

Aspects and Words

The problems arising through a misinterpretation of our forms of language have the character of *depth*. They are deep disquietudes; their roots are as deep in us as the forms of our language and their significance is as great as the importance of our language. (*PI*, sec. 111)

M EMBERS OF THE ASPECTS family, while related, do not necessarily share anything that makes them all aspects. Experiencing a change of aspect is characterized by our recognition that something has altered and nothing has altered. This is important, but our examples are as noteworthy for their differences as for this common feature. I can see the duck-rabbit now as a duck, and then as a rabbit. The Necker cube flips in orientation from this way to that, and I see this flip. What do I see, however, when I notice a resemblance between two people or between someone in front of me and another who is absent or between this friend now and the way he was forty years ago? Do I stop noticing the resemblance after a while? Where does it go, or does it become part of my everyday seeing? When I finally see the man in the puzzle-picture, he never goes away. I even forget what the picture looked like when I could not see him.

Is my seeing of him the seeing of an aspect, when I cannot again see the original, inchoate mess? Consider, too, the so-called "double cross" in figure 23 (*PI*, p. 207).

We can see the black cross as on top or the white cross as on top. The cross is more purely optical than the Necker cube or the duck-rabbit, both of which seem to require a conceptual element. Wittgenstein sug-

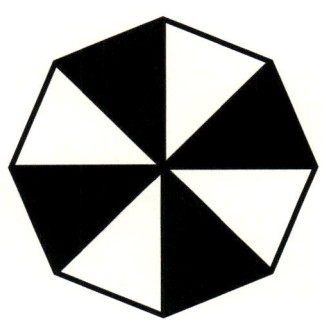

Figure 23. The double cross.

23

gests that the double cross might even be seen in its two aspects by very young and even pre-linguistic children (*PI*, p. 207). Seeing the Necker cube demands that we know something about cubes, and we need to be familiar with ducks and rabbits to see the duck-rabbit. It would sound odd to say, "I see the picture as a duck and something else, but I have no idea what." And when we try to see a drawn triangle as a wedge or a toppled Christmas tree, we must exert some effort. It doesn't just happen for us.

You might object that I have no right to call all these examples "aspect-seeing" if they differ so widely. What justifies my considering them together? Well, for one thing, it *seems* right that these examples, and similar ones, should be thought of together as providing a special kind of visual experience. Unlike illusions, aspects cannot be uncovered—revealed for what they really are. We can't measure them and discover that in fact the duck-rabbit is really a duck, or the Necker cube really has only one orientation. We can't explode them as deceptive because they are not deceptive. They are a true form of seeing. Our responses to these different visual experiences show some common features, just as we might respond similarly to all members of a family or talk about them in a similar way just because they are related to one another.

Wittgenstein compares the "picture duck-rabbit" to a "picture-rabbit":

> If I saw the duck-rabbit as a rabbit, then I saw: these shapes and colors (I give them in detail)—and I saw something like this: and here I point. . . . This shows the difference between the concepts. (*PI*, pp. 196–7)

The concepts he distinguishes here are *seeing* and *aspect-seeing*. When I notice an aspect of something, I will never be able to describe what I see simply by giving the details of the raw perception. Even a drawing—a perfect copy—of the duck-rabbit would not capture *what I see* when I see the duck-rabbit as a rabbit. I am compelled to point to a picture-rabbit, a real rabbit, or to describe what I see by referring to something that is not contained in the drawing itself. In a slightly different way, Wittgenstein also distinguishes two senses of the word "seeing":

The one: "What do you see there?"—"I see *this*" (and then a description, a drawing, a copy). The other: "I see a likeness between these two faces"—let the man I tell this to be seeing the faces as clearly as I do myself.

The importance of this is the difference of category between the two "objects" of sight. (*PI*, p. 193)

In this example the two objects of sight differ because in the first case, but not in the second, *the drawing will do*. I can point to a picture-rabbit or a real rabbit while I'm seeing the duck-rabbit as a rabbit. This will help clear up what I'm seeing. But in the case of facial resemblances, there is *nothing like it* to which I can point. Yet I can say that my response to the duck-rabbit and the face have this in common: that I cannot expect someone else to see "what I see" by my merely indicating what I'm looking at. He simply may not see an aspect that I am seeing, even though he *sees* in another sense exactly *what I see*.

Another important feature of my reaction to seeing an aspect is how I respond to a sudden change in what I see. "I contemplate a face, and then suddenly notice its likeness to another. I see that it has not changed; and yet I see it differently. I call this experience 'noticing an aspect'" (*PI*, p. 193). I'm aware that the face has not changed—in fact, I can even say that I *see* that it has not changed. And yet at the same time I am forced to acknowledge that something is different, that I see it differently. In such a *eureka!* moment, where has the change occurred? In the face in front of me? In my head? In my eyes? I am seeing something that *is*, something in front of me, yet I am tempted to say the essential part is in my mind. I have had a perceptual experience almost like one I'd have if something new came into my line of vision. Yet simultaneously with this, I realize that nothing has changed. When Menelaus struggles with Proteus, he *knows* that despite the changes the sea god undergoes he is still wrestling with Proteus. When we struggle with changes of aspect, we *see* that nothing has changed, while we *see* that something is different.

Seeing aspects is voluntary. I don't mean that you can produce aspect changes at will (though you might be able to do so with some figures like the duck-rabbit and the Necker cube). I mean that it makes sense to ask someone to try to see something differently, whether he succeeds or not. Where an effort is possible, the request to try makes sense. What exactly do we do when we try? Take the simple case of the black and white cross. Try to see the black arms of the cross covering the white. Then try to see the reverse, the white covering the black. Can you describe what you do in each case? I can do no better than repeat the command. I think about the one on top of the other—or better, I imagine it so. I can say no more than this.

Maybe it shouldn't be surprising that we find it hard to articulate what we do. After all, if I'm ordered to walk across the floor, can I say more about what I'm doing than simply that I am walking? I can't easily give details of what muscles I use or in what sequence. Anyway, would this be *what I am doing*? I simply walk, and I correctly describe what I am doing in just those terms. Should we be satisfied with such a description in the case of seeing the black and white cross? When we met the Necker cube in chapter one, I gave some hints on how to see the reversal of perspective for those who might have been having a hard time. One can learn to make the cube reverse at will by means of these devices. In the end, all I said was that you ought to imagine first the black dot as closer, then the white dot as closer. I gave no indication that this action of imagining was reducible to other, simpler acts. No, you simply imagine one dot as closer just as you simply imagine the black cross on top of the white, or the duck-rabbit as a duck. To imagine something seems to be a fundamental voluntary human activity, related to other such mental actions as thinking. ("Think of the black dot as closer to you, then you will see the cube as if from below.") We might even say that imagining is a form of thinking.

Imagining is voluntary, which suggests that its role in seeing aspects is akin to thinking. It is also true that when we look at the duck-rabbit or notice a friend in a crowd, we are seeing. This places aspect-seeing on the side of perception. Seeing is involuntary, and so aspect-seeing has an involuntary side as well. We cannot see whatever we want. Nor does it make sense to ask someone to *see* green grass as red, though we might ask him to *imagine* it as red. Seeing aspects combines the sensory and the intellectual. Wittgenstein says:

> Now, when I know my acquaintance in a crowd, perhaps after looking in his direction for quite a while,—is this a special sort of seeing? Is

it a case of both seeing and thinking? Or an amalgam of the two, as I should almost like to say? (*PI*, p. 197)

Amalgams are usually formed by dissolving silver, tin, or other metals in mercury. The resulting substance is a mixture, not a compound—a physical, not a chemical, union. It nonetheless possesses properties that neither metal possesses separately. The word "amalgam" has also come to mean any combination of diverse elements that go into making up a person's character or personality. The effect is more than the simple sum of the effects of the elements. When we see an aspect of something or experience a change of aspects, something new seems to come into existence; we might call it a sight-thought. It helps carry home the message that the concept of seeing is broad and complex. We say that we can see, in a proper sense, not only colored shapes and physical objects, but also the friendliness of a face, or its resemblance to another face, the glance one person throws at another or the one a painted figure casts at the viewer. We can see a posture as hesitant, or we can see black marks on the moon as craters.

When I see something *as*, I do not issue a simple report of what I see because my description must make use of something that is not contained in what I see. In describing what I see when I see a chair, I need not refer to anything but the chair, and I can easily show someone the chair that I am seeing. If I'm asked, however, what I'm seeing when I look at the duck-rabbit, I can't simply show my questioner the picture I'm viewing, because if I'm seeing it as a duck, showing him the picture won't convey that. I need to add to my description of the duck-rabbit itself: "and something like a picture-duck" or "and something like that."

Changing aspects is not like changing clothes, because an aspect is not a covering or disguise. An aspect doesn't hide or misrepresent the way an illusion does. There is no *true* way of seeing the duck-rabbit or the Necker cube, no way that would show itself on closer inspection or through measurements. When I recognize a facial resemblance or find the man in the chaos, I am struck by things belonging together that previously did not seem to do so. What strikes me—what gives me that "aha!" feeling—has always been there in front of me, but the way things hang together changes. I make connections that before I had not. The same lines in the Necker cube seen one way are now grouped differently, and I see the cube from another perspective. What was the inside is now the outside, and the outside the inside. Sometimes when the terms in an algebraic equation are grouped differently, when the parentheses are moved, for example, or a variable shifted from one side to the other, I might suddenly recognize an equation for, say, a circle, whereas before it was all a bit of a jumble.[1] The imagination can contribute to knowledge even without our performing a proper experiment. Just rearranging things on our to-do list can sometimes clear the air and help us distinguish what is important from what isn't. A re-ordering of our priorities can give new shape to our day or week. The dawning of a new aspect, however, is not mere housecleaning. Rather, it seems to be the arrival on the scene of something new, almost as if we'd done an experiment or made a discovery. In Einstein's 1905 paper *On the Electrodynamics of Moving Bodies*, which presents his special theory of relativity, he performs only thought experiments (*Gedankenexperimente*). The central argument for his theory involves imagining clocks positioned all along a railway platform. Sounds easy, doesn't it? We don't even have to leave the room. Yet by means of this thought experiment, Einstein creates a radically new way to see the entire universe, a way that leads to unexpected truths. Has Einstein *discovered* something?

Finally, when I am struck by a changing aspect, like a face or the solution to a puzzle picture, I occupy myself with what I am noticing. I attend to it; it absorbs me. In that respect experiencing a change of aspect is similar to an action. When I notice an aspect or experience a change of aspect, I am doing something. But what? No doubt I will describe what I see differently when asked, but what have I done to get to get to that point?

A. Introspection and Experiment

If it is the case that in coming to see new aspects of things, something changes but everything stays the same, we might naturally be tempted to conclude that what changes must be *in me*, in my head. The duck-rabbit picture doesn't change, nor does the face of the old friend in front of me. The triangle remains a triangle, no matter how

I interpret it. Since I can't point outside to the picture and say, "See, now it's a duck!" I feel I ought to be able to point at the *it* in my head and say, "Now *it's* a duck!" "Actually you should point to your own visual impression when you say: 'I see this,' then you would really be pointing to what you see" (*LWPP I*, 148).

Psychologists and philosophers have tried two main approaches over the years in attempting to expose the contents of the mind: introspection and experiment. Can they help us understand what happens when we experience a change of aspect? The French rationalist philosopher René Descartes (1596–1650) is considered the founder of introspection as a way of knowing what's in the mind and recognizing the limits of the mind's self-knowledge. In his *Meditations on First Philosophy* he attempts to consider as doubtful and untrustworthy any belief, experience, sensation, or idea about which he cannot be entirely certain: "[I]f I am able to find in each [opinion] some reason to doubt, this will suffice to justify my rejecting the whole" (Meditation I). He scans the catalogue of his mental states and sets aside all those about which he can entertain the least uncertainty. Later, the Scottish empiricist philosopher David Hume (1711–1776) came to conclusions much different from Descartes's. He begins his *Treatise on Human Nature* by saying that

[a]ll the perceptions of the human mind resolve themselves into two distinct kinds, which I shall call *impressions* and *ideas*. The difference betwixt these consists in the degrees of force and liveliness, with which they strike upon the mind, and make their way into our thought or consciousness. Those perceptions, which enter with most force and violence, we may name impressions: and under this name I comprehend all our sensations, passions and emotions, as they make their first appearance in the soul. By ideas I mean the faint images of these in thinking and reasoning; such as, for instance, are all the perceptions excited by the present discourse, excepting only those which arise from the sight and touch, and excepting the immediate pleasure or uneasiness it may occasion. (Vol. I, Book I, I.1)

He follows Descartes's apparently reasonable suggestion that, if you want to know what knowledge or any other mental condition is, you ought to begin by examining the contents of your own mind, where you can expect to find such things. In the end, he and Descartes don't find the same things there, or they understand differently what they do find.

More recent debate about what we might find in our minds through introspection has centered on the notion of "qualia" (singular, "quale"), which comes from a Latin word meaning "what sort" or "what kind." One of the simpler, broader definitions is "the 'what it is like' character of mental states. The way it feels to have a mental state such as pain, seeing red, smelling a rose, and so forth." C. I. Lewis (1883–1964), in his book *Mind and the World Order*, was the first to use the term "qualia" in its generally agreed modern sense: "recognizable qualitative characters of the given" (p. 121). Frank Jackson later defined *qualia* as "certain features of the bodily sensations especially, but also of certain perceptual experiences, which no amount of purely physical information includes" (Jackson 1982, 127–36). These features of my bodily and mental experiences and states might be thought of as accessible to me alone. They cannot be communicated or apprehended except through direct experience. They are private in that people cannot directly compare their *qualia* with those of another. When I am conscious of a *quale* (such as "the what it is like to see red"), I am conscious of it in its entirety. That is, it is directly and completely apprehensible by consciousness, and I can make no mistake about it (except the seemingly minor mistake of getting the word I use for it wrong).

Of the many thought experiments that philosophers do, there is one about Mary, the brilliant color scientist (Jackson 1986).[2] Mary has been imprisoned from birth in a black and white room. She has never left, but has had access to all possible information about colors, except what they look like. When she is finally released from her laboratory prison, armed with a hand-held device to measure wavelengths of light, she sees a red rose. Once she has determined that the wavelength of the light reflected from the rose is approximately 650 nanometers, she remarks, "Ah, now I know what red looks like, and I know what it is like to see red." Mary rushes back to her twin sister, Jane, who has been raised and educated just like Mary but has not yet been liberated. She tries to tell Jane all about something they didn't have before, an experience. She tries to persuade her that though they possess all possible physical knowledge about colors, until now they lacked an important piece of (non-physical?) knowledge. Mary tries to pass this knowledge on to her sister, but it is quickly evident to her that there is only one way to do so: show Jane something red. Until Jane is freed from her learning tank, she will remain woefully ignorant of what it is like to see red.

This thought experiment has been used and reused on both sides of the debate about *physicalism*—the belief that all the knowledge we can have about the world is reducible to knowledge about physical properties such as weight, temperature, electrical states of brains, and so forth. Mary has all of this knowledge about colors before she leaves her prison. If she comes to know something after she leaves (what it is like to see red), then not all knowledge can be physical. That's the whole argument. This is a fun experiment, which like all thought experiments, need not be carried out in real life in order to make its point—namely, that there are things, call them "qualia," that exist and cannot be understood except by direct, private experience. "If you don't get it, you don't get it."[3]

As the debate over the nature and importance of qualia rages, some have tried to enlarge the family of qualia. Galen Strawson has suggested that such experiences as understanding a sentence, suddenly thinking of something or remembering something, and so on, are also not reducible to sensory experiences. Each of these "thought-experiences," Strawson claims, is a distinctive experience in its own right. He says that "each sensory modality is an experiential modality, and thought experience (in which understanding-experience may be included) is an experiential modality to be reckoned alongside the other experiential modalities" (1994, p. 196). By "experiential modality" I think he means what it is like to experience whatever is under question—in this case, thought.

I don't want to suggest that those who write about qualia have come to some agreement about their nature. People can't even agree on whether they exist or not, though they are supposed to be immediately present to us. They are not revealed by experiment, but by private, personal experience. If I have them, I can know I have them by examining the contents of my mind through something like introspection. I have introduced them here in order to raise the following question: Might my experience of a change of aspect constitute what could be called a quale? That is, when I experience a shift in the Necker cube or suddenly recognize a facial similarity, might my experience satisfy some of the important conditions for qualia? I cannot draw a picture for you of what I am seeing. I can't communicate to you what I am seeing in any direct way, as for example by saying, "I am seeing a duck," because I am not seeing a duck, but rather am seeing the duck-rabbit as a duck. I would like to point at my head and say that now I see *this*, but that would only underscore the apparently private nature of the experience of a change of aspect. Noticing a resemblance between two faces or seeing the duck-rabbit as a rabbit cannot be reduced to particular perceptions of parts of what I am seeing. When I show you the picture of the duck-rabbit, you are in one sense seeing all that I am seeing, but in another sense you are not. Mary and her naïve sister share everything there is to know about red except what it is like to see it. We share everything about seeing what is in front of both of us, except the "what it is we are seeing." This latter sense, the aspectual sense, might be thought of as satisfying some of the criteria for qualia.[4]

If this is true—if, that is, the dawning of an aspect is like what Mary experiences when she sees something red—we might say (depending on how we weigh the debate about qualia) that experiencing a change of aspect is not a publicly accessible event. It also might not be a physical event. Mary knew all about the physics of color but still did not know how red looks. I may know all about a drawing of the Necker cube. I may even know the algebraic equation for the drawing, yet never have had the experience of the Necker cube's flipping suddenly while I look at it, just as I cannot read from a map the sublimity of the view from a scenic overlook. Perhaps, then, aspects are known through introspection. As with other qualitative characteristics of perceived things, this may be the only way we can fully understand them in the end. At least this is a possible approach to what aspects are. Wittgenstein, however, rejects introspection as a path to better understanding aspects. If I can know about qualia and aspects only through introspection, and if such knowledge must be radically private, then according to Wittgenstein I am only fooling myself that I know what I am experiencing. If I can't let you in on my experience, maybe I don't know what I'm talking about when I purport to describe it. Wittgenstein's claim that private language is impossible lies at the heart of his rejection of introspection as a way to come to know anything. We'll see in detail later why he believes this. For now it is enough to say that to the extent that qualia can be known only to me, they cannot help us understand aspect experiences, because in a very real way, aspect experiences *can* be shared.

Maybe by experiments we can better understand the nature of aspects and of changes in aspect. Psychologists have long studied ambiguous figures, such as the duck-rabbit and Necker cube, as a door into how the mind engages in "a series of inferential processes" in order to "perceive a consistent and stable environment" (Mitroff, Sobel, and Gopnik 2006, 709).[5] If what takes place in the eyes and brain when we look at ambiguous figures is not a conscious experience that we can describe, unconscious brain processes may be responsible for how we see. Most psychologists—and not only psychologists—believe that the causes of psychological states and processes, when not apparent to an observer, must be brain and neural activities that are unconscious, somewhat hidden and perhaps difficult to measure. This principle has become so well established that we would be hard-pressed to find researchers who doubt it seriously, never mind deny it. If not conscious, then unconscious, processes can account for seeing aspects, as well as for intending (Haggard and Libet 2001), thinking (Damasio 1994), and consciousness (Humphrey 2006).

Over the last 170 years, psychologists have shown an enduring interest in ambiguous (or reversible) figures (Long and Toppino 2004). They have believed that "these phenomenally unstable figures . . . offer a unique window to the involvement and interplay of critical underlying processes in the visual system" (p. 778). The vast majority of proposals for exactly which processes are at work when we perceive ambiguous figures can be divided into two suggestively-named classes: bottom-up and top-down. Bottom-up theories of perception view the eye and brain as more or less passive receivers of visual stimuli, to which the reaction is rapid and involuntary. The brain is organized in a kind of functional hierarchy. "Processing" begins with the "raw data" of the eyes and proceeds upwards in complexity to recognition of objects and the initiation of action.[6] One kind of bottom-up theory explains the duck-rabbit by *satiation*. When we see the duck-rabbit as a duck for a while, the neurons that represent the duck interpretation will fatigue and give way to those that represent the rabbit interpretation. A similar type of fatigue is hypothesized to account for what happens when we stare at a green patch for an extended period, then turn to look at a white patch. The after-image is red, because the green neurons (those responsible for our seeing green) will have become tired (unable to operate normally) by the previous viewing, and so the neurons responsible for seeing red dominate. Top-down, or *cognitive*, theories claim that knowledge, estimates of probability, anticipation, and other "higher order" brain functions can influence what we see, and in particular, which aspects of pictures we recognize and to which illusions we are susceptible.[7] Richard Gregory claims that it makes evolutionary sense that perception would be "a matter of looking up stored information of objects and how they behave in various situations." An animal would be able to determine quickly and with limited information whether what it sees ought to be avoided, approached, or disregarded. Gregory cautions, however, that there will "also be errors, possibly gross errors, when the wrong model is selected" (Gregory 1968).[8]

Necker, who first reported on the rhomboidal crystal in 1832, favored an optical rather than a mental explanation for why the figure reversed. He thought eye-movements were important, because that part of the figure which fell on the fovea of the eye was naturally taken by the observer to be closer. As the eye moves and focuses on one corner or another, that corner appears closer, as in figure 9 in chapter one. This version of a bottom-up account found support in experiments.[9] But the discovery that an afterimage would also show reversals seems to raise doubts about the necessity of eye movements at all, since one can view an after-image without moving the eyes (Gregory 1970). Try this for yourself. Stare at the white dot in the middle of the cube in figure 24 while counting to ten, then shift your gaze to a blank piece of white paper. The afterimage you have shows the same character of reversing as the original figure. If eye movements are a necessary part of the Necker cube reversal, afterimages should show no evidence of flipping.

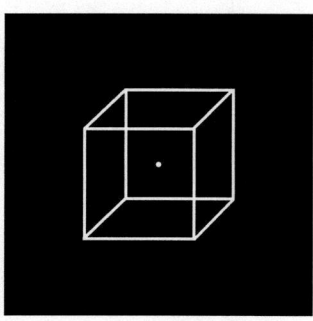

Figure 24. Necker cube afterimage experiment.

Subsequent bottom-up research has centered on the concept of neural adaptation. Long and Toppino (2004, 751) write: "On the basis of both physiological and psychophysical evidence, it is now believed that continued stimulation of selective neural channels temporarily alters their response profiles, thereby reducing their sensitivity and altering their ability to respond to subsequent stimuli until they have recovered from this adapted state." Research tools have even allowed investigators to locate some of the parts of the retina and brain supposed to be undergoing fatigue or adaptation. One sort of neural adaptation evidence that supports sensory (or optical) bottom-up theories is the distribution of pattern reversals over time. It has been shown (and you might try this yourself) that the rate of reversals that occur when one views something like the duck-rabbit or the Necker cube increases over the viewing time. This is interpreted to mean that fatigued neural channels (say the duck channels) are not given sufficient rest time before other channels (rabbit channels) are fatigued. When we now see the duck-rabbit once again as a duck, it will be for a shorter period because the processes by which we see it are less energetic than they were at first. This all sounds automatic and beyond the reach of any conscious attempt one might make to see the figure as one or the other. Another sort of argument stems from localization of reversal patterns. If the figure is allowed to fall on a non-fatigued part of the retina, reversal times return to the starting point. This suggests again that automatic, physical responses (in this case, by portions of the retina) are responsible for seeing reversals. There are other experiments to support bottom-up, optical, or purely sensory processing.[10]

Research, however, has also been directed recently at top-down influences. What happens when observers simultaneously view multiple reversible figures? When we look at two Necker cubes at the same time, either one within the other or side-by-side (fig. 25), we can see the cubes reverse independently of each other. These results again raise doubts about how eye movements could be the source of reversals, because while viewing these figures the eyes move together in only one way while the figures reverse in different ways. However, these results also suggest that no single, globally-configured, top-down process such as "perceptual learning, attention, rhythmic metabolic processes, and a central decisional or

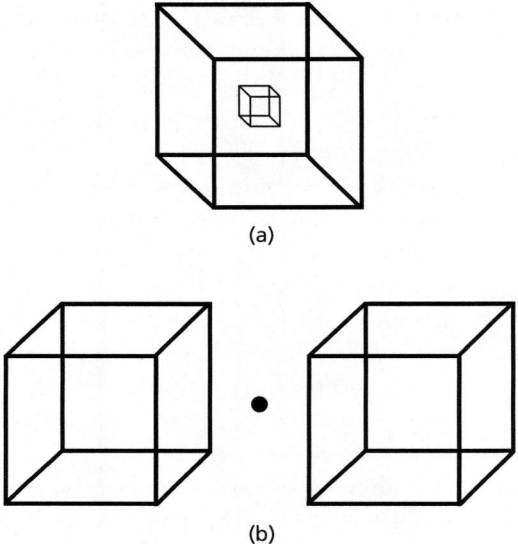

(a)

(b)

Figure 25. Independent reversals of Necker cubes.

problem-solving process" causes figures to reverse. If one process—of whatever kind—was entirely responsible for the reversals, the two cubes could not reverse independently of one another (Long and Toppino 2004, 754–5).

There are, however, other arguments in support of a top-down view, even if it might not be the case that one process controls all reversal experiences. One early source of evidence for top-down or cognitive influence in perceiving reversals comes from volition or attending. It is in keeping with Wittgenstein's observation that we have greater control over the seeing of aspects than over the seeing of, say, color. We can ask another to try to see a figure, a face, a painting, or hear a piece of music in a new way, even if in the end she cannot succeed. But we can't ask someone to try to see this red as blue. (One might try to imagine it to be blue, but that request would make sense only if it meant something like "Imagine if this were blue, then would it go with the wallpaper?") In volitional studies, observers are sometimes simply instructed to try to maintain one aspect of what they are seeing as long as possible, or to switch it on a given signal. It seems that such instructions can have a significant effect on reporting figure reversals even when allowance has been made for the possibility that a subject might change the points on a figure he or she focuses on to facilitate the switch.[11]

Prior knowledge that a figure is reversible ("it can be more than one thing") also seems to affect reports of reversibility. Those who know that a presented figure is ambiguous are much more likely to see both its aspects than those who do not know. If passive, bottom-up processes were alone responsible for figure reversals, we would not expect knowledge (or "higher" brain functions) to play such a striking role in seeing these aspects.

Spontaneous reversals, those that occur without prior knowledge of the figure's ambiguity, are possible in people who display certain cognitive abilities. In a recent study of young children who were presented with the duck-rabbit, researchers concluded that a person must be able to raise questions about the validity of his or her own representations in order to experience a spontaneous reversal. Spontaneous reversals require a particular skepticism about one's own percepts. The heart of ambiguous meaning lies in the awareness that pictures and words need not be simply what they appear to be. Psychologists tested groups of five- to nine-year-old children for cognitive ability, then showed them the duck-rabbit without telling them that the figure could be seen in more than one way. They used the "ice-cream test" to gauge cognitive ability. In this task, the experimenter showed the child a model of a town and identified its relevant landmarks. Next, the child was read a story about an ice-cream vendor who talks to two town children and then goes somewhere else in town. Finally, the child is asked a question about where the ice-cream man is. The test is supposed to measure "theory of mind capabilities." These include an understanding that a single image can represent more than one thing, and in addition further "metacognitive" abilities that will lead a person to see that recognizing possible ambiguity can help solve a problem. The psychologists discovered a significant correlation between high cognitive test scores and ability to experience spontaneous changes in the duck-rabbit figure, as measured by what the children said. It's worth repeating that the change of aspect we experience while viewing the Necker cube can be considered largely a perspective reversal, and that experienced while viewing the duck-rabbit might be called a meaning reversal. In both cases we experience a change, while also knowing that nothing has changed.[12]

Learning and expectation effects have also been measured as forms of top-down processing. Even when sessions are separated by intervals as long as a week, observers report more reversals at subsequent trials than at initial trials. This indicates that some "learning" takes place at the early sessions and that it carries over to the later ones.[13] Expectancy (including the context in which a figure appears and the context of the psychological experiment itself) also influences perception of reversibility. Subjects shown or given a verbal description of one of the two possible interpretations of a figure were more likely to see the biased aspect than the unbiased, as in figure 26, where the center can be seen either as a "B" or a "13," depending on whether the context is numbers (vertical) or letters (horizontal).[14]

Figure 26. What is in the middle?

In the past decade, electrophysiological studies of brain activity during reversal experiences have also provided evidence. Scientists seem to recognize increased activity in areas of the brain usually considered the seats of higher cortical functions, suggesting that these areas and processes have something to do with experiences of aspect changes. In the end, however, Long and Toppino conclude that only a "hybrid perspective" will be able to account for figure reversals: "Although observers can voluntarily maintain a hold on a particular interpretation of a figure to a significant degree, they cannot eliminate reversals" (2004, 259). It's not within the scope of this book to explain in detail the various hybrid proposals that psychologists have recently made. We can say, however, that these conclusions reflect what might be called the experimental side of Wittgenstein's observation that seeing an aspect and experiencing a change in aspect are "amalgams" of seeing and thinking. Psychologists have found reversible figures a door into brain processes, but Wittgenstein finds them a door into our *conceptual* world—the world that discloses what seeing really is.

Face recognition is another aspect-related area where there is rich experimental data. For Wittgenstein, the sudden recognition of the similarity of one face to another (whether both are present or not) fully represents the "dawning of an aspect." How do psychologists talk about such moments? Current debate centers on whether we recognize and remember faces differently from the way we do other objects. Some evidence indicates that we do and that the manner of recognizing faces is holistic rather than constructed piecemeal from facial features. This question is of interest also to those concerned with developing security devices that utilize face recognition by machine. Of course, a machine need not remember and recognize faces and similarities the way a person does, but we humans are the best face recognizers around, and knowing how we do it might help those developing face recognition tools.[15] There has been much research into the recognition of facial expressions. The fact that facial muscles do not move bone, like virtually every other muscle, but rather move skin suggests to some people that facial expressions (which depend only on the movement of facial muscles) may have always played an important role in social relationships. Facial muscles may have been developed or selected primarily for this reason.[16]

Scientists have been able to localize the part of the brain most responsible for the recognition of faces, the amygdala, and have measured increased neural activity in that area during episodes of facial recognition (Nelson 2001). While it is less clear *what* is happening, it has become pretty clear *where* it's happening. Your response to an angry face (whether a real face, a photograph, or a schematic) may differ depending on circumstances (in a play or at a playground, for example), but you surely are able to recognize a wide range of emotions in a face (Ekman 2007). This seems to be true across cultures, as well. However, the orientation of a face can be an obstacle to recognition. The expression on an inverted face is difficult to read. The aspect the face presents seems to require normal, or almost normal, orientation to be identified correctly. "Perhaps you can see that it is smiling, but not exactly what *kind* of smile it is. You cannot imitate the smile or describe it more exactly" (*PI*, p. 198). And I can bring myself to see a smiling face as menacing or friendly by imagining suitable contexts. The facial expression itself has aspects.

Introspection and experiment might both teach us something about aspects, changes in aspect, and seeing in general. Introspection might reveal the more ineffable, private features of aspect-seeing, while experiments focus on its causes. Does either of them, however, help us learn what aspect-seeing *is*? What kind of question is that anyway? Wittgenstein says some disturbing things about both introspection and experiment as ways to understand seeing aspects. About introspection he writes:

> Introspection can never lead to a definition. It can only lead to a psychological statement about the introspector. If, e. g., someone says: "I believe that when I hear a word that I understand I always feel something that I don't feel when I don't understand the word"—that is a statement about *his* peculiar experiences. Someone else perhaps feels something quite different; and if both of them *make correct use of* the word "understand" the essence of understanding lies in this use, and not in what they may say about what they experience. (*RPP I*, 212)

Concentrating on what goes on in us while we view the duck-rabbit or Necker cube, or when we are noticing a similarity between two faces, or while a puzzle figure emerges from some chaos, will not tell us what an aspect is, what seeing an aspect is, or what it is for an aspect to dawn. No matter how closely I attend to what is going on in me, that is all I will observe. In *The Principles of Psychology*, William James (1842–1910) tries to come to a resolution about what "the self" is through introspection:

> In *effort* of any sort, contraction of the jaw muscles and of those of respiration are added to those of the brow and glottis. . . . In a sense, then, it may truly be said that, in one person at least, the *"Self of selves" when carefully examined, is found to consist mainly of the collection of these peculiar motions in the head or between the head and throat.* I do not for a moment say that this is all it consists of, for I fully realize how desperately hard is introspection in this field. But I feel quite sure that these cephalic motions are the portions of my innermost activity of which I am *most distinctly aware.* (Vol. 1, p. 300 f.)

Wittgenstein remarks on this passage: "James's introspection showed, not the meaning of the word 'self' (so far as it means something like 'person,' 'human being,' 'he himself,' 'I myself'), nor any analysis of such a thing, but the state of a philosopher's attention when he says the word 'self' to himself and tries to analyze its meaning. (And a good deal could be learned from this.)" (*PI*, sec. 413). What *cannot* be learned in this way is what the self is.

Wittgenstein is also skeptical of the value of experiments in psychology. He thinks they do not help us to understand ordinary psychological terms, including seeing and seeing aspects. In fact they are likely to lead us far astray: "In psychology one is completely uncertain of the fruitfulness of the experiments. Rather, in psychology there is what is problematic and there are experiments which are regarded as methods of solving the problems, even though they quite by-pass the thing that is worrying us" (*RPP I*, 1039). What Wittgenstein means by this remark[17] can begin to become clear only after we have taken a close look at what he says about language and how we do things with words. Language must itself become an object of wonder before we can see past its appearances. Wittgenstein believes that until we do, we shall remain hopelessly muddled as to what seeing is, and what in particular aspect-seeing is. He makes the remarkable claim that an appreciation of how we learn and use words is a prerequisite to our being able to weigh the value of psychological experiments about seeing and, by extension, experiments about most of the other areas psychologists currently investigate. Until we sketch out what these concepts are, that is, how these words are taught and used, we cannot know what we are investigating when we experiment. Conceptual or philosophical investigation comes first.

Wittgenstein believes that language can be compared to an ancient city,

> a maze of little streets and squares, of old and new houses, and of houses with additions from various periods; and this surrounded by a multitude of new boroughs with straight regular streets and uniform houses. (*PI*, sec. 18)

It is difficult to command a perspicuous, surveyable view of this city. Consequently, maps of its streets and terrain can be misleading, directing us one place while leading us to believe we are somewhere else. In ordinary, day-to-day discourse, we have no need for such maps, because we generally know our way around without them. But it is our fate to persist in map-drawing while we are enmeshed in the "labyrinth of paths" that is our language (*PI*, sec. 203). Wittgenstein contends that much of contemporary psychology is a misleading map of this kind. Now, however, we must take a detour, "the long way around."[18] We need first to take a look at what Wittgenstein says about words so that we can return to aspects with a fresh appreciation for the role language plays in seeing.

B. How We Do Things with Words

[Humpty Dumpty said] ". . . [T]here are three hundred and sixty-four days when you might get un-birthday presents—"

"Certainly," said Alice.

"And only *one* for birthday presents, you know. There's glory for you!"

"I don't know what you mean by 'glory,'" Alice said.

Humpty Dumpty smiled contemptuously. "Of course you don't— till I tell you. I meant 'there's a nice knock-down argument for you!'"

"But 'glory' doesn't mean 'a nice knock-down argument,'" Alice objected.

"When *I* use a word," Humpty Dumpty said, in rather a scornful tone, "it means just what I choose it to mean—neither more nor less."

"The question is," said Alice, "whether you *can* make words mean so many different things."

"The question is," said Humpty Dumpty, "which is to be master— that's all." (Carroll 1946, 93–94)

What is the connection between language and reality? How does speech *connect* with the outer and inner worlds? Such enormous and venerable questions will have no simple answers, we know. At the very beginning of *Philosophical Investigations*, Wittgenstein cites one answer that might occur to us. It comes from St. Augustine's *Confessions*. Augustine likely did not fully subscribe to this view, but it paints an enticing and simple picture of the way language originates and how it operates. Augustine describes how he thinks he must have come to learn language as an infant. He writes:

[W]hen people called an object by some name, and while saying the word pointed to that thing, I watched and remembered that they used that sound when they wanted to indicate that thing. Their intention was clear, for they used bodily gestures, those natural words which are common to all races, such as facial expressions or glances of the eyes or movements of other parts of the body, or a tone of voice that suggested some particular attitude to things they sought and wished to hold on to, or rejected and shunned altogether.

In this way I gradually built up a collection of words, observing them as they were used in their proper places in different sentences and hearing them frequently. I came to understand which things they signified, and by schooling my own mouth to utter them I declared my wishes by using the same signs. (Augustine 1997, I. 8)

Augustine's words offer a particular view of human language: namely, that the individual words in a language name objects, perhaps also actions and qualities, and that sentences are combinations of such words. Words such as "soon," "not," "perhaps" take care of themselves. In this picture of language, Wittgenstein finds an example of the belief that every word has a meaning that is correlated with it. The meaning is the object for which the word stands, or an idea which is connected by the word to the object.[19]

To contrast with this image of language, let's place ourselves in a simple situation. Imagine that I send someone shopping:

I give him a slip marked "five red apples." He takes the slip to the shopkeeper who opens the drawer marked "apples"; then he looks up the word "red" in a table and finds a color sample opposite it; then he says the series of cardinal numbers—I assume he knows them by heart—up to the word "five" and for each number he takes an apple of the same color out of a drawer.—It is in this and similar ways that one [actually] operates with words.—"But how does he know where and how he is to look up the word "red" and what he is to do with the word "five"?— Well, I assume that he *acts* as I have described. Explanations come to an end somewhere.—But what is the meaning of the word "five"?—No such thing is in question here, only how the word "five" is used. (*PI*, sec. 1)

In this thought-experiment, Wittgenstein turns our attention to the possibility that the meaning of a word is the use we make of it, not some object to which the word "refers," or an idea which gives the word its power: "For a *large* class of cases—if not for all—the meaning of a word is its use in the language" (*PI*, sec. 43). Wittgenstein doesn't attempt to clarify or explain what exactly he means by "use in the language." Elsewhere he says that "the concept of use is flexible and varies along with the concept of activity" (*LWPP I*, 340). The word "five" in the example is not used like the word "red." The shopkeeper does not consult a sample with the word "five" written on it. "Red" is not used like "apple," for there is no sample for "apple" as there is for "red." These three simple words, "apple," "red," "five," begin to illuminate how words function in various ways. To postulate a meaning for each word—apart from its uses in particular circumstances—misconstrues how language works, and how we work with it. Wittgenstein rejects any question about what the meanings of these words might be apart from their uses. Such questions would already presuppose a certain view of what gives words their value, a kind of theory of meaning, before a description of how words are actually used has been articulated. Once we describe how they are used, we will find that we have no need for a theory. Instead, Wittgenstein invites us to "think of words as instruments characterized by their use" (*BB*, 67).

> Think of the tools in a tool-box. There is a hammer, pliers, a saw, a screwdriver, a rule, a glue-pot, glue, nails and screws.—The functions of words are as diverse as the functions of these objects. (*PI*, sec. 11)

No single use characterizes all words. Traditional functional categories, such as noun, verb, adjective, adverb—in each of which all members act in basically the same way—are useful categories for some purposes, but they can be overemphasized. When we become confused about the meaning of a word or the sense of a sentence, Wittgenstein wants us to ask: "On what occasion, for what purpose, do we say this? What kind of actions accompany these words? . . . In what scenes will they be used, and what for?" (*PI*, sec. 489). The variety of the purposes for which we use words is bounded only by the variety of human activities in which language plays a part.

The kinds of things we do with words, together with the contexts or circumstances that allow us to operate with them, Wittgenstein calls *language-games*. He hopes that the image of the game will give us a perspicuous view of parts of language and emphasize features of language that are more important than we generally recognize. He means to "bring into prominence the fact that the *speaking* of a language is a part of an activity, or form of life" (*PI*, sec. 23). Wittgenstein does not believe language is a game; our linguistic activities are less trivial than games because of the way they are interwoven into our lives. He does, however, think that we can achieve some measure of clarity about language by comparing it to games. It is also true that children often learn how to speak in the context of word games.[20] The game of chess highlights some of the features of language Wittgenstein wants us to notice.

We play chess according to rules that determine what moves are permitted. They allow us to play the game—but not necessarily to play it well because the rules do not tell us what moves are best. The rules tell us how the individual pieces can move, something that cannot be determined by an examination of the shapes of the pieces or their positions on the board. Each piece is defined by its use, that is, by its role in the game. (One would not say, for example, "I know what a bishop *does*. Now tell me what it really *is*." What it does is what it is.) In language, too, rules of what Wittgenstein calls "grammar" widely conceived determine the limits of what it makes sense to say. Like moving a piece in chess, saying is always a kind of doing. The rules demarcate the region of the sensible in which the activities of language can take place—in which, that is, we can successfully do things with words. The function of individual words and sentences can be determined only by observing how they are in fact used in the various games of our language, and in what circumstances and for what ends we use them.

Chess can be taught, and one can learn it. In the process of teaching, it must be possible for the teacher to correct the learner, to tell him, for example, that a pawn that has reached the last row cannot be promoted to a king (*BB*, 67), or to remind him that a bishop cannot jump over other pieces. These moves are not allowed in the game. We can imagine a variant of chess in which these moves are permitted. We would have to experience it to decide if such a game was worth playing, but it might no longer be considered chess. We teach and learn language, too. We correct children when they say ungrammatical things, in the narrow, school-book sense of grammar, as when the subject and verb of a sentence don't agree in number. We also correct them in other contexts when they speak ungrammatically in a wider sense of grammar. For example, a child who awakens at home in the morning and says he has been on a boat during the night might be told that he's had a dream. He quickly learns to append "I dreamed" before such statements. We might suspend this rule of saying "I dreamed." We could imagine children doing this as a kind of game: "Where did you go last night?" The context would then make clear that their travels were dream travels and that they were not speaking nonsense. When Wittgenstein uses the word "grammar," he generally means it in this wider sense, into which are incorporated the circumstances in which something is said. A sentence, therefore, may be grammatical in the narrow sense, but not grammatical in the wider sense. This reminds me of the joke about a man who comes running into his doctor's office, dragging a friend by the wrist, crying, "Doctor, doctor, I think I have Parkinson's disease—and he has mine!"

Chess is also autonomous. That is, we are not tempted to think that we must look for the meaning of the game outside the game. While chess contains elements reminiscent of battle, church, and state, one need not know anything about real battles, churches, or states to play chess. If you follow rules other than those of the game, you do not play chess *badly*; you simply do not play chess. This might have consequences, but not for chess. In contrast, consider rules of cooking. They are not autonomous, because their purpose depends on something outside the rules—namely food. If you break the rules of cooking, you might very well still cook, but you might do so badly (*Z*, 320). Language, too, Wittgenstein wants to say, is autonomous. It requires no justification. We do not read off its rules from nature. In that sense, the rules of language are arbitrary. If you follow rules other than those of your language, you do not say something *wrong*, you say something nonsensical. Or you might say nothing at all. To call the rules of our language arbitrary, however, is not to say that they are whimsical or pointless. To call them arbitrary is to say that "the *aim* of grammar is nothing but that of the language" (*PI*, sec. 497). Grammar rules—the rules we use for describing reality—may therefore be conventional, but this does not imply that in some sense reality is itself conventional. The *rules* for describing reality are arbitrary, but nonetheless the *description* of reality is determined by reality.

Among the many games that people play are board games, ball games, card games, Olympic games, war games, related in various ways, with various concepts of winning, various rules of what is permitted, various contexts in which they are played and with various pieces of equipment. The multiplicity of language-games is no less; Wittgenstein mentions the following:

> Giving orders and obeying them—
> Describing the appearance of an object, or giving its measurement—
> Reporting an event—
> Speculating about an event—
> Forming and testing a hypothesis—
> Presenting the results of an experiment—
> Making up a story, and reading it—
> Play-acting—
> Singing catches—
> Guessing riddles—
> Making a joke; telling it—
> Solving a problem in practical arithmetic—
> Translating from one language to another—
> Asking, thinking, cursing, greeting, praying. *(PI,* sec. 23)

Our expectation of what is appropriate, what is sensible, and what is nonsense varies among language-games. "Come back soon!" when said in the context of the language-game of "giving orders and obeying them" plays a different role from the one it plays in the language-game of greeting or asking or praying. We usually grasp the use in its context without much thought, but it would be wrong to say that "come back soon" has "its own meaning" apart from the different uses to which it can be put in different language-games. These language-games, and myriad others, belong as much to "our natural history as walking, eating, drinking, playing" (*PI,* sec. 25). They are part of the weave of our lives, and so the observation and description of language-games, if it is sensitive and detailed, can constitute a study of human life (Malcolm 1994, 77).

At this point someone might quite properly object: "You take the easy way out."

> You talk about all sorts of language-games, but have nowhere said what the essence of a language-game, and hence of language, is: what is common to all these activities, and what makes them into language or parts

of language. . . . And this is true. . . . I am saying that these phenomena have no one thing in common which makes us use the same word for all,—but that they are *related* to one another in many different ways. And it is because of this relationship . . . that we call them all language. (*PI*, sec. 65)

Just as we shall find no one thing common to all games, so, too, the various boroughs of language need not share a common street plan. We see instead "a complicated network of similarities overlapping and criss-crossing" (*PI*, sec. 66). As I mentioned earlier, Wittgenstein characterizes these similarities as "family resemblances," because the resemblances between members of a family in particular traits overlap and intersect in the same way. Games—and language-games—form such families.

Music also has many of the features of games that Wittgenstein finds important for understanding language. Different forms of music (such as Gregorian chant, harmonic, twelve-tone, raga, jazz) are defined in part by the rules that circumscribe the bounds of what is musically possible. These rules can be taught and learned, and mistakes can be made and corrected. Music rules can also be stretched and new forms of music invented, though perhaps not at will. Individual notes or note groups derive their meaning from their use in the piece and from the context in which they appear. The same note might be heard as the tonic in one measure, the dominant in another, as the beginning a twelve-tone row or the end, and so forth. Music, too, is autonomous. A melody or a piece of music does not derive its meaning from something outside. When we attempt to explain a musical theme to someone or how to play a piece better, we do not point to some thing or idea outside the music, but rather say things like "'At this point of the theme, there is, as it were, a colon,' or 'This is . . . the answer to what came before'" (*BB*, 166), or "'tell yourself that it's a *waltz*, and you will play it correctly'" (*BB*, 166). Wittgenstein would like to say that what the melody tells us is itself, but in order to understand the melody, one must already be familiar with music, just as understanding a sentence requires understanding a language: "Understanding a sentence is much more akin to understanding a theme in music than one may think" (*PI*, sec. 527). When we are tempted to say that understanding a sentence points to a reality outside the sentence, we should instead say, "Understanding a sentence means getting hold of its content; and the content of the sentence is in the sentence" (*PI*, sec. 167). We cannot "get hold of" what it is for a piece to be a bishop in chess or a tone to be a dominant in music without already knowing chess or music. So, too, we must already be masters of a language—of a certain kind of *technique*—before we can understand a sentence. When we do understand, it is not because we see how the sentence points away from itself, but because we know how it is used, which is to say, what we can do with it.[21]

By the analogy between language and games and other rule-directed human activities, Wittgenstein highlights the social quality of language, just as he emphasizes its pragmatic quality by comparing words with tools. At root, the social and pragmatic qualities of language are the same, though they provide different views of the functioning of language in our lives. In an effort to explore language's social side and its implications, Wittgenstein draws us more deeply into the problem of what it is for someone to follow a rule. Games, music, and language are all rule-governed human activities, and their social character derives in important ways from rules. Following rules is involved in every important human activity, in every activity where there can be correct and incorrect, or better and worse, ways of doing things. Rules can, of course, be stretched, reinterpreted, changed. Rule-governed activity is not lockstep activity to which we must adhere at any price. Rather, following rules allows us to do things, in much the way that the restrictions imposed by the rules of tennis let us play a game we find worthwhile (at least I do).

Wittgenstein's discussion of rules leads him to talk about what understanding a rule is and eventually to his extraordinary claim that private language is impossible. He asks, "Is what we call 'obeying a rule' something that it would be possible for only *one* man to do, and to do only *once* in his life?" (*PI*, sec. 199). This question, like the vast majority of the questions Wittgenstein asks, is a conceptual one, that is, "grammatical" in the broad sense. It is not an empirical or experimental question. He is not asking something like, "Is it possible for only one man, and only once, to swim the Atlantic?" Rather, he's asking, "Does the concept of obeying a rule make sense if applied just once?" Wittgenstein answers himself as follows:

> It is not possible that there should have been only one occasion on which someone obeyed a rule. It is not possible that there should have been only one occasion on which a report was made, an order given or understood; and so on.—To obey a rule, to make a report, to give an order, to play a game of chess, are *customs* (uses, institutions). (*PI*, sec. 199)

Elsewhere, Wittgenstein extends this claim, with modification, into the area of the psychological: "Why does it sound queer to say: 'For a second, he felt deep grief'? Only because it so seldom happens?" (*PI*, sec. 148). "Could someone have a feeling of ardent love or hope for the space of one second—*no matter what* preceded or followed this second?" (*PI*, sec. 583). Deep grief and ardent love are not sensations like pain or perceptions like that of a bright light. They require a wider context in which to show themselves. This is another way of saying that the language-games we play with these words prohibit our using them to represent momentary or brief experiences. This is not a fact of psychology but of "grammar." Kant says something similar about making promises in the *Groundwork of the Metaphysics of Morals* (55/422). A universal law that dictated that I could break my promises whenever it was to my advantage to do so "would make promising . . . itself impossible." Under such conditions, no individual, no matter how sincere, could promise anything because the institution for promising could itself no longer exist. To promise requires not a certain *state of mind*, but a web of words and customs. When I say "I promise," I have promised. In general, obeying a rule is an institution much like promise-making.[22]

What goes on when we learn rules and follow them? Is a rule an abstract entity that allows for all possible workings-out, as we might imagine an algebraic expression to be? Is a rule a kind of "mental mechanism" that goes through its motions whenever it is turned on? For example, when we speak, we more or less follow the rules of English grammar automatically without needing to think about them. (Compare how we hesitate as if searching for the rules when we speak a foreign language we are just beginning to learn.) Or does following a rule consist in intuiting what your teacher wants you to do, as when you continue a number series correctly? Even though I haven't made explicit even to myself why I think this number is the next one in the series, if my teacher acknowledges that it is, then perhaps I am really following a rule. Wittgenstein rejects all three of these proposals. Take reading as an example of rule-guided activity. Wittgenstein has in mind what we might call "automatic reading" in which comprehension of the text is not important—the sort of reading you don't want to encourage in your children, your students, or the readers of your book! In this way we could be said to "read" a language we don't know, say ancient Greek, once we've mastered the sounds of the letters, diphthongs, and accent marks, even before we learn any grammar or vocabulary. Reading in this way seems to be rule-guided. Not just any sounds I utter will be correct, but only those that are connected in some way with the written words on the page. The possibility of making mistakes and being corrected makes sense here, as it does in learning how to play a game. Whether I am reading correctly or not depends only on the relationship between what I say and the marks on the page, not on any outside reality to which the words might refer.

In exactly what way must the sounds I make relate to the written words for what I am doing to be correctly called "reading," in the sense of "rendering out loud what is written or printed"? When one reads, says Wittgenstein,

> his eye passes . . . along the printed words, he says them out loud—or only to himself; in particular he reads certain words by taking in their printed shapes as wholes; others when his eyes have taken in the first syllables; others again he reads syllable by syllable, and an occasional one perhaps letter by letter.—We should also say that he has read a sentence if he spoke neither aloud nor to himself during the reading but was afterwards able to repeat the sentence word for word or nearly so.— . . . Now compare a beginner with this reader. The beginner reads the words by laboriously spelling them out.—Some however he guesses from the context, or perhaps he already partly knows the passage by heart. Then his teacher says that he is not really *reading* the words (and in certain cases that he is only pretending to read them). (*PI*, sec. 156)

Wittgenstein tells us that if we focus on the reading of the beginner and use it to determine what *reading* consists in, we may be inclined to say that reading is a "special conscious activity of the mind." Wittgenstein, however, does not want to say this. "The same thing may take place in the consciousness of the pupil who is 'pretending' to read, as in that of the practiced reader who is 'reading' it. The word 'read' is *applied differently* when we are speaking of the beginner and of the practiced reader" (*PI*, sec. 156). The application is different because the context is different, just as a pawn that has reached its opponent's back row can now be used differently. Still, we are tempted to go on and say that if the difference between the beginner who is pretending to read and the skilled reader does not lie in some conscious activity, it must lie in an unconscious one— another mechanism to distinguish reading from not reading. "But," Wittgenstein replies, "these mechanisms are only hypotheses, models designed to explain, to sum up, what you observe" (*PI*, sec. 156). They are nothing that we can easily know and, consequently, they can never be used to teach someone how to use the word "read." This is to say that they cannot figure in the concept of reading, cannot be what counts as reading. When I teach a child how to read, I don't look into her mind to determine what, if anything, is going on there. I listen to her, watch her, and determine if she is actually reading.

Wittgenstein's interlocutor persists: "But isn't that only because of our too slight acquaintance with what is going on in the brain and nervous system?" (*PI*, sec. 158). If we knew more, we'd be able to say, "Now he has *read* this and now the reading connection has been set up." But ask yourself, how much do you know about these things? Aren't you approaching the concept of reading with certain requirements, such as that whatever connection is set up between the printed word and the read word spoken out loud must be a connection set up *inside* the person doing the reading, a mental connection, perhaps a physiological one? But maybe the connection is *outside*, in the context in which the reading takes place, in the teaching situation, and in the common language. If you are wearing an analog watch, not a digital one, try this experiment:

> say the numbers from 1 to 12. Now look at the dial of your watch and *read* them.—What was it you called "reading" in the latter case? That is to say, what did you do to make it into *reading*? (*PI*, sec. 161)

Wittgenstein says that "nothing else happens when one says the [numbers] than just saying them while looking" at the numerals on the watch face (*BB*, 149). It is not necessary, he thinks, that certain peculiar experiences more or less characteristic of reading take place while we are reading. I might say that when I am really reading, "the words I utter *come* in a special way" (*PI*, sec. 165). But in what way? "Read the letter 'A'.—Now, how did the sound come?—We have no idea what to say about it" (*PI*, sec. 166).

The difference between reading and not reading does not lie in conscious or unconscious mental processes. It does not lie in states of the brain and nervous system, nor in some special feeling. For Wittgenstein, the difference lies in the circumstances that make it correct in the one case and incorrect in the other to say of someone that he or she is reading. If reading is a rule-generated activity, like playing games, speaking, and playing music, it must be possible to teach someone how to do it. This means it must be possible to correct his mistakes when he is wrong, to encourage him when he is doing well, and thereby to teach him not only how to read, but at the same time, what counts as reading. We must expect that sometimes we will only vaguely understand how to apply the rules. In some situations, we will not know what to say about how the rule should be applied or we will have to decide how to apply it. An inexact rule is not necessarily unusable, as when I instruct someone learning tennis to "toss the ball about this high on your serve."

Any social, rule-governed activity hangs on what the person does, not on what he feels or what he thinks he is doing. In teaching someone how to read, we never point to our head or his and say, "This is reading." We never correct what might be going on in his consciousness or his brain. We correct what he says, and we do so in the context of particular circumstances and particular ends. If we know that Mr. Smith has never before seen the Greek alphabet, yet on the first day of ancient Greek class can recite the opening lines of Homer's *Iliad* with perfect Greek pronunciation while his eyes run across the lines of printed text, we know he is not reading. We know this, not because we have special access to his mind or brain, but because we know he has never before studied Greek. That is, we know something about his life, about his education and experience, not something about his present mental state. This knowledge justifies us in saying, "He is only pretending to read." What we might have been tempted to take as a mental activity (that of "reading" or "pretending to read") Wittgenstein suggests we view as a public condition, available to all, because it is a rule-governed public activity, and rules are essentially teachable and learnable, even though the rules are not taught and learned *explicitly* while we master our native language. We might say that concepts, like people, require society.

Still, you might object that automatic reading cannot be the paradigm of rule-governed activity. Following a rule often (and perhaps in the most important cases) requires that we also *understand* the rule before we can follow it. We are inclined to say that without understanding, we are no better than mindless machines that act in a regular way. Wittgenstein agrees that there is all the difference in the world between saying a sentence with understanding and saying it without understanding, but in what does the understanding consist? Understanding is neither a mental nor a physical event, process, or state, though there may be "more or less characteristic *accompaniments* or manifestations of understanding" (*PI*, sec. 112).

Wittgenstein offers at least two arguments for this somewhat remarkable claim that understanding is no sort of mental or physical phenomenon. First, no mental or bodily phenomena are necessary to my understanding a word, a sentence, or a mathematical formula, any more than they are necessary for my understanding how to play chess. For example, let's suppose that in order to understand a sentence, I must first have some kind of mental image. This image would serve the function of connecting the sentence to the world. Wittgenstein writes:

> Suppose I teach someone the use of the word "yellow" by repeatedly pointing to a yellow patch and pronouncing the word. . . . I make him apply what he has learned by giving him the order, "Choose a yellow ball out of this bag." What was it that happened when he obeyed my order? I say "possibly just this: he heard my words and took a yellow ball from the bag." Now you may be inclined to think that this couldn't possibly have been all, and the kind of thing that you would suggest is that he imagined something yellow when he *understood* the order, and then chose a ball according to this image. (*BB*, 11 f.)

Wittgenstein then asks if imagining the yellow is also necessary when we command him to "imagine a yellow patch"? "Would you still be inclined to assume that he first imagines a yellow patch, just *understanding* [the] order, and then imagines a yellow patch to match the first?" (*BB*, 12). Answering "yes" to this question leads us into an endless series of imagining a yellow patch so that we can imagine a yellow patch so that we can. . . . Why not just stop with "he heard my words and took a yellow ball from the bag"? Wittgenstein does not deny that we sometimes do imagine colors, shapes, and so forth when we understand a sentence, but such imaginings are not necessary to the concept of understanding. They are not part of the way we teach or correct the use of the word "understanding." One might understand without having any mental images at all, or any other kind of experience that could be said to constitute the understanding.

Nor are such mental images sufficient to my understanding a sentence. Any image might cross my mind, or I might feel something when I hear or read a sentence, yet I still might not understand what I have heard or read. Wittgenstein says:

> Suppose that a picture does come before your mind when you hear the word "cube," say a drawing of a cube. In what sense can this picture fit or fail to fit a use of the word "cube"? (*PI*, sec. 139)

The picture alone lacks what we might call its "method of projection," that is, a *rule* which would connect the image with the use of the word "cube." The image alone cannot tell us how it is to be applied or used. That is, the image cannot tell us *what it means.* According to Wittgenstein, it is no more sufficient grounds for saying "I understand" than would be a drawing or model in front of me:

> What is essential is to see that the same thing can come before our minds when we hear the word and the application still be different. Has it the *same* meaning both times? I think we shall say not. (*PI*, sec. 140)

What, then, does Wittgenstein say understanding is? When do we say of someone that she understands? Wittgenstein wants us to keep in mind that the word "understand" is itself teachable and learnable. A learner, or even a fluent speaker, can make mistakes in applying it and be corrected. Understanding a word signifies an activity that manifests itself in at least three ways: in how one uses the word, in how he responds to its use by others, and in how he shows others its use (Glock 1996, 373). Understanding a sentence or a rule is an ability to do something, such as get a yellow ball when asked, recite the alphabet, continue a number series, translate a Greek passage, help carry on a discussion. Understanding a language is knowing what expressions of the language mean, that is, knowing how to use them in accordance with the rules for their use, even if these rules cannot be made explicit by the speaker. ("That sounds wrong to me" is enough of an indication of the speaker's suspicion that a rule is being broken.) This requires knowing the difference between right and wrong ways of using words and gestures and tones of voice. In this sense, understanding is an ability to do something in accordance with rules.

You might say that this still does not sound like enough, for mere activity in accordance with a rule can't be equivalent to following a rule. If the difference between the two does not consist in what goes on in the mind or brain, then what is the difference? Anything that acts in a regular way acts according to some rule, even if it acts without understanding, as perhaps the heavenly bodies do. To address this concern, Wittgenstein once again calls our attention to the social nature of language and other rule-governed activities. We use rules as standards of correctness in practice. The relation between a rule and what counts as following a rule is given by how we employ the rule, how we would explain or justify our use of it, and how we would teach it or learn it or correct misapplications of it:

> A rule for the use of an expression and the acts that [follow] it are not independent of each other, but two sides of the same [conceptual] coin, two aspects of a *practice*. . . . There is no such thing as a rule without a technique of application that is manifest in action. . . . The phenomenon of language is part of the web of human action and interaction in the world. It presupposes as its stable framework certain pervasive regularities of the physical world and of human nature. Understanding a language is not a mental state but a capacity or array of capacities to employ symbols in accord with rules in a myriad of speech activities. This conception of language as *Praxis*, this emphasis upon the pri-

macy of the deed is a fundamental aspect of Wittgenstein's philosophy. (Baker and Hacker 1983, 250)[23]

All this may be true, you say, but can language be simply rule-following language-behavior, which Wittgenstein's emphasis on action and practice might lead one to think? What about my inner life, my thoughts, feelings, hopes? What about my experiences of aspect changes, as when the Necker cube flips or I finally see the man in the picture-puzzle or my friend in the crowd? I know that *something* has changed while what is outside has stayed the same. These are obviously private experiences, you say, because others may not see "what I see" though they are looking along with me. They are mine or yours, and Wittgenstein hasn't yet told us how language as activity can have any connection to them or how we can talk about them at all with any but subjective certainty.

Wittgenstein takes this question very seriously. His response lies at the heart of his reflections on language, psychology, philosophy, and seeing aspects. He asks:

[C]ould we . . . imagine a language in which a person could write down or give vocal expression to his inner experiences—his feelings, moods, and the rest—for his private use?—Well, can't we do so in our ordinary language?—But this is not what I mean. The individual words of this language are to refer to what can only be known to the person speaking; to his immediate private sensation. So another person cannot understand the language. (*PI*, sec. 243)

The question can also be put this way: How can you ever come to talk with someone about your sensations and thoughts—about your inner life in all its complexity—if they are fully yours and if language depends on what we all can share, as Wittgenstein has implied? Isn't it obvious that I cannot express what is essentially inner by means of words whose meanings rely entirely on what is outer? The question can also be applied to recognizing changing aspects, where what is outer (the picture, the faces, and so forth) does not change, but something else does. This something is a radically inner something, we might at first think. Wittgenstein believes these deep concerns rest on a deep misunderstanding of how we actually use words. In his argument against the possibility of private language, he uses pain as an example, but he means to include sensations in general, visual impressions (*PI*, sec. 227), imaginings (*PI*, sec. 280), and states of mind and mental processes (*PI*, secs. 290, 305–6).

Wittgenstein believes that certain philosophical and psychological conceptions of self-consciousness and the mind are incoherent. This is especially true of knowledge of other minds and what goes on in them. The incoherence rests on a fundamental misunderstanding of the way language works and what exactly we can do with words. Our attempts to understand mental life—our own and others'—are undermined, not fostered, by an Augustinian view of language, namely, that the purpose of words is to name and of sentences to describe. Ordinary language is okay when we let it do its work and don't try to neaten it up, summarize it, and extract theories from it. Otherwise we can unwittingly let ourselves be led into confusion. We know our way around perfectly well until asked to draw a map. Then we let the difficulties we have with figuring out how all the roads and landmarks are situated infect the confidence we otherwise ordinarily feel.

As WILLARD IS LEAVING his logic class, he runs into his friend, Galen, who asks him how he is. Willard: Okay, except for this pain in my shoe. Galen: In your shoe? Willard: Well, yes. We were just learning about logical syllogisms in class. I have a pain in my foot, and my foot is in my shoe. Therefore, I have a pain in my shoe. Galen: Ha, ha.

When Galen, who is not so clear-thinking as his friend, tries to retell the joke, no one finds it funny. He forgets exactly how it goes but remembers its gist. He begins the syllogism with "My foot hurts," thinking that this means the same as what Martin had said. And it does, except for its "grammar." And on that hangs the point of the joke.

WITTGENSTEIN BEGINS HIS DISCUSSION of "private experience" by asking his interlocutor,

> [I]n what way are my sensations *private*?—Well, only I can know whether I am really in pain; another person can only surmise it.—In one way this is wrong, and in another nonsense. . . . It can't be said of

me at all (except perhaps as a joke) that I *know* I am in pain. What is it supposed to mean—except perhaps that I *am* in pain?

Other people cannot be said to learn of my sensations *only* from my behavior,—for I cannot be said to learn them [at all]. I *have* them. The truth is: It makes sense to say about other people that they doubt whether I am in pain; but not to say it about myself. (*PI*, sec. 246)

If by "private" I mean that I have a knowledge of my sensations available only to me and that others only surmise or infer my sensations while I can know them, then I have committed a grammatical or conceptual error. I have misdrawn the map of my own neighborhood. Since it makes no sense for me to say I doubt that I am in pain, then it makes no sense for me to say that I know that I am in pain.[24] Where there can be no grounds for doubt, neither can there be grounds for knowledge, says Wittgenstein, and he believes our ordinary way of speaking accords with this. We can always ask someone who claims to know something, "How do you know?" This is a call for his grounds or reasons, just as we might request reasons when someone expresses doubt. The expression of my grounds for knowing something can take many forms. Sometimes "because I have done this many times before" is sufficient, other times we require more, or something different. Each case needs to be considered separately, with sensitivity to how words are actually used in ordinary language, which is, after all, the language we learned. Wittgenstein does not suggest that we revise the way we ordinarily speak about doubt and knowledge. Rather, he describes what he takes to be the actual use of words in the language-games in which they are at home. We can rely on our linguistic intuitions to confirm this by acknowledging what sounds right and what sounds funny. In describing the use of the words "doubting" and "knowing," Wittgenstein is describing the concepts of doubting and knowing themselves. We, too, would recognize this if we paid attention to how we use the words in ordinary life and how we might teach others how to use them, or how we correct them when they are wrong. (Even the skeptic does not teach his young child, "Perhaps that's a chair."[25]) Words are learned within families of similar and contrasting words; they are learned in relation to their various opposites. I learn "knowing" and "doubting" together. Where there is no room for one, there is no room for the other. The head of a coin may be forcibly separated from its tail, but the result is only to remove both pieces from circulation:

> When I talk about language (words, sentences, etc.) I must speak the language of every day. Is this language somehow too coarse and material for what we want to say? *Then how is another one to be constructed?*—And how strange that we should be able to do anything at all with the one we have! . . . Your questions refer to words; so I have to talk about words. You say: the point isn't the word, but its meaning, and you think of the meaning as a thing of the same kind as the word, though also different from the word. Here the word, there the meaning. The money, and the cow that you can buy with it. (But contrast: money, and its use.) (*PI*, sec. 120)

While language is doing its work—while we are at work with it— we generally do not make the kinds of mistakes that might lead a philosopher to suggest that while she *knows* she is in pain, she can only infer that others are.[26] In jokes we laugh at such mistakes. That reminds me of this exchange between Blondie and Dagwood:

> Blondie: Oh, I feel so blumpy today!
> Dagwood: "Blumpy?" That word's not even in the dictionary!
> Blondie: That's because no one has ever felt blumpy before! (Fann 1971, 109)

As soon as I disengage the gears of ordinary language and allow its engine to idle, I'm tempted to imagine that when I have a pain I possess some *thing* to which no one else can have access and that my inner life is available only to me for my own viewing. But the truth is that "no one can have my pain" is a rule of grammar, just as is "no one can play solitaire with a friend."

A thought that may have occurred to you at some time or other offers another avenue of approach to clarifying the connection between language and our inner lives. Wittgenstein has his interlocutor say the following:

> The essential thing about private experience is really not that each person possesses his own exemplar, but that nobody knows whether other

people have *this* or something *else*. The assumption would then be possible—though unverifiable—that one section of mankind had one sensation of red and another section another. (*PI*, sec. 272)[27]

Wittgenstein believes that the tempting suggestion of the possibility of an unverifiable "inverted spectrum" is not empirically false, but rather conceptually incoherent. It is a paradigm for bewitchment that can be worked on our intellects by language and by theories of language. We can acquire a perspicuous view of one part of the landscape of our language by understanding why the alleged possibility of an inverted spectrum is no possibility at all. Our success will also relieve us of a pack of other temptations that can make themselves felt when we let language take a vacation.[28] Surely, though, it makes sense to say that the road sign that I see as green you might see as red.[29] After all, I can imagine the same sign as being red, and when I do, I am imagining what you are seeing, though I cannot see it that way myself. Of course we can never know this, because we both learned to use color words in basically the same way, and so we now both call the color of that sign "green." Wittgenstein says this is as if "when I uttered the word I cast a sidelong glance at the private sensations, as it were in order to say to myself: I know all right what I mean by it" (*PI*, sec. 274). But "imagine someone's saying: 'I know how tall I am!' and laying his hand on top of his head to prove it" (*PI*, sec. 279). Children sometimes do just that until they learn that they really have not shown how tall they are by this charade. We make no use at all of a concept of private height, which each person might have for himself and which is independent of measured height. The claim that my private sensation of green can be known only by me is analogous to the claim that I am *this* tall. Just like that claim, it is not in dispute because it is a misuse of language. One can't accomplish anything—except perhaps to make a joke—by such utterances. Both statements do no work but still make a lot of noise, like a car engine revving in neutral.

Wittgenstein continues:

Look at the blue of the sky and say to yourself "How blue the sky is!"—When you do it spontaneously—without philosophical intentions—the idea never crosses your mind that this impression of color belongs only to *you*. . . . And if you point at anything as you say the words you point at the sky. (*PI*, sec. 275)

But how is it even possible for us to be tempted to think that we use a word to *mean* at one time the color known to everyone—and at another the "visual impression" which I am getting *now*? (*PI*, sec. 277)

The temptation arises in part because of misleading analogies in the forms of our expressions. These analogies don't bother us when we let language do its ordinary business, but when we tamper with them or inspect them too closely, they can lead us into trouble, that is, to philosophy or to humor. If we allow ourselves to think of "attending to a sensation" as an inner pointing (as one might consider introspection to be an "inner inspection"), we might then begin to mix the rules of one language-game with those of another. We do, after all, often direct our attention to things people point out to us. Even the phrase "direct your attention to" leads us to imagine attending as having a direction. I turn my head and look. If in attending I am pointing, then by attending I can name, just as by pointing to something I can tell you what it is called. It would seem I could thereby give my sensation a place in my private language. Wittgenstein's argument against the inverted spectrum and private language turns on the impossibility of my pointing to or naming my sensations for my own exclusive use. I can point to someone else, or the traffic sign, or the blue sky, but attending to my sensations is not a kind of pointing, nor a preliminary to naming. My effort to point to my private sensation is a sham, because "to point" and "to name" take their meanings from their use in our language, the language I learned by being taught by others and which in its everyday use is governed by rules of correctness. When my speech is corrected, it is on the basis of what my teacher sees me do, hears me say, and the circumstances in which I do them. He does not correct me on the basis of what is going on in my mind. I can't give a private name to my private sensations for my private use because nobody could have taught me how to do so. If I try to teach myself how to do it, my only rule of correctness is what appears correct to me at the time, and that is no rule at all. No *use* can be made of a private word. The view that words stand for things or ideas lies behind the inverted spectrum puzzle. If my private sensation is a something, I ought to be able to give it a name. (Recall Augustine's account of how he thinks he learned to speak.) I can point to the pain in my foot, can't I? Yes, we say that, but we also say, "my foot hurts," or "it hurts me there." Once we remind ourselves of the different ways we talk about sensations (and by extension about the vast panorama of our inner life), we will be less inclined to consider them objects to which we can privately point, which can be privately named, and which can take their places in a private language.[30]

Wittgenstein compares the idea of a private sensation to a box with something in it. He says:

> Suppose everyone had a box with something in it: we call it a "beetle." No one can look into anyone else's box, and everyone says he knows what a beetle is only by looking at *his* beetle.—Here it would be quite possible for everyone to have something quite different in his box.—But suppose the word 'beetle' had a use in this people's language?—If so it would not be used as the name of a thing. The thing in the box has no place in the language-game at all, not even as a *something*: for the box might even be empty. . . . That is to say: if we construe the grammar of the expression of sensation on the model of "object and name" the object drops out of consideration as irrelevant. (*PI*, sec. 293)

If the word "beetle" has a use in these people's language, what is the use? Can the word be used as the name of some object, namely, what is in each person's box? Well, "beetle" does not get its use from any identity or similarity between the contents of the boxes because the contents are not shared. Whatever is in each person's box can be anything, even something that changes constantly. It can even be nothing at all. This is not to say that the boxes *are* all empty, but rather that as far as the usefulness of what is in them, they might as well be empty. It is at least imaginable that they all are empty and yet that "beetle" still plays the very same role in their language. So "beetle" can't refer to any object.

The parallel with sensations is exact. "Sensation" has a use in our language. Can it be as the name of some object, namely, what each person privately *senses*? Well, "sensation" does not derive its use from any identity or similarity between different people's sensations, because these sensations—whatever they are—are not shared.

What I have might be different from what you have. You might have nothing at all. Yet "sensation" still plays a perfectly useful role in our language. So it cannot be as the name of some object: "[T]he object drops out of consideration as irrelevant." When we are tempted to say that the sensation must be something that we *have*, we ought to remind ourselves that we have thus far said nothing, unless we go on to say what is involved in this having: "To have" doesn't always mean "to possess," just as "with" does not always mean "to accompany." It is "as if I were to say of someone: 'He *has* something. But I don't know whether it is money, or debts, or an empty cash register'" (*PI*, sec. 294).

Wittgenstein believes a private language makes no sense even if I am concerned simply about talking to myself. My inner life is essentially shareable, and it can be mine only if it is possible for others to know about it. The real incoherence of the private linguist is that he cannot achieve what he thinks he is achieving—namely, referring (even for himself) to a private sensation (or private inner life). What gives the lie to one who claims he can construct a private language is that whatever use he makes in the future of a sign he creates now (say one to denote *this* particular sensation) will be correct. He cannot in any ordinary sense make a mistake. This suggests that private language is not rule-governed, and to the extent that language must be so, a private language can't be a language at all.[31]

Before resuming the thread of our investigation of aspects, it might be helpful to list the most salient features of Wittgenstein's thinking about language as I have outlined it in this section:

1) *The meaning of a word is its use in our language.* When we want to know what a word like "seeing" means, we ought to look to its use in actual circumstances, and not presuppose that these uses will necessarily fit into a neat, circumscribed definition. To know what counts as seeing requires that we lay out, in all its complexity, how "seeing" words are used. (A good dictionary can help if used with care, but our own instincts about what "sounds right" usually prove more reliable.) The meaning of a word is not an ethereal intermediary that connects word and object. In this sense, words are like tools—they *are* tools—and their functions are "as diverse as the functions of these objects" (*PI*, sec. 11).[32]

2) *Language-games* are the contexts in which we do what we do with words and the rules by which we use them. Just as a game is an activity, so too words get their life and meaning from how they are used. These activities are rule-governed, just as the activities we call games are. We might not always be able to articulate the rules governing the language-game (or games) in which we are engaged. Still, just as we might know how to do a complex dance but be unable to say how to do it, so too most of us speak our native language with a fluency that transcends our ability to articulate the very rules we are following. The rules of language, while arbitrary, are not whimsical. Nor are they laws of nature: they are invented, not discovered. But they allow us to operate in the natural and social world. The variety of language-games is vast. Wittgenstein mentions the games of "lying" (*PI*, sec. 249), of "repenting" (*PI*, sec. 190), of "physical objects" and "sense impressions" (*RPP I*, 289), and others. All are "patterns, strands, moments that go into the making up of our conversations or even into the making up of a single utterance" (Baz 2000, 97).[33]

3) *Language is taught to children and learned by them.* Children are not born speaking their native language. They must learn that there are right and wrong ways of speaking, which is not to say true and false ways, but sensible and nonsensical ways. When a child makes an error in speaking, she can be corrected. What is corrected is what the child *says* in a given context. Sometimes when we are stuck on how to think of the use of a word (like "consciousness" or "thinking" or "time"), we can ask ourselves: How does one teach a child how to use these and related words? In what contexts are these words "at home"? "[I]f the words 'language,' 'experience,' 'world,' have a use, it must be as humble a one as that of the words 'table,' 'lamp,' 'door'" (*PI*, sec. 97).[34]

4) *Family Resemblance.* When we use the same word for a range of phenomena, we should not assume that all uses possess some common feature by virtue of which that one word is always used. Once we have laid out the various uses of a word, we most often find instead that these are connected by family resemblance, shared traits but not necessarily any one trait possessed by all, except the family

name. In this sense the search for, say, what consciousness is will not result in a definition ("the what it is to be consciousness"), but rather something more like a map of or guide to the various contexts in which we find the word and related words and the uses they have in those contexts. ("He has lost consciousness." "Were you conscious of her presence in the room?" "It was a conscious decision on my part.") This may seem unsatisfactory to those who want to "get behind the words to the essence," but for Wittgenstein, "essence is expressed by grammar" (*PI*, sec. 371), that is, by how a word is used.

5) *"Private language" is impossible.* We cannot talk meaningfully to ourselves alone about anything—sensations, perceptions, feelings, thoughts—that cannot *in principle* be shared with others. We have no other tools to express what we feel and think than the words we were taught in a social environment. Our language follows rules. We cannot give rules to ourselves, correct our own errors, or acknowledge our own achievements. Whatever we thought was correct would be correct and whatever we thought wrong, wrong. There can be no private language because the very notion of it abolishes the sense of a standard of correctness that is required by any language. This does not mean that we can't talk to ourselves, keep our feelings hidden, or pretend in our natural language. We can, and do.

In the next section, we'll look at exactly what Wittgenstein says about aspects and why the work of psychologists on seeing ambiguous figures, faces, and puzzle pictures fails to address an issue critical to Wittgenstein: the place of seeing aspects in our *conceptual* world.

C. How We See Things with Words

I want you to perform a brief experiment. First read it through from start to finish before beginning. (You'll see why.) Close your eyes. Move your head to some other position than it is in while you are reading. Now open your eyes and say exactly what you see. When I did this experiment, I saw drapes, a radiator, a piece of wall, a desk lamp with a pleated shade, and, you know, other things, just as you might have seen. But having gone to graduate school in philosophy and having read David Hume's *Treatise on Human Nature* and works on "sense-data" by writers like G. E. Moore (1873–1958) and A. J. Ayer (1910–1989), I quickly grew suspicious of my simple-minded description.[35] Perhaps what I was really seeing were shapes and colors arranged in a certain way. The real object of my sight, I wondered, might be simply those. And having studied some psychology and physiology, I know a bit about how our visual apparatus works, with light streaming into the eye and falling on the retina, producing electrical currents that flow to the optic nerve, lateral geniculate nucleus, and then to the visual cortex in my brain. I thought maybe it was merely colored light that I was really seeing. The drapes, wall, radiator, and so forth are inferences that the brain or mind makes somehow, based on the light input. But then (you can see that I have read too much) I remembered that light consists of electromagnetic waves or packets of energy called photons. (No one seems to know for sure.) These have no color, and they are certainly not shaped like drapes and radiators. Perhaps then I was really seeing electromagnetic waves or photons. By this point, I didn't know what I was really seeing. Wasn't I also seeing objects that serve particular human purposes? They are called "drapes" because they drop down or can hide things, and they are called "radiators" because they radiate heat, though the one I looked at was not doing so then. To complicate things further, I realize that the objects I've seen are also products of human labor, "congealed labor," as Marx calls them, products of civilization.[36] If my eyes happened to light on a drawing of the Necker cube or the duck-rabbit, or a family portrait, my problems would be further deepened. What do I see in these cases? "Colored patches" seems inadequate, "civilization" seems extravagant, and simply "pictures" seems to sidestep the question. And so I am left wondering if "what I see" has any single complete and correct description at all.

Wittgenstein asks:

> What is the philosophical importance of [experiencing an aspect]? Is it really so much odder than everyday visual experiences? Does it cast an unexpected light on them?—In the description of it (the) problems about the concept of seeing come to a head. (*LWPP I*, 172)

What problems does he have in mind? As the experiment we just performed suggests, one problem is simply figuring out what I see when I see anything at all. What is the proper object of seeing? It's not so easy to say, and we may want to throw up our hands and say that all of these objects might, simultaneously, be what we see: "It is here quite as it is with talk of physical objects and sense impressions. We have *two* language-games, and their mutual relations are complicated. If one tries to describe these relations in a simple fashion, one goes wrong" (*RPP I*, 289). Another problem he might have in mind concerns mental images, visual impressions, and an inner picture. When we open our eyes and see, do we always have a mental image in consciousness? What is the connection between what's out there and what's in here—that is, in my brain or mind? Do I *see* mental images the way I see pictures? And how in the world could *this* (my mental image) be produced by *this* (my brain)?! What can psychological experiments tell us about all this? "Where do we get the concept of the 'content' of an experience from? Well, the content of an experience is the private object, the sense-datum, the 'object' that I grasp immediately with the mental eye, ear, etc. The inner picture.—But where does one find one needs this concept?" (*RPP I*, 109). A third problem arises when I begin to think of the connection between what I see and how I describe what I see. How are what I see and what I say related? Is my saying a *report* of my seeing, something that follows the actual visual experience and can be transmitted to others through speech, as a picture can be sent over the Internet?[37] These are some of the problems Wittgenstein has in mind. He thinks that thinking hard about seeing aspects and changes of aspect will help us approach these questions about seeing in general with a more cautious eye.

When we experience a change of aspect, something strikes us. When we first notice that the duck-rabbit is an ambiguous picture, that it can be seen either as a duck or as a rabbit, we might say, "Aha! Now it's a rabbit!" or something like that. My words express my surprise; they express that something has struck me, something not entirely in my control. "I want to say that the natural, primitive expression of the experience of an aspect would be such an exclamation; it might also be a lighting up of the eyes. (Something strikes me!)" (*RPP I*, 862). If I thought the picture itself had changed, or if I saw a rabbit run across my path when I was not expecting anything of the sort, I might be surprised, but there my surprise could be traced to something's having really changed in the world. In the case of a change in aspect, however, "What is strange is really the surprise; the question 'How is it possible!' It might be expressed by: 'The *same* and *yet* not the same'" (*LWPP I*, 174).[38] We ought to find this strange because our experience of the change is one of *seeing*, yet of seeing an unchanging object. I am surprised by the dual nature of the experience, by my awareness that there both is a change and is not a change. In normal situations when the object I'm looking at changes, I'm not surprised to see a change. Similarly, when it does not change, I'm not surprised not to see it change. Some optical illusions rely on apparent changes in the object of sight when we know there can be no change in the figure we're observing. What distinguishes these illusion-experiences from experiences of aspect changes is that in the case of illusions I can discover what is really on the paper and trace what I "see" to essentially subjective sources. The dark shadows flickering at the intersections of the white lines in Hermann's grid (fig. 18) are an example. Something is happening in the observer's retina to produce this illusion. In the case of noticing a change in aspect, the situation is very different. There is no "real" object other than the ambiguous one, no third face which could be the resemblance between the two faces I see, or the one I see and the one I remember. All I seem to be able to say is that what I see is *there* and *not there*. To help describe my experience, I could make exact drawings of what I saw before and what I saw afterwards, but these drawings would be of no help because they would be congruent.

In the case of the duck-rabbit, I could point to pictures of rabbits and say that I also saw something like that, but not in addition or next to it. A three-dimensional model that could be shifted in space might serve as an aid to describing what I see in a drawing of the Necker cube. The puzzle picture, the one that after the dawning of its new aspect looks like a medieval representation of Jesus, could be supplemented by a real picture of Jesus in that style. In chapter one, it was a verbal description of what I saw that supplemented the original picture and helped to reveal its hidden aspect. Even then, not all people will have seen the human form. They might have been helped by a real picture. These are the best sorts of descriptions one can give of what one sees. They might all still be inadequate to help someone who does not experience the change of aspect. He might in a sense see exactly what I see, namely, the drawing in front of us, but not see what I really see: the rabbit, the cube in its new orientation, Jesus. Seeing a resemblance between two faces is more difficult to supplement. I cannot point to some third thing and say that in addition to the two faces, I also see something like *this*. Yet when such a resemblance strikes me, I experience a change of aspect.[39] Nothing has changed, yet I see something new. In a sense something new has come into my world, something not illusory or hallucinatory or purely imaginary, but rather an object of real seeing.[40] If you can't see it, and you are not blind or don't misunderstand my words, there is no method for getting you to see it. By contrast, if I were standing on a hill and could see a town stretched out below, in which I noticed a church steeple, I could get you to see the steeple by putting you in my place and directing your eyes with the help of landmarks we both could see. I could physically point you in the right direction, tell you what I see around the steeple, even set up a telescope or tube through which you could look. Nothing similarly objective can be done with aspect changes. Because of that, we want to locate the change when we experience a change in aspect in the imagination of the looker. This seems right. Many acts of the imagination are voluntary; they are a form of thinking. I can ask you to imagine being at the beach on a beautiful day, or shoveling snow on an ugly day, and you can do it. You can often imagine what you are asked to imagine. Even when you cannot succeed in imagining something, it makes sense to ask you to try. If someone stops you on the street and asks you for directions, you may try to give them, but fail for any of several reasons. So, too, in noticing changes of aspect. There are ways to *try* to see the duck-rabbit as a rabbit or to see the Necker cube flip. The imagination is always engaged when we are seeing aspects, and that is why we think of the experience of a change of aspect as something at least partly subjective, or inside me.

Aspect changes, however, also strike us as real seeing. It is as if the concept of *seeing* rises to the surface of our description of what is going on when we see an aspect. "Seeing" fits; any description that falls short of "seeing" just doesn't work. I don't imagine an aspect, or hallucinate it, or dream it. Aspects aren't illusions because we know that when we experience a change of aspect, we are not being taken in or deceived. In fact, just as in normal seeing, we feel that we have come to know or understand something when we notice an aspect. Real seeing, however, is not voluntary, as aspect-seeing can be. I cannot at will see whatever I want. I cannot look at this patch of green grass and see it as red, nor can I resist seeing the duck-rabbit as a rabbit when it is shown to me in a field of rabbits: "The dagger which Macbeth sees before him is not an imagined dagger. One can't take an image for reality nor things seen for things imaged. But this is not because they are so dissimilar" (*RPP II*, 85). It is because imagining is voluntary, while seeing and hallucinating are not. The language-games played with all these are different, though they are closely related. (In *Don Quixote* by Miguel Cervantes [1547–1616] Don Quixote sees giants where Sancho Panza sees windmills. It makes all the difference in the world to our understanding of the story whether we think Don Quixote is lying, hallucinating, or seeing an aspect.) My expression of a change of aspect is the expression of seeing something, in fact, *seeing* it *as*. The *seeing* is the involuntary part, the *as* is the voluntary part that engages the imagination or thought: "Hence the flashing of an aspect on us seems half visual experience, half thought" (*PI*, sec. 168).

Wittgenstein distinguishes "change in aspect" from "continuous seeing of an aspect." If I am shown the duck-rabbit and see only a rabbit in it, he tells us:

> I should not have answered the question "What do you see here?" by saying "Now I am seeing it as a picture-rabbit." I should simply have described my perception, just as if I had said "I see a red circle over there."—Nevertheless someone else could have said of me: "He is seeing the figure as a picture-rabbit." (*PI*, sec. 166)

It would have made no more sense for me to describe what I'm seeing by saying "Now I see it as a picture-rabbit" than it would for me to describe a knife and fork by saying "Now I see them as a knife and fork." If someone else were to say of me, "Now he sees it as a knife and fork," all that one could assume was that in some contexts this knife and this fork could be seen as something else. That is certainly possible, though in ordinary circumstances, such a remark would be nonsense, or perhaps part of a joke. I cannot say that I see the knife as a knife, or the duck-rabbit as a rabbit, when that is all I see, without implying that I know that it is possible for me to see the knife as something else, or the duck-rabbit as something else. We don't ordinarily see things as themselves. (This is a grammatical point.) The language-game I play with seeing-as does not permit this sort of move. That is, it sounds funny to us and somewhat suspect: "If you say 'Now it's a face for me,' we can ask: 'What change are you alluding to?'" (*PI*, p. 195). But if you say simply, "It's a face," then my question evaporates. I don't know what to do with an aspect-expression when uttered by someone who cannot see the two aspects of the duck-rabbit, or who only sees the knife and fork or the face in the usual way. His remark idles, it doesn't move, though it has the sound of moving. If someone else, however, could say he is seeing it as a rabbit, he would be implying that he knows the duck-rabbit is an ambiguous figure, and that he himself has seen both aspects. He might even believe it's possible to lead the other to experience a change of aspect. The picture itself seems to contain both aspects, but one seems hidden or perhaps invisible to one of the observers. In experiencing a change in aspect, we notice that what we had been viewing was itself an aspect. This is what others knew and I did not.[41]

A change of aspect has duration because it is an experience. It makes sense to ask, for example, "How long did the resemblance between the faces strike you?" It would be odd to respond that the resemblance has struck me continuously since I first noticed it, even if I have now incorporated it into my way of looking at the faces. The aspect finds its place in my ordinary perceptions. It becomes itself ordinary, no longer striking or astonishing. Some of you have no doubt already come to this position with regard to the puzzle picture of the medieval Jesus (fig. 22). When I now see the picture, I cannot see it as a puzzle. I see in it only the figure, clear as day. But I know others will not see that at first. Am I seeing an aspect of the picture, now that I cannot see it in its original, disorganized condition? Well, there is a way in which what is at first surprising or new becomes less so but doesn't disappear, as the dawn is to the sun during the day. "I should like to say that what dawns here lasts only as long as I am occupied with the object in a particular way. ('See, it's looking!')— 'I should like to say'—and is it so?—Ask yourself 'For how long am I struck by a thing?'—For how long do I find it *new*?" (*PI*, p. 210).

How I express what I see when I see an aspect has all the world to do with the place of aspect-seeing in our pantheon of concepts. How I express what I see tells us what I see and what I call seeing. Let's say I'm looking through a telescope at the moon and my friend asks what I see. I tell him, the moon. I can let him look and he will see what I was seeing. I don't even need to say anything, because in a very real sense he will see just what I did. But if I say that I see the man in the moon, then putting him in my place might not allow him to see what I saw. He might not see the moon as a face. I could draw a face for him or tell him what I see and let him look again. If he comes to see what I see, if he sees the man in the moon where he did not see it before, how exactly did my expression of what I saw (either the face drawing or my words) help him to see? What is the relationship of my expression to his seeing, and what is its relationship to my own seeing?

When Wittgenstein talks about the experience of a change of aspect, he calls attention to the fact that someone might be able to figure out that this picture can serve as either a picture-duck or a picture-rabbit, or that in this painting, the horse is to be taken as galloping. Yet for the one who must figure these things out, the aspects do not dawn, they do not strike her or surprise her.[42] To experience a change in aspect is precisely not to figure it out, but to see it. We have many different experiences, and there are characteristic expressions for them. When I have a bad toothache, I might grimace, put my hand to my face near the painful tooth, moan, complain, and so forth. Similarly when one is experiencing other kinds of sensations, there may be expressions that normally accompany them. They have duration and content. Visual impressions are also experiences. Experiences have duration and content, and can be described in words or by pictures or even gestures: "'I just saw a shadow flitting by.' Isn't that the expression of a visual experience?" (*LWPP I*, 556).[43]

When children learn to use the words that will come to express their experiences of sensations and of visual impressions, they can only do so by being taught the correct use of those words by another person. They do not invent words for themselves to express their toothache or describe what they see. When they make the gestures characteristic of toothache, a parent might tell them how to talk about their experience. The teacher does not feel the pain of the child, whatever that could mean. He or she observes behavior and teaches correct use accordingly: "A child has hurt himself and he cries, and then adults talk to him and teach him exclamations and, later, sentences. They teach the child new pain-behavior. 'So you are saying the word "pain" really means crying?'—On the contrary: the verbal expression of pain replaces crying and does not describe it" (*PI*, sec. 244). If we think of pain as a *something* the child has in his tooth, like a filling—or something he has in a box, like a beetle— then we might be inclined to say that the parent can only infer from the child's behavior that she has a pain in her tooth. (We know that humans can later learn to simulate pain.) When we look at how the word "pain" is taught, however, in what circumstances and how it is learned, we really can't discover any inferences at work at all. Try to imagine that the young child showing all the signs of toothache is really not in pain, but is inwardly smiling. We just can't do it: "But isn't it still *possible* that the child gives all these signs, yet feels no pain?" What can we do with this thought? Doesn't it have merely the appearance of sense in this context? "But if we can imagine this possibility, doesn't that tell us that pain and these behaviors are different?" Of course they are different. Pain is not the same as screaming. But neither is it something else, like a cause. Pain and pain-behavior are different because the latter is the expression of the former, not because it is an effect or a symptom of it.

If I want you to have the same sensation I have had, for instance, that which comes from a pin prick, I prick you with a pin. I put you as it were in my place. I know that you have felt the same thing I have when you respond more or less the way I did. If you do not respond that way—say a pin prick makes you giggle—not only would I be surprised, but I also would unable to teach you how to use the expression "how a pin prick feels" the way others can use it. If you do react in the normal way, you also learn what the sensation is, and your behavior is the criterion by which others determine that you had this experience. (You didn't use criteria in your own case because you didn't *determine* that you had the experience. You had it.) Once a child has learned language, his behavior can also become simply what he says. That is, the words *replace* the pain behavior.

Let's now consider ordinary visual experiences. How do we know someone is having visual experiences, and how do we teach a child to talk about them? We know someone *has* visual experiences, that is, is not blind, by how he makes his way around. If he can move around a room with confidence, if he can avoid obstacles, pick up objects, be drawn toward a distant light, then we say that he sees. All these activities involve being able to do something: get around. This can be done well or badly. That is, a judgment can be made that some-one has correctly navigated a space, picked up a cup, or moved in the direction of a light. There are purely neurological tests that can be performed, too, which don't involve any sort of activity, but require merely a response to a stimulus, such as pupil dilation in the sud-den presence of a bright light. A baby can be tested in this way before it has learned to do much of anything. Still, that we can see fully is expressed by our ability to do something, to be masters of a kind of activity. When a child learns a language, it also learns how the word "seeing" and related words are used. That is, it learns "what seeing is," which for Wittgenstein is equivalent to "what is called 'seeing.'" It learns this along with the description of what it sees. It doesn't first learn what seeing is and then learn about the objects of sight. When it learns that it is "seeing a cup," it learns both what a cup is and what seeing is.

The criteria for someone's seeing something are what is there and where he is. That is, it is enough for us to say that a sighted person sees the church steeple if it is actually there and if he is in a position to see it.[44] If I want him to see what I have seen when I looked out at the steeple, all I need do is put him in my place and he will see it. That's how this language-game with seeing works. I know he sees what I see because these conditions are met. If I want to see what he sees, I do the same: I put myself in his place and I see the steeple. If both conditions are satisfied but he cannot respond in ways that show he is seeing, something is wrong with *him*, with his vision. If I take his place and don't see what he said he did, then apart from the possibility that he is lying or hallucinating, I can conclude only that either the steeple is no longer there or that I'm not in the right place. I don't conclude that I am blind, because the two criteria I use to judge that *he* sees are not criteria for me. I don't use criteria in my own case. That is, it would not be correct for me to say that I *know* that I see the steeple. This could mean no more than that I see the steeple. "I know" adds nothing in my own case.

What's important about all this is that in teaching others how to talk about seeing, it is not their *seeing* that we observe and to which we respond. We respond to what they *do*. In a sense seeing is not a *phenomenon*. It is not something we observe, not something that appears apart from the expressions of seeing. In teaching the concept of seeing, there is no way to separate the seeing from the doing. If a child does not behave in a certain way, she cannot learn what seeing is and we cannot correctly say that she is seeing at all. The child's actions justify our saying that she sees. These actions include what she says. (During an eye exam, our acting consists mainly of saying.) I can also express what I see by a picture; but this does not mean that what I see is a picture, any more than what I see is words because I can express it in words.

To learn how to use "seeing" words, I must be taught by others. Their teaching is based on what *they* see of both me and what else is around them (like the steeple). Wittgenstein's argument against a private language precludes the possibility that a precocious child might succeed in teaching himself what seeing consists in, entirely independently of what others say. All he would be able to do is to say what he is inclined to about one experience and another, with no possibility of correction or guidance. Nothing he said to himself could be wrong, and therefore nothing he said to himself could be right. Not even he himself could know what he was seeing unless he had mastered how to use the words associated with both seeing and the ordinary objects of sight. This mastery, this ability to get around in a room and in language without bumping into things, is a condition for his seeing at all. The mastery is not a symptom of seeing, nor an effect of it, but a criterion for it. If in the absence of such mastery we insisted on saying that someone was sighted, we would be changing the meaning of what it is to see. The ability and the experience go hand in hand, because of how we teach and learn how to do things with words.

It might seem odd that a logical condition for having a visual experience is mastery of a technique. We would not say the same about the experience of pain, for example. The characteristic expressions of pain are pain-reactions—grimacing, moaning, and so forth—that eventually are replaced in part by our words. No technique is involved in those reactions. Ordinary visual perception is something like that, too, but the responses are more in line with using an ability than reacting to a stimulus. That is why we say that people see better or worse. This ability is not something we have in addition to seeing, as I said earlier, but is part and parcel of it. We detect colorblindness, for example, by showing someone a card with a pattern in a color and asking him to say what he sees, that is, to do something. If he cannot, we conclude that he is colorblind. "But isn't it possible," you may counter, "that psychologists will be able to determine color blindness without asking someone to do anything? Then there would be a sort of seeing (or non-seeing) detached from mastery of a technique." It may be true that all and only colorblind people show a certain activity (or lack) in an area of the brain when shown a test card or stimulated in some other way. This would be interesting to learn. But what we *mean* by color blindness depends on what people can and can't do. The neurologist may have located the cause of color blindness, but he hasn't yet said what color blindness is. And in fact if someone exhibited this brain activity, but reacted normally on a test when he had to respond, we would accept the results of the visual test, not the brain data.

Things get really interesting when we turn our attention to aspect-seeing and experiencing a change of aspect. The experience of a change of aspect requires mastery of a technique in every case. Most often this technique is the ability to speak a language. What we see and what we say are so intimately connected in the case of aspects that we can no more separate them than we can separate thought from words or the smile from the Cheshire cat. And yet we are forced to consider the experience of a change of aspect to be genuine seeing, even though seeing as we normally talk about it need not involve language at all. Differences in visual experiences, therefore, need not correspond to differences in what is presented, because our concept of *visual experience* is connected to ways of behaving. That is, the criterion for distinguishing one visual experience from another is not something that goes on inside of me, but what I do. When we see aspects, this behavior is largely linguistic. It is as if our eyes reflect our words. Wittgenstein believes that it takes effort to see how we in fact use words, though we usually use them effortlessly: "We speak, make utterances, but only *later* do we form a picture of their life" (*RPP II*, 486). And that is what he is up to: describing the learning and use of words connected to seeing. This tells us what seeing is. Psychological words in particular form a tangled web leading off in all directions, and we're not well prepared to describe their many uses. Why should we be? These uses are not easily surveyed (see *Z*, 113).

To get a better handle on how we see with words, let's begin with a case of aspect-seeing that doesn't obviously involve language but still requires that someone know his way around. Consider a two-dimensional figure that represents a three-dimensional object (fig. 27). This is a drawing from proposition 16 of Book XIII of Euclid's *Elements*.

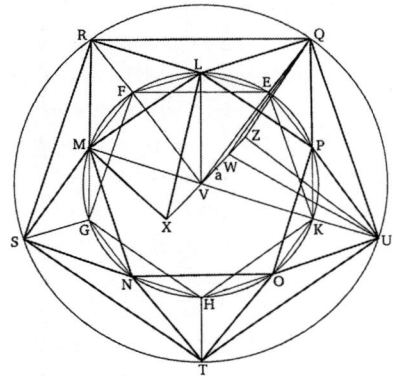

Figure 27. Euclid XIII, 16.

What does it mean for me to look at a drawing in descriptive geometry and say: "I know that this line appears again here, but I can't *see* it like that"? Does it mean a lack of familiarity in operating with the drawing, that I don't "know my way about" too well?—This familiarity is certainly one of our criteria. What tells us that someone is seeing the drawing three-dimensionally is a certain kind of "knowing one's way about." Certain gestures, for instance, which indicate the three-dimensional relations: fine shades of behavior (*PI*, p. 204).[45]

What someone says and does—including how he emphasizes certain lines when explaining the drawing or simply drawing with matching colors—tell us that he sees the three-dimensional aspect of the drawing. "But couldn't he *see* the three-dimensional aspect, yet simply not be able to point it out or explain to others how it fits into the entire drawing?" It's certainly true that he might very well see it, yet not be able to get *me* to see it. If, however, he showed none of the characteristic signs of seeing, such as knowing his way around the figure as if it were three-dimensional, we would have no reason—and no right—to say he saw it. If we have no reason, neither does he. His ability to make his way through the figure, to point out this and that, to raise and answer appropriate questions is a criterion for his seeing it as a three-dimensional figure. Whatever is going on with him, it cannot be a case of seeing the figure three-dimensionally if he does not know his way around. Mastery of a technique, being able to do something, is a condition for having this kind of visual experience. Once again, my ability is neither an effect nor a symptom of my seeing, but a criterion for it. It makes it what it is: "Just as in chess a move with the king only takes place within a certain context, and it cannot be removed from this context.—To the concept there corresponds a technique. (The eye smiles only within the face.)" (*RPP II*, 150).

You still might hesitate. "Isn't *seeing* one thing, and *doing* another? Can't I see the picture three-dimensionally without doing anything at all?" And this is right. To be master of a technique is to be *able* to do something, not necessarily to be doing it right now. I must be capable of moving within the figure, talking about its orientation, outlining its faces, even if I don't actually do these things. I, an adult who has learned to do things with lines and words, can *see* without actually engaging my ability to move the pencil a certain way. But if I lacked this ability, it would not make sense to say that I might have seen. The reason is to be found once again in how we teach and learn language. If I had never shown the characteristic signs of seeing flat figures three-dimensionally, I would never have been able to learn how to use words associated with such seeing. My teacher would not have known when to correct me, when to encourage me, how to teach me. I would not be justified—nor would anyone else be justified—in saying that nonetheless I was seeing the drawing three-dimensionally. The language-game that we play in assigning visual experiences to others (and to ourselves) requires that we be able to *do* things in order to be able to *see* things: "Why does it seem so hard to separate *doing* and experiencing?" Wittgenstein asks

(*LWPP I*, 585). We might say it is because they are united in our language and in that part of our natural history related to how we learn to talk and act and think.

When I wanted you to have the same visual experience I had, I put you in my place, literally, and pointed your head toward whatever it was I had been perceiving. What happens when I try to do that with the cases of aspect-seeing we met in chapter one? Consider the duck-rabbit. I show it to you in ordinary light, your eyes are open, and so forth. The criteria for ordinary seeing are met, and so I want to say that you see something. But these criteria are no longer enough to assure me that you see what I saw. I may have seen only a duck, you may see only a rabbit. I may have seen a duck and then a rabbit, while you see a rabbit and then a duck. Even if we gaze at the picture together, there is no guarantee, as there would be with ordinary seeing, that the two of us see the same thing. I am not inclined to fall back on your inner experience or mental images, which are hidden from me, as an explanation, though I've not ruled them out. It must be possible to teach the use of words like "aspect," "first duck, then rabbit," and so forth. I describe to myself what *I* see in these terms. I know that I didn't invent them. How did I learn them? Somewhere along the line in learning language, I became able to describe my visual experience of things like the duck-rabbit, or express my sudden recognition of an old acquaintance. In the psychology experiment by Mitroff *et al.* mentioned earlier, some children who were presented with the duck-rabbit were told simply that it could be a picture of more than one thing. This was enough to allow the vast majority to experience a change of aspect in this picture.

If I want to know what you are seeing, I need to ask you. A drawing won't do, because it, too, would be ambiguous or weighted to duck or rabbit. Your words, however, will tell me what you see. In fact, only your words can let me know what you see. They are not the next best thing to being there, as they might be when ordinary seeing is in question. They are not a symptom, but rather the expression of what you see. I know that you are seeing what I am seeing if you describe what you see in a way that is similar to my description:

> What is the criterion of the visual experience?—The criterion? What do you suppose?

The representation of "what is seen."
The concept of a representation of what is seen, like that of a copy, is very elastic, and so *together with it* is the concept of what is seen. The two are intimately connected. (Which is *not* to say they are alike.) (*PI*, p. 198)

Your description of the duck-rabbit is the representation of what you see. "I see it as a rabbit" tells me exactly what you see in a way that drawing a picture-rabbit would not—for, after all, you are not seeing a rabbit, but you are seeing the duck-rabbit *as* a rabbit. You wonder: What if I didn't know the word "rabbit" but was familiar with the animal? Couldn't I show you a rabbit or a picture of one to let you know what I was seeing? Couldn't I escape the need to say anything? I agree that you could do this, but only if you could tell me that you see what we both see (the drawing of the duck-rabbit that is in front of us) *and something like this* (while you point to the rabbit or rabbit-picture). It's to words that you must turn to convey that it is an *aspect* you see. This is why an ability with words is a criterion for your seeing the duck-rabbit as a rabbit.

The Necker cube appears to flip. I can describe what I see in different ways. For example, one aspect is roughly a view from slightly above, the other is a view from slightly below. Or I might describe it as Necker did for his drawing (fig. 11): point A forward and point X back, or point A back and point X forward. If you are inclined to agree with these descriptions or offer one of your own that makes sense to me, then we are seeing the same thing, having the same visual experience. If, however, you see only one of these—that is, the figure does not flip for you—that will come out in your description of what you see.

When I see the cube move between its two different aspects, am I really having two different visual impressions? As we've seen, if how I would draw what I see were the criterion for what I see, it wouldn't be right to say I'm having two experiences, because the drawings would be the same:

In order to answer this I should like to ask myself whether there is really something different in me. But how can I find out?—I *describe* what I am seeing differently. (*PI*, p. 202)

You object. "Yes, I see the cube flip and then describe it differently. But I'd have seen it flip even without the subsequent descriptions. The descriptions are for *your* sake, so you know what my visual experience is. They don't tell me anything. And so we are back to the question: Am I having two distinct visual experiences, as I would if I turned my gaze from one physical object to another? That is, are my two descriptions of two different things?"

Wittgenstein says this:

> "Is it a *genuine* visual experience?" The question is: in what sense is it one? Here it is difficult to see that what is at issue is the fixing of concepts. A *concept* forces itself on one. (This is what you must not forget.) (*PI*, p. 204)

Here he means that I can describe my experience of a change of aspect while viewing the Necker cube in no other way than as seeing. I see it in one orientation and then I see it in another. In that sense, the concept of seeing (of "genuine visual experience") is the natural way to think of what I am doing while I look at it. There may be causes for this "forcing" of the concept, but Wittgenstein is more interested in the fact of our feeling compelled to describe our experience a certain way than in what its cause might be.

If the concept of *seeing* is forced on me here, what about the descriptions I give? Where do they come from, since what I'm looking at on the page is unchanging? One might just say that they are the descriptions of what I see in each aspect, just as I'd give different descriptions of two chairs in a room. I just look and describe. This sounds right because seeing the two aspects of the Necker cube consists in two visual experiences. I am seeing something—or some things. The drawing on the page does not change, yet my description of it does. In a sense, there is only one object that I see, namely the drawing of the Necker cube, but I see it in two ways: "'Nothing has changed' means: Although I have no right to change my report about what I saw, since I see the same things now as before—still, I am incomprehensibly compelled to report completely different things one after the other" (*RPP II*, 474). Or simply: I describe what I see in two ways. Two different descriptions make themselves available to me and provide me with two different visual experiences—but of only one object. The descriptions are themselves part of the visual experiences: one object, two descriptions, two visual experiences. "The substratum of this experience is the mastery of a technique" (*PI*, p. 208). In this case the technique is language, and it allows for alternative descriptions of what I see. The descriptions are in a sense brought to bear on what I see, providing me with a new experience, *creating* a new experience.

To be a master of one's language includes the ability to describe the same thing differently, to find multiple ways of talking about the same thing. The peculiarity of what happens when we experience the change in aspect of the Necker cube is that the ability seems to find its way into our eyes: "It is only if someone *can do*, has learnt, is master of such-and-such, that it makes sense to say that he has had *this* experience. And if this sounds crazy, you need to reflect that the concept of seeing is modified here" (*PI*, p. 209). Thought, in the form of words, of descriptions, of language as a learned skill, shapes our sight.

Wittgenstein believes that how language is taught and learned is at the root of our seeing aspects and experiencing changes of aspect:

> Don't I see the figure sometimes this way, sometimes otherwise, even when I don't react with words or any other signs?
>
> But "sometimes this way," "sometimes otherwise" are after all words, and what right have I to use them here? Can I prove my right to you or to myself? (Unless by a further reaction.)
>
> But surely I know that there are two impressions, even if I don't say so! But how do I know that what I say then, is the thing that I knew? (*RPP I*, 5)

Language is taught publicly and teachers can correct their students in what they say. I cannot invent a language of my own that could amount to anything more than what I am inclined to say at a given time. Wittgenstein's question to his objector in this passage underscores that I cannot even refer to the visual experiences I claim to have unless I rely on a language I have learned from others. I cannot tell myself anything about my present experiences because I cannot know what I mean without using the technique of a language that I have mastered. Language, however, is full of ambiguities. The same word will take on different meanings, different nuances, depending on the form of the sentence and the circumstances in which the sentence is spoken or written, that is, the language-game in which it is used. Could it be that the ambiguity of language makes for the ambiguity that we see in things? Rather than reflect an inherent ambiguity in nature, mightn't language instill in our relation to the world the ambiguity that makes human experiences what they are?

The puzzle picture in chapter one (fig. 22) was of interest because a verbal description could turn a collage of black and white patches into a human figure. Unlike the duck-rabbit or the Necker cube, which are ambiguous (that is, they can be more than one thing) and reversible (that is, they can shift back and forth between aspects), the puzzle picture tends for most people who solve it to remain thereafter always the same. It does not shift back to the chaos of the black and white blotches once it has attained the coherence and unity of a recognizable form. We might say that a meaningless picture has become meaningful through a description. (The duck-rabbit and Necker cube are meaningful in both their aspects.) Some people see the man in the puzzle picture without any help, others only with help, and others never see it. The help I gave in chapter one was linguistic, but we could also outline the figure with a pointer without saying anything at all. On the television game show *Camouflage*, the audience knew the contestant had detected the object hidden in the picture if she could outline it. (That constituted winning in that game.) When the contestant could do this, do I know that she had *seen* the whole object—the coherent whole in the mass of lines? Well, if she named it and could outline the figure, she had seen it.

The difference between finding Jesus in the puzzle picture and finding the teapot in *Camouflage* lies in the sudden shift from meaningless to meaningful that the puzzle picture undergoes for me. As a whole it becomes something I now view as a representation, perhaps even as a work of art. When I see the human figure, I am not simply picking out an object hidden amongst others. It is not camouflaged in any ordinary sense. The original picture lacks unity. When I experience a change of aspect in it, my visual impression changes from chaotic to organized. I now give a different description of what I see, fully aware that in the purely perceptual sense, nothing has changed. Once again it seems correct to say—and this is exactly what people do say—that I see the man. Seeing is exactly what I am doing, though I certainly was also seeing before I saw him. My description and my seeing once again walk hand in hand.

For Wittgenstein, the paradigmatic case of experiencing a change in aspect—the example he gives first and returns to frequently—has to do with faces, with seeing the similarity between two faces or recognizing a familiar face in a crowd after I have been looking in that direction a while or seeing the teenager in the old man. These examples all seem somewhat different from ambiguous figures, reversible figures, and puzzle pictures. It is easy to see why. In the latter three cases I am looking at something when I experience a sudden aspect shift, the "aha!" moment. I am looking at a drawing of the duck-rabbit, or at the Necker cube, or at the blotchy puzzle picture. What I am seeing is not in any obvious sense a relation between the aspects of the pictures or anything else. They just seem to change. It is Wittgenstein's claim, however, that all aspect perceptions involve relation: "[W]hat I perceive in the dawning of an aspect is not a property of the object, but an internal relation between it and other objects" (*LWPP I*, 516). An "internal relation" is one that is essential to one or both of the things related (the "relata"). For example, an arc of a circle is internally related to the center of that circle. It could not be an arc of the circle without that relationship to the center of the circle. An external relationship exists between, say, the ". . ." of Morse code and the letter *S*. The three dots would still be three dots without that relationship. The relation must be established independently of what the three dots are or what the *S* is.[46] When the duck aspect of the duck-rabbit dawns for me, I perceive a relation between the drawing and a duck (or a picture-duck). What I see when I see the duck aspect could not be the duck aspect unless it had that relation to a duck (or a picture-duck). This relation is established through language. Just as the hearing of harmonic relations in music is mathematics for the ear, so too, the seeing of aspects is language for the eye.

This is also the case when, after looking at someone for a while, I suddenly notice the resemblance between her and her mother. My experience is essentially one of a relation between two faces. I am struck by this similarity at least for a while, after which I am no longer struck, but the resemblance remains with me. The aspect can become incorporated, I might say, into my ordinary perception, much as the puzzle-man is now simply a man to me. Perhaps now if someone points out the resemblance of the faces to me, I won't be struck by it because I've already noticed it.

The question then is: What is the object of my visual impression when I notice a resemblance between two faces in front of me? Once again, I can ask how I would describe my visual impression. I would simply say that I see a resemblance between these faces. I might be able to point out details (shape of nose, eye color, and so forth), but I might not.[47] These would not constitute the resemblance anyway, since someone might be able to see all of these details yet not see the resemblance. ("I see that they have those traits in common, and if you want to say that means they resemble one another, I'll go along with you. But I don't see the resemblance.")

The concept of resemblance between two objects (not human faces) requires that we ask in what way they resemble each other or for what purpose they are similar. An ordinary screwdriver looks much like a screwdriver made of chocolate, but the resemblance ends there. And this would be correct. We're more willing to call many things similar if we are also free to say how they differ. Their resemblance may be in shape, size, color, function, any of the countless attributes they have or uses to which they can be put. It is imaginable that a child comes to begin using the words "like," "similar," "resemble," in contexts like this, dealing with objects in the world.[48] Both objects are in front of us, and we can give our reasons for saying what makes them similar, if reasons need be given. (Only as a joke would I offer a chocolate screwdriver to someone who needed a screwdriver to work a screw. I would fulfill his command better if I brought something that did not look at all like a screwdriver but could do the work of a screwdriver better than the candy one, assuming it was work he wanted to do.) With both objects present, I learn to talk of them as similar or dissimilar. I can even draw a picture of a screwdriver—it need only be a line drawing, nothing fancy—and expect someone to bring me a real screwdriver. If I require that the one he brings be just like the one drawn, I would do well to specify in what respects I mean the similarity to be understood, or else I might run the risk of the jokester's returning with another drawing. Does the duck-rabbit seen as a duck resemble the duck-rabbit when seen as a rabbit? They are congruent, but what we see in the two cases is different enough that we might not even notice they are the same figure: "Nor has the head seen like *this* the slightest similarity to the head seen like *this*" (*PI*, p. 195). (Identity does not entail similarity in the case of aspect-seeing.)

That the same picture or face or screwdriver can be described in different ways indicates that it is capable of multiple relations. This is the heart of ambiguity. Language creates the ambiguity of things by offering more than one way to talk about what we see. The ambiguity of things—their potential to bear different relations to one another and be described differently—comes out in how we see aspects. If there is one essential character of aspect-seeing, it is the possibility of ambiguity.

Wittgenstein mentions at least four cases of seeing a resemblance between faces or noticing a face in a crowd. He begins by distinguishing two uses of "see":

> The one: "What do you see there?"—"I see *this*" (and then a description, a drawing, a copy). The other: "I see a likeness between these two faces"—let the man I tell this to be seeing the faces as clearly as I do myself. (*PI*, p. 193)

Here both faces are in front of me, and yet another person standing with me might not see what I see: the resemblance between them. A second case could involve only one face present to me: "I contemplate a face, and then suddenly notice its likeness to another. I *see* that it has not changed; and yet I see it differently" (*PI*, p. 193). A third example is similar to the second, but involves a person now and the same person years ago: "I meet someone whom I have not seen for years; I see him clearly but fail to know him. Suddenly I know him, I see the old face in the altered one. I believe I should do a different portrait of him now if I could paint" (*PI*, p. 197). In the fourth case, resemblance is not even mentioned, yet we see that this case, too, belongs with the others: "Now, when I know my acquaintance in a crowd, perhaps after looking in his direction for quite a while,—is this a special sort of seeing? Is it a case of both seeing and thinking?" (*PI*, p. 197).

All four cases of seeing or noticing have two things in common. First, they all strike me. I don't figure them out or reason them through from cues or evidence. ("This must be old Jack because of that hairy mole on his neck.") I suddenly simply see the resemblance or recognize the person. Second, I cannot draw or point to anything to help another see what I see in these cases. When I see the duck-rabbit as a duck, I can describe what I see by doing a drawing and then pointing to ducks or pictures of ducks and adding that I also see "something like that." Here, when I notice a resemblance between two faces, while I can draw the faces, I can't point to anything like what I see when I see the resemblance. Maybe all I do is notice the resemblance, and perhaps this is entirely an act of the mind, not a real seeing at all. My mind might be completely engaged in ways I am not aware of to lead me to notice these things. Here too, however, the concept of "seeing" seems forced on us. Yes, I do see a resemblance, and the resemblance seems to be really there. Once again, however, I know—I see—that the face I am looking at has not changed. It has acquired a different look because it has been related to other faces, present or past. Thought has been engaged to alter the visual impression. What I see changes along with the description of what I see. I want to describe the face I see as "like" another, and this description seems to come from no effort that I notice myself making. Nor do I derive the description from the resemblance I see. The description of similarity is the expression of my visual experience, not a report about it, just as in the cases of the duck-rabbit and the Necker cube.

To say that the concept of similarity has "forced" itself on me, made its way into my eyes where it had not been before, suggests that what I am seeing is not true of the world in the same way as my seeing a tree that everybody can see and acknowledge. There may well be people who have no concept of similarity between faces, much as I hear certain isolated tribes cannot see a human face in a black and white photograph.[49] These people who lack a concept of facial similarity would find it more important to emphasize the differences between people. Do they, then, fail to see something in the world that I see? This is badly put. I should ask instead: Is similarity between faces important to them? And need it be so (*RPP II*, 638)? Concepts, Wittgenstein says, "are the expression of our interest, and direct our interest" (*PI*, sec. 570). To the group I'm considering here, individual facial differences are much more important than similarities, to the degree that it has no use for a concept of facial similarity. "Well," you may say, "can't these people still see similarities in faces? We can. There must be something there." Yes, of course, this is how we express it. But they would never describe their visual experience of two faces this way, and if their experiences are not expressed this way, we would be wrong to say that they have them. This may seem odd, but is it so odd?

Once again I see a hand raised in the audience. "The argument you present on Wittgenstein's behalf—that the seeing of aspects involves language and is essentially a grammatical or conceptual event—is interesting but a bit suspect. Why can't all of the experiences of aspect changes you've shown us boil down to images in the mind rather than the surreptitious imposition of words and their meanings? When I see the Necker cube flip, it is my mental image that flips. When I see the duck-rabbit as a duck, I have an image of a duck in my mind. When I notice a similarity, one image ties up with another, perhaps with one that I remember, and I experience the similarity. And when I see the puzzle picture become the picture of a man, the organization of my mental image changes and reveals the orderliness I hadn't been seeing. These processes might be a combination of *bottom-up* and *top-down* processing as you discussed earlier. Many psychologists studying these phenomena talk about 'representations' and 'processes.' Why should we not say that their accounts in the end are more understandable, more believable than Wittgenstein's account, and besides have the weight of experiment on their side?[50] In addition, your suggestion that the seeing of aspects is at root a linguistic event and that aspect changes exist only for beings with language seems like a testable, empirical claim, not a bit of conceptual analysis alone. Can't we devise an experiment to determine if, say, pigeons or rats experience the flip of the Necker cube? Is it inconceivable that they do? Wittgenstein seems to neglect all of the psychological research done in recent years. Of course, he died in 1951, so he's to be forgiven for that. But you seem to suggest that he wouldn't have made much use of this research anyway. What's the problem with psychology?"

Well, it's always useful to hear from a friendly and articulate skeptic. One's thoughts get nowhere without some resistance.[51] The objector makes some good points. The tug of the mental image explanation is still very strong. As long as we say that some*thing* changes when we experience a change of aspect, we seem committed to search for the thing that changes. The temptation is great to believe that, if not an external object, then an internal object must have changed. This internal object, call it the "mental image," would be something very much like the external object, or rather like a picture of it. When we suddenly notice that the duck-rabbit, which we've seen only as a duck, can also be seen as a rabbit, perhaps our mental image emphasizes the rabbit qualities of the picture, such as where the eye is placed relative to the ears or beak, or in which direction it is looking. Or maybe we subconsciously compare the duck-rabbit to a memory-image of a rabbit. In the case of the Necker cube, our image of the flat drawing seems three-dimensional already, which suggests that our mental image is something other than a copy of what our eyes are looking at. We can almost see our image of the cube flip through mental space. When the aspect changes, it is as if Necker had held his original crystal first in one position then in another. When we notice a resemblance between two faces, perhaps we literally see that the daughter's nose is just like the mother's, the eyes the same color, and so forth until, with enough traits registered as the same, we want to say, "See! They look so alike!" When I see the young friend in the old man, perhaps I am comparing what I literally see before me with the memory image I stored away in my mind years ago.

The seductiveness of these arguments rests on the belief that we have mental images that are like pictures and that we compare mental images with objects the way we compare pictures with objects. We can also compare mental images with other mental images or with pictures the way we compare pictures with other pictures. Wittgenstein's grounds for challenging this purported similarity between mental images and pictures are "grammatical" or conceptual, not empirical or experimental. Wittgenstein believes that if we pay attention to how we use words when we talk about images and the imagination, we will discover that when we imagine something or have a mental image, we do not have something that is just like a physical picture, only private rather than public. Nor is imagining a case of non-sensory perception. Wittgenstein does not deny that mental images exist or that we can see things "in the mind's eye." He does, however, deny that we do the same kinds of things with mental image words that we do with picture words or with sense-perception words or with aspect words. We play different language-games here, but ones that he says "hang together" (*Z*, 625). The functioning of the imagination does not need mental images, even when I imagine something that I might express in a rough drawing. That is, I might draw something from imagination that is in no sense a copy or likeness of any image I have in my mind. I might have no image at all in my mind. Regardless of whether or not someone had a mental image, we would still say that his drawing came from his imagination. It might in fact turn out that having mental images facilitates doing certain things for some people, such as making drawings, but the absence of those images has no effect whatever on how we employ the word "imagination." If I want to know if you can play chess, I don't try to discover what's going on inside you. I watch you play chess.

Wittgenstein says that images are not a private sort of physical picture. The concepts of *mental image* and *picture* are not alike, though they are intimately connected. We do not see, look at, or otherwise observe our mental images. This is not an empirical remark that experiments might someday disprove, but a conceptual one about how we actually think and speak about pictures and mental images. I can look at a photo of the Statue of Liberty, I can look at the same photo again, or I can look at it more closely or under different light. I can compare it with other photos of the statue. But only as a sort of joke would I say that I was doing any of these things with my mental image of the Statue of Liberty: "As if someone were to buy several copies of the morning paper to assure himself that what it said was true" (*PI*, sec. 265).

Saying that a picture is unchanged differs from saying that a mental image is unchanged. We say about a photo "that it remains the same not only on the ground that it seems to us to be the same. . . . In fact we shall say under certain circumstance that the picture hasn't changed although it seems to have changed" (*BB*, 171). We say it hasn't changed because we know something about how it has been kept, how photographic images fade over time, and so forth. This of course doesn't prevent us from talking about imagining the same thing from one day to the next or saying things like: "A picture of him flew before my mind." But from such usage we should be slow to infer either that pictures can fly or that mental images are pictures. "In part of their uses the expressions '[mental] image' and 'picture' run parallel; but where they don't the analogy which does exist tends to delude us" (Hallett 1977, 372).

For at least two reasons, imagining differs from straightforward seeing but also somewhat resembles seeing aspects. First, mental images are voluntary, says Wittgenstein, while sense-perceptions are not. He says:

> When we form an image of something we are not observing. . . . The coming and going of the pictures is not something that *happens* to us. We are not surprised by these pictures, saying "look!" (*Z*, 632)

While we don't always succeed in conjuring up the images we want or bringing about an aspect change at will, "trying to imagine something which isn't present," and "trying to see the duck-aspect in the duck-rabbit" both make sense. "Trying to see something that isn't present" doesn't make sense. Second, because images are voluntary, they tell us nothing about the world; that is, they have no cognitive content. To the degree that seeing aspects does inform us of the world—and we've yet to consider to what extent it does—it is more like true perception and less like imagining.

Some experiments by psychologists might be construed as indicating that Wittgenstein was simply wrong about the cognitive content of mental images, and that in fact mental images can tell us about the world, just as pictures and sense-perceptions do. Roger Shepard published an influential study in 1971 on the speed of mental rotation of figures.[52] The subjects were shown pairs of drawings such as those in figure 28 and asked whether or not the two were different views of the same shape. Shepard varied the angular distances between the two figures so that some were only a few degrees different, while others much more. He then measured how long it took people to tell whether the two figures were the same or different. He found that their reaction times were proportional to the angles that separated the figures. It took twice as long to decide that one figure was the same or different from the other if the angle of separation was twice as great. Many studies have produced similar results,

(a)

(b)

(c)

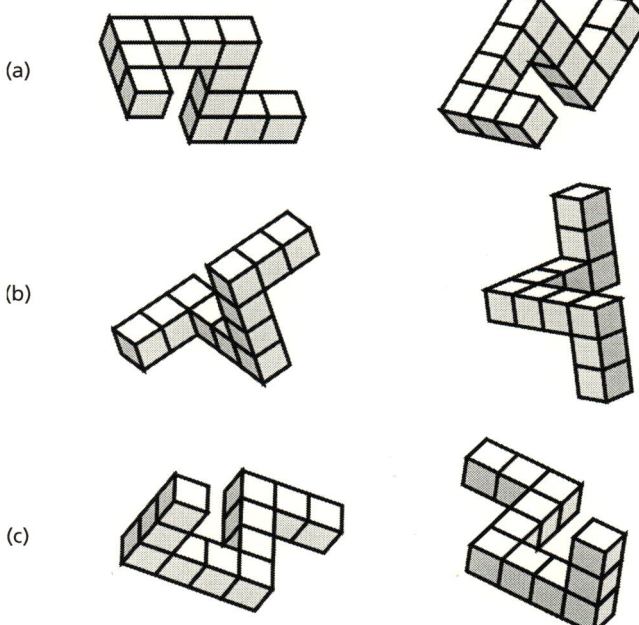

Figure 28. Mental rotation.

some even providing evidence for inertia and momentum effects.[53] Other experiments seem to indicate that mental images take place in a mental medium that possesses texture and boundaries.[54] Shepard's results have been interpreted to mean that, in an effort to solve the problem, subjects rotate a mental image through mental space in a way remarkably like the way a real figure might be rotated through real space. In this case at least, it seems that mental images can tell us something about the world, very much as our eyes can, and are therefore like real perceptions and pictures. How might we understand these experiments?

Wittgenstein describes the uses of words and the puzzles, paradoxes, and dangers that await those who fail to heed their uses. He offers no explanation of these uses, for there can be no theory of language as he understands it. This is not a failure on his part, or settling for second best. Language, especially about what is psychological, is like an old, complex city, with all sorts of curving, intersecting streets, where names change unexpectedly. To draw a map of such a place is a daunting task, but absolutely necessary if we are not to get lost when we try to do philosophy or psychology. A map that straightens the curves and regularizes the streets would be virtually useless. Though it would certainly look like a map, its connection with our city would not be at all clear. The problems that engage Wittgenstein "are solved, not by giving new information, but by arranging what we have already known" (*PI*, sec. 109). These problems revolve around the essential nature of things, because "[g]rammar tells us what kind of object anything is" (*PI*, sec. 373). This implies that questions like, "Can mental images tell us something true or false about the world?" and "Are aspects mental images or qualia?" will not be answered by experiments such as Shepard's, but by reminding ourselves how we use words like "mental image," "seeing," and "imagination": "Every sign *by itself* seems dead. *What* gives it life?—In use it is *alive*. Is life breathed into it there?—Or is the *use* its life?" (*PI*, sec. 432).

I cannot observe a mental image because, like a pain, it is not the kind of thing it makes sense to say I am observing. I don't observe my pains and mental images: I *have* them. You can observe the expression of my pain. You can listen to what I say about my mental image or of my experience of a change of aspect. But you cannot observe any of them. A mental image is unobservable not because it is too small or hidden or fleeting, but because the *grammar* of the expression "mental image" is not the grammar of a word that can refer to an observable object or event, like a picture, though a picture might be used to express or represent a mental image. Wittgenstein believes we have a deep prejudice in favor of considering the meaning of a word to be not its use, but some kind of intermediary between object and thought. "This is not a stupid prejudice" (*PI*, sec. 340), but it gets in the way of our understanding how words are really used. One cannot guess how they are used, but must lay out the complex and interweaving patterns of their use, the intersections of uses with one another, the birth of new uses and the death of old. This amounts to saying that the psychologist must know what he is looking for before he can know where and how to look, or whether looking of the sort he does—through experiment—can be helpful at all.

This demands first of all asking questions like, "How does one learn to talk about mental images?" and "What applications do we make of words like 'image' and 'imagination'?" Only then shall the psychologist know what a mental image is. Wittgenstein believes the psychologist will then no longer be faced with questions like, "Do mental images exist and what are they like?" Rather, the psychologist will be more concerned with the causes and effects of the phenomena he is investigating. (It might be of interest to discover, for example, that whenever people report having a certain mental image, their blood pressure drops. This would be a useful result.)[55]

What connects an image with the object of which it is an image? What makes an image of him into an image of him? Wittgenstein's oblique reply is, "Not its looking like him" (*PI*, p. 177).

> The same question applies to the expression "I see him now vividly before me." . . . What makes this utterance into an utterance about him?—Nothing in it or simultaneous with it ([or] "behind it"). If you want to know whom he meant, ask him. . . . His answer [will] be decisive. (*PI*, p. 177)

I imagine a building on my campus, McDowell Hall, and I imagine that it is on fire. Someone asks me how I know it is McDowell Hall. Couldn't it be some other building very much like it? The question makes no sense in this context. "Imagine an equilateral triangle. Did you do it? How do you know it's an equilateral triangle?" "Imagine two unequal parallel straight lines. How do you know that they aren't equal, but instead one is closer than the other?" Two of my brothers are identical twins. If I show a friend a photo of one and tell him it is a picture of my brother Homer, he can ask me how I know it is Homer and not my other brother, Virgil. When I tell him that I took the picture, the matter is settled. But if I say I am *imagining* my brother Homer, the question "How do you know it's Homer and not Virgil you're imagining?" makes no sense. I cannot answer simply, "It looks like Homer," because it would also look like Virgil if it "looked like" anyone at all. Not even God, could he look into my mind at that moment, would be able to tell of which brother I was thinking (*PI*, p. 217). Yet no one would question *my* authority in the matter.[56]

Wittgenstein's criticism of the claims of experimental psychology runs deep and broad. Good work can be done in psychology, especially when psychologists link causes and effects.[57] But without preliminary conceptual clarification—in effect, the laying out of the subject matter of psychology—experiment can often lead down dead-end paths that prevent real progress:

> The confusion and barrenness of psychology is not to be explained by calling it a "young science"; its state is not comparable with that of physics, for instance, in its beginnings. (Rather with that of certain branches of mathematics. Set theory.) For in psychology there are experimental methods and *conceptual confusion*. (As in the other case conceptual confusion and methods of proof.)
>
> The existence of the experimental method makes us think we have the means for solving the problems which trouble us; though problem and method pass one another by. (*PI*, p. 232)

It would be good to ask what psychologists think they are studying, and compare this to what physicists think *they* are studying, to get a better sense of the point of Wittgenstein's critique.[58]

When we look at some of the psychological studies I cited earlier in this chapter, we would find that the psychologists who study what Wittgenstein has called aspect changes (which they call by a variety of names) talk about such things as 1) visual perception, 2) interpretation by the brain of retinal images, 3) bits of information, 4) cognition, 5) representations, 6) attention, 7) consciousness, and 8) phenomenal experience.[59] Virtually no psychological study begins by asking how such words are normally used in ordinary language, which is their home. The writers might not believe that these concepts are crystal clear, but no one seems to feel the need to explore exactly what he or she is talking about before beginning to suggest causal theories of how such experiences, actions, intentions, and so forth can come to be or how they are related.

Well, perhaps psychologists don't need to talk about these things in that way. Physicists don't explain the common use of terms that they employ, like "force," "momentum," "charge." They don't ask how the word "mass" is used in ordinary language before studying the relationship between mass and weight. The physicist, however, appropriates these words—or invents new ones like "quark" and "meson"—and thereby creates new concepts. He does not pretend to be explaining what "force" is in its ordinary employment. This is similar to medicine's use of words like "shock," which have an employment in ordinary life that differs from their use in medicine. The doctor knows this, and generally no confusion arises because a word's use in medicine is circumscribed.

Well, you say, isn't the psychologist doing something much like the physicist or physician? His sphere is not the physical world, except to the extent that a lot of recent work in psychology relies on observations and measurements of brain and nerve activity. His goal is to understand the psychical and what underlies it, in fact, what causes it. This is not so very different from the goal of the physicist, who can learn about what can't be seen (subatomic particles, for instance) on the basis of what can be seen (instrument readings and such things). Shepard's rotating mental cubes are a good example of just this sort of work. We come to know more about moving bodies through observations of bodies in motion, and more about electricity by observation of the phenomena of electricity. We don't explore how we use the words "motion" and "electricity" in our ordinary language to come to understand what motion and electricity are, do we? Shepherd and countless other psychological investigators do work that is no different from Galileo's and Faraday's, except in the objects they study.

Wittgenstein thinks this comparison is flawed:

Misleading parallel: psychology treats of processes in the psychical sphere, as does physics in the physical.

Seeing, hearing, thinking, feeling, willing are not the subject of psychology *in the same sense* as that in which the movements of bodies, the phenomena of electricity, etc., are the subject of physics. You can see this from the fact that the physicist sees, hears, thinks about, and informs us of these phenomena, and the psychologist observes the *external reactions* (the behavior) of the subject. (*PI*, sec. 571)

While the physicist observes and reports on the phenomena he is investigating, the psychologist observes human behavior, for example reaction times and verbal reports, not mental images, intentions, or consciousness. You might object: "Scientists often draw conclusions about what they are investigating, but cannot see, from what they *can* see and measure. They devise experiments to trick, cajole, or torture nature into revealing its secrets. William Harvey, for example, by his experiments on the heart and blood, could come to know what he could not directly see—namely, that the blood circulates through the veins and arteries. And Galileo could discover the acceleration of a freely falling body, which he could not measure directly, by using inclined planes to slow the acceleration to a measurable rate.[60] Even though the psychological experimenter can't see his subjects' mental images, observe their intentions, or measure their consciousness, she can still learn facts about their nature."

This argument, however, assumes that all psychological words refer to phenomena. That is, it takes for granted that psychologists study what at least in principle can appear or be seen, if not by the experimenter then by the subject himself.[61] If this were true, the subject matter of psychological research would be similar to that of research in physics. But Wittgenstein believes that many psychological words do not refer to phenomena in any way at all. They are not used that way: "I would like to say: psychology deals with certain . . . phenomena.—But the words 'thinking,' 'fearing,' etc., etc., do *not* refer to these phenomena" (*RPP II*, 35). In the list of psychological terms that do not refer to phenomena, and so, *a fortiori*, cannot in principle be subject matter for experimental psychological investigation, Wittgenstein includes "imaging," "hoping," "seeing," "remembering," "intending," and more.[62]

> To close one's eyes in order to form an image of something is a phenomenon; to strain in looking another; to follow a thing in motion with one's eyes yet another.
>
> Imagine someone saying: "Man can see or be blind!" One could say that "seeing," "imaging," and "hoping" are simply not words for phenomena. But of course that doesn't mean that the psychologist doesn't observe phenomena. (*RPP II*, 77)

The psychologist observes phenomena but cannot in principle observe *seeing* because seeing is not a phenomenon. The psychologist studies the phenomena of seeing, but tends to treat them as *symp-*

toms of something underlying, rather than as *expressions* of seeing. But the phenomena of seeing are not symptoms at all, but inseparable from what we mean when we say of someone that he sees, or is blind:

> I said there were phenomena of seeing—what did I mean by that? Well, for instance, everything that can be portrayed in pictures, and that would be described as "seeing." Exact observing; looking at a landscape; someone blinded by light; the look of joyous surprise; turning away so as not to see something. All the kinds of behavior which distinguish a sighted man from a blind one. (*RPP II*, 132)

If Wittgenstein is right that the psychologist studies not *seeing* but only its phenomena, what about thinking? Aspect-seeing is an amalgam of ordinary visual perception and thinking (*PI*, p. 197). Can the psychologist study thinking? What goes on when someone thinks? When I recognize my friend in a crowd after having looked in his direction for a while, in a sense I both see and think. It is as if thought is brought to bear on seeing, producing the experience of recognition. This does not happen ordinarily, or at least we don't feel compelled to speak that way. When I look at a tree I see a tree, I do not suddenly recognize that it is a tree. The "cognize" in "recognize" points to the element of thinking in such visual experiences.

Anyone who attempts to study *thinking* by observing it in himself, however, runs into the same conceptual dead end as the one who purports to tell us what *seeing* is:

> In order to get clear about the meaning of the word "think" we watch ourselves while we are thinking; what we observe will be what the word means!—But this concept is not used like that. (It would be as if without knowing how to play chess, I were to try and make out what the word "checkmate" meant by close observation of the last move of some game of chess.) (*PI*, sec. 316)

When one looks at the last move in a chess game, one is in a sense seeing a checkmate. But there is much else that one has not seen if he observes only this last move. He cannot know the meaning of what he witnesses because he witnesses only it and not the context in which it occurs, the chess game. We cannot get clear about what "thinking" is (that is, how the word "thinking" is used) by any sort of observation of an event, either by introspection or by collecting information about what goes on in the brain or about the phenomena associated with thinking. We can come to understand what thinking is only by broadening our study to include the circumstances in which we use that word and related words. Learning how a machine is made won't tell us how it is used. Just so, learning about what goes on in the brain when someone says he is thinking, or what he says goes on in himself when he thinks, won't tell us what thinking amounts to. For this we need to understand the *concepts* of thinking, not the causes of some of their manifestations.

Thinking forms a family of concepts with various meaning. Wittgenstein says:

> Remember that our language could possess a variety of different words: one for "thinking out loud"; one for thinking as one talks to oneself in the imagination; one for a pause during which something floats before the mind, after which, however, we are able to give a confident answer. One word for a thought expressed by a sentence; one for the lightning thought which I may later "clothe in words"; one for wordless thinking as one works. (*Z*, 122)

Thinking is definitely not some sort of accompaniment to thoughtful activities: "While we sometimes call it 'thinking' to accompany a sentence by a mental process, that accompaniment is not what we mean by a thought" (*PI*, sec. 332):

> If thinking and speaking stood in the relation of the words and the melody of a song, we could leave out the speaking and do the thinking just as we can sing the tune without the words. (*BB*, 42)

But can't I do just that? Can't I think without speaking? I often know in an instant what I want to say but the saying of it takes much longer than my prior thinking did. Wittgenstein agrees that we can think without speaking, even without speaking to ourselves. This does not imply, however, that thinking is necessarily a mental process, one which may or may not accompany other processes like talking. "Thoughtful talk" is not distinguished from "thoughtless talk" by any kind of mental process accompanying the one and not the other. Wittgenstein asks us to ask ourselves when we would say of someone or something that he, she, or it is thinking.[63] How would we teach someone the rules for using the words "thinking," "thought," "thoughtfully," and so forth? Not by pointing to a mental activity, distinct from other kinds of activities. We don't teach a child what thinking is by referring to brain processes. We would not do so even if we could make brain processes visible to the child by means of some kind of "brain activity reading device."[64]

Wittgenstein gives us a rule of thumb to use whenever we are tempted to say that there *must* be a mental process of thinking, one that psychologists can study: substitute for "thinking" or "thought" the expression of the "thinking" or "thought" (*BB*, 42). This is not to say that a thought is identical with its expression, for instance, a spoken sentence, because we do all too often speak thoughtlessly, as when we read aloud automatically or when we think about something else and don't pay attention to what we are saying. Wittgenstein says, however, that "speech with and without thought is to be compared with the playing of music with and without thought" (*PI*, sec. 341). When I play a piece of music with thought, there may be no "thoughts" accompanying my playing. My playing can be described in ways that playing without thought cannot. ("Notice how he phrased that passage to bring out its connection with the opening theme.") To say I played the piece with thought is to say something about how I played the piece; that is, in this context, "with thought" performs an adverbial function, even though "thought" is grammatically a noun. My actions express my thought, just as my gracefulness is expressed in my dancing and my anxiety in my pacing.

True, we often speak as though thought and speech were separate activities and we might do one without the other, as we might hum the tune of a song and not sing the words. "Think before you speak!" "What I just said didn't quite express my thought." "The English language uses words in the order in which we think them" (*BB*, 148). What "accompanies" speech in those cases might be modulation of tone of voice, certain gestures, and the context in which the remarks are made. We are not tempted to call *them* the thinking. No, what allows me to say of someone else that he is thinking includes what he is doing now, what has led up to it, and what he would be willing to say when asked. The psychologist who hopes to learn more about thinking by asking people what goes on when they think or by observing their reactions to certain kinds of problems or by studying brain activity while they are thinking has involved himself in a hopeless conceptual muddle. We discover more about what thinking is by reminding ourselves what we mean when we say that someone is thinking.[65]

Wittgenstein's argument against thinking as a phenomenon is far-reaching. It applies to virtually all psychological concepts, including hoping, intending, willing, and remembering. These concepts are everyday concepts, used in our common discourse with others to help do the work of ordinary language. Their uses depend on the circumstances in which they occur. They are "messy," which does not prohibit their functioning perfectly well in the contexts in which and for which they are taught and learned. Empirical investigation in psychology requires that these concepts be tidied up because experimental situations demand clear parameters for measurement. In effect the researcher defines a usable concept in a new way for the experimental context. The physicist, the chemist, and the biologist generally invent concepts for their purposes, such as quark, valence, and mitochondria. When these concepts are no longer useful, they can be changed or replaced, as happened with conatus, phlogiston, and vital fluid. The physicist, chemist, and biologist begin with phenomena; the concepts they use seem to help unify their observations.

An Augustinian view of how language operates promotes the psychologist's misunderstanding of concepts such as thinking, intending, and consciousness. If every word stands for something, whether it is an object, action, process, or state, it makes sense to attempt to try uncovering exactly the things to which these words refer in reality. To the psychologist, the brain and nervous system—or at the very least, the human body—is the seat of psychological action. It is there that one would look for what psychological words refer to. But language doesn't work that way. Most psychological terms cannot be understood without spelling out their various uses in different contexts. Experiments in psychology condense context into brain states and concepts such as mental image and seeing into unitary internal conditions. Rather than search outside the individual person to get clear about what thinking is, the psychologist, like the observer of the last move in a chess game, looks inside. Wittgenstein suggests that if we "pretend humans don't have nervous systems, then it will be clearer how to come to understand the concepts" (*RPP I*, 1063). If human beings are viewed under the aspect of machines—and there is nothing in principle wrong with this view; a nervous system might be thought of as a kind of mechanism—then machine concepts would make sense. Machine concepts help us understand how a machine works, without heeding how the machine is used. They look to the *workings* of the machine, not to the *work* of the machine.

Still, a sense of wonder comes over us when we try to imagine how the lump of matter that is the brain can produce *this*, be it our perceptions, aspect changes, or consciousness. This feeling occurs when I "turn my attention in a particular way on to my own consciousness, and, astonished, say to myself: THIS is supposed to be produced by a process in the brain!—as it were clutching my forehead" (*PI*, sec. 412). There seems to be an unbridgeable gulf between brain processes and our conscious experiences, yet we think that there must be a solution, a theory that can show how these are connected. We might wonder how a piece of photographic paper can produce a picture, or marvel at the workings of a television. We know that these can be explained, perhaps by our learning how film and televisions are made and by knowing a bit about chemistry and electronics. We can look inside these objects and discover how they produce the effects they do because these effects are phenomena. Our search for a similar account of our conscious experiences in terms of the functioning of the brain and nervous system seems to be more challenging. Nevertheless, it ought to yield to scientific investigation in the end, or so we believe. And it will, if we will be satisfied with such things as the relationship between light shined in the eye and neural activity in certain parts of the brain. We will not, however, find mental images in the brain as we find photographic images on film and television images on the television screen. This is not because the problem transcends our ability to experiment or to understand. Rather, it is because mental images are not pictures, just as thinking is not a brain process, nor consciousness a brain state.

Earlier, one of you raised the question: "Couldn't an experiment be devised to test whether or not animals, who have no language, experience changes of aspect when viewing, say, the Necker cube? If they do experience such changes, wouldn't that be evidence that language is not a necessary part of either the experience or the concept of aspect change as Wittgenstein seems to be suggesting, at least on your interpretation?" One study on pigeons, for example, by Vetter, Haynes, and Pfaff (2000) claims to show that pigeons experience visual multistability when presented with a certain kind of ambiguous figure. They summarize their research as follows:

> Perceptual multistability refers to cases where perception alternates between two or more interpretations of an unchanging sensory stimulus. In a first experiment we trained 8 pigeons to discriminate horizontal and vertical apparent motion stimuli and then presented a multistable display. In five cases their behavior showed alternations similar to human experiments. . . . This is the first evidence of visual multistability in animals confronted with classical ambiguous figures. (p. 2177)

Based on how the animals respond, the researchers conclude that pigeons experience an alternation in their visual perception. In a similar situation, humans might respond similarly, but if we want to know what they see, we must *ask them*. Their verbal response tells us what they see. The psychologists in this study treat the responses of both the humans and the pigeons as symptoms of an underlying perception and perceptual change, whereas Wittgenstein has argued that what we say when we experience a change in aspect is not a symptom at all, but an expression of what we see. The same argument cannot be used of pigeons because we can't ask them what they see. To say that they see what humans see in a similar situation is to alter the concept of experiencing a change of aspect, a concept that we learn to use by learning how to describe what we see, not by our own nonverbal responses. Something *is* going on in pigeon brains, no doubt about that. And it may be similar to what goes on in the human brain. But that does not make the *concept* of pigeon perception any more like the concept of human perception. To know what aspect a person is seeing, we ask him. That is essential to the concept.[66]

If Wittgenstein's critique of psychological research is valid, what exactly do psychologists learn by their research? Their experiments and statistical analyses must mean something. Exactly what is the subject matter of psychology? This question is hopelessly broad as put and can likely only be answered in bits and pieces by looking at what particular experiments do and what their designers think they do. The concepts that interest many psychologists are everyday concepts, such as seeing, thinking, and remembering. They are snatched from their everyday use, defined anew, and examined experimentally. There is nothing wrong with this, as long as it is clear that the psychologist *changes* the concepts with which he begins. As a consequence, his investigations cannot easily be returned to the everyday employment of these concepts and be expected to have illuminated them. When someone says that "the word is on the tip of my tongue," no one would look at the speaker's tongue and expect to find the word there. The psychologist, however, might be tempted to look into the brain (or mind) to locate the source of this "feeling" and how we came to have it. This is simply to misunderstand the use of such expressions as "on the tip of my tongue," "in a flash," "I remember it all very clearly"—that is, what they mean. Concepts guide our investigations and so we ought to be very careful how we handle them, especially at the beginning of research when we don't yet know our way about. It is then, more than at any other time, that humility about the complexity of our language must dictate how we go on.

Conclusion

In experiencing a change of aspect—in fact in the very possibility of our being able to see aspects—the problems of seeing come to a head. Human seeing is suffused with the techniques of speech that we learn before we are even aware that we are speaking. When we are struck by a change of aspect, we become aware of a new sort of belongingness. That these lines could go together or that this face could be thought of along with that: such noticings reshape "what we see," without changing "what we see." While it is true that, in some sense, the imagination can tell us nothing about the world, it is also true that the imagination contributes to knowledge by bringing new concepts to bear on our timeworn perceptions and thereby bringing us to see differently. Knowledge does not consist simply in what works in the world, but also in what is *possible* in the world. Human seeing retains the potential to cast the old as new if we do not let our pre-established concepts and secure knowledge prevent us from experiencing the change that a new aspect can bring about. People's concepts show what matters to them and what does not. They also help shape what matters to them and what doesn't: "But it's not as if this *explained* the particular concepts they have. It is only to rule out the view that we have the right concepts and other people the wrong ones. (There is a continuum between an error in calculation and a different mode of calculating.)" (*RC*, 293).

In beginning to explore what it is to see aspects and experience aspect changes, Wittgenstein thinks he has helped us find our way about in the complicated net that is our talk about seeing, thinking, and imagining. This help consists entirely in getting a clearer view of how we do things with these words (*PI*, sec. 125). "The work of the philosopher consists in assembling reminders for a particular purpose" (*PI*, sec. 127). We are reminded of how we do speak and how we teach others to speak. Wittgenstein offers no theories of seeing, only descriptions, because in describing how we use words, the "what it is to be" of things is revealed. In a sense, all that is hidden is right in front of us. Our problem in understanding aspects turns out to be an aspect problem itself.[67]

If Wittgenstein is right, we might be able to increase our chances of experiencing aspect changes by becoming more sensitive to how we use words, by expanding our ability to use them, and by reading and listening to others who use words in ways that don't at first seem quite right to us. We might then come to appreciate better that the job of language is not to be a "mirror of nature."[68] Perhaps language also shapes how we see and what is possible for our eyes. Wittgenstein takes seriously that jokes can help accomplish this. Jokes often turn on ambiguities, and the recognition of ambiguities (the feel for them) is essential to our ability to experience aspect changes. Ambiguity—its recognition, its resolution, our tolerance for it—is a hallmark of human experience.

When Wittgenstein says that we are "compelled" or "forced" to use a certain word or expression in a given context, he is pointing to the manner in which the way we learned to use words makes itself felt even when we cannot articulate how it does so. A word feels right in a certain context, or is forced from us. When the Necker cube flips, I *see* the new orientation. No word describes it better. You say:

"But can't my experiences transcend my ability to talk about and describe them? The lesson of seeing aspects is not that language is the hinge on which changes of aspect swing, but rather that language cannot reach to all my experiences, many of which precede or elude it both descriptively and logically. How is one to define a feeling? It is something special and indefinable. One can only recognize it within oneself." Yes, something about that sounds right, but "it must be possible to teach the use of words!" (*LWPP I*, 394). How do I know that I have a "feeling" or have experienced an "aspect change" if I haven't learned how these words are used in the first place? I learned them in a public way, and when I use them, even to myself, they carry along with them their origin out in the open. If I can't tell *you* what's going on with me, I can't tell *me* either. In an important way, there is no radical privacy about personal experience, no great divide between inner and outer. If I can call what I now have an experience, it is the same sort of thing you have when you have an experience. The very general fact of nature that we teach and learn language as we do provides the sort of unity to our possible experiences and expressions that we might have feared was lacking. In the next chapter we'll explore a way in which there can be a real division between people and their experiences of seeing. I'm talking about *aspect blindness*.

CHAPTER THREE

Aspect Blindness

How can it be nonsense to say, "There are people who see," if it is not nonsense to say, "There are people who are blind"? But suppose I had never heard of the existence of blind people and one day someone told me, "There are people who do not see," would I have to understand this sentence immediately? If I am not blind myself must I be conscious that I have the ability to see, and that, therefore, there may be people who do not have this ability? (*RC*, I 87)

A. Imagination

When I look at the duck-rabbit against a background of ducks, I see it only as a duck. It likely will not even enter my mind that it could be seen as something else. The context of ducks hides its rabbit aspect and prevents me from seeing it. Similarly, if I were to view the duck-rabbit against a background of rabbits, its duckness would not appear to me. The context seems to lock the duck-rabbit into one aspect or the other, transforming it from an ambiguous figure into an ordinary one. In the words of the psychologists, the background "disambiguates" the duck-rabbit. It forces the picture to become one thing or another to my eyes and keeps it from alternating between its two forms. Something seems to be gained in the clarity that the background provides, a stability in appearance lacking when the duck-rabbit is seen out of context. The disambiguation of the duck-rabbit, however, can also strike us as a loss: where did the rabbit go in the field of ducks? The freedom we had of seeing the duck-rabbit as either duck or rabbit is replaced by the security that it will be only duck or only rabbit.

When I see the duck-rabbit out alone, without a context that would determine which one of its two aspects I see, I might experience a change of aspect spontaneously. That is, the duck-rabbit might go from duck to rabbit for me without my being told that the figure is ambiguous.[1] Or I might see both aspects only after I'd been told that the figure could be seen in more than one way, or after I'd been asked whether or not I saw anything else in the figure. We can then say that

I can see both aspects and can experience the change from one to the other when prompted. Some people who can see both a duck and a rabbit in the duck-rabbit can nonetheless not see the switch from one to the other, either spontaneously or when prompted. For example, if the same figure were to be used in a book to illustrate a duck on one page and a rabbit on another, these people would see a duck on the first page and a rabbit on the second, but not recognize that it was the very same picture on both pages. They can see each aspect when it is pointed out but cannot see the aspects changing.

When we see both aspects of the duck-rabbit and experience a change in aspect without help from the background or context, the result seems to be something like what would happen if the background changed. When we disambiguate the duck-rabbit on our own, do we in some way provide a background against which to see or imagine the ambiguous figure? Is what we do internally like what gets done externally by a real change in background? When someone tells us that this figure can be seen as both a duck and a rabbit, are his words as good as background in helping us to see?

The two cases, the prompted and the spontaneous, seem different. When I am prompted, I am given a hint that I might expect to see more than just one figure. When the aspect changes spontaneously, I don't know what I ought to do. I may have no clue what other sort of context to provide, if any. Why not a background of roses or grasshoppers or skyscrapers? How can I provide anything when I have no idea what is needed? Yet many adults, but not all, can see the duck-rabbit as ambiguous without prior warning or guidance (Doherty and Wimmer 2005, 407–421). If I need some sort of context or background in order to see an ambiguous figure in one or the other of its aspects, then in some way or other I am providing it because this background is not part of the ambiguous picture itself.

In chapter two, I examined Wittgenstein's reasons for saying that some experiences require that we be able to *do* something in order for it to be correct to say of us that we have had the experience. Seeing a change of aspect is one of these experiences. In order to be able to say that we have experienced a change in aspect, and that we now *see* something different, we must be masters of a technique. It may have surprised us at first that in the case of aspects our ability to see depended on our ability to speak. When we ask another what he sees when he looks at the duck-rabbit, we expect him to be able not only to say "first a duck, then a rabbit," but also to point out where the bill is, where the ears are, in which direction the eye is looking, and so forth, in answer to our questions about these things. If he cannot, we can't be justified in saying that he has experienced a change in aspect while looking at the duck-rabbit. Our being justified in what we say is important to the very concept of the experience of such a change because otherwise we cannot teach a child what it means to say something like "first I see a duck, then I see a rabbit." I cannot correct her errors or applaud her successes. If I cannot be justified in attributing an experience to another, then she cannot learn how to use these and similar expressions correctly. This is more or less what we said in the last chapter.

If I am doing something like providing a background when I look at an ambiguous figure, can I say that my ability to do something is responsible for my disambiguating it? Does my ability to make my way around English help to disambiguate the duck-rabbit while I view it? Having this ability, I could explain to another exactly how the picture now looks like a duck, now looks like a rabbit. If I did explain it, I would be placing the aspects of the picture into contexts. I would describe what I see, and in so doing I would be relying on my listener's knowledge of what ducks and rabbits look like, where the bills and ears go, how the eyes of animals look in a direction, and so forth. I'd be doing this by saying things and perhaps pointing to parts of the picture while I did so. I needn't explain it, not even to myself, in order to see it. But I could. That's what an ability is: I could do something if the occasion called for it. A tennis player who can serve a tennis ball at 120 miles per hour has this ability whether he is actually serving the ball or not. In a similar way I, as an avid observer of tennis—one who knows the rules, has watched many games, and has played regularly—can *see* things in a tennis match that the novice observer cannot see. I can see aspects of what is happening on the court to which the new viewer would be more or less blind. I can *see* when a player has made a difficult shot, when her strategy has changed, when she is getting tired. I needn't say to anyone, not even myself, what I see. My familiarity with the game, my knowing my way around it, suffuses my seeing. I could say what I am seeing, and I might even be able to say why I see these movements on the court in the way I do. I could try through hints and tips to get you to see what I am seeing, but you might never graduate beyond the ability to figure out what is going on to actually *seeing* it.

In this and similar ways, having certain kinds of visual experiences requires that I be master of a technique, that I have an ability. If under normal circumstances, I could not explain what I see when asked, another person would not have the right to say that I see it. He could not say of me, "Well, he sees it anyway, even if he can't explain it." And if another person lacks that right, so do I. If I can't *say* it, I can't *see* it. If this ability amounts to providing a background or context for what I see, then indeed I do provide it. These are not empirical or phenomenological claims about what I see. They are conceptual because they concern what it means to say of someone that he sees, say, the duck-rabbit first as a duck, then as a rabbit, or of Galileo that he first sees dark spots on the moon, then sees craters. If Galileo could not have explained why he saw craters, then even though there were craters on the moon, no one would have been correct in saying that Galileo saw them. Seeing new aspects and experiencing changes in aspect tie up closely with ability and with what it makes sense to say of someone else.

You may object that an ability as I've described it is not really a background or context against which to see the duck-rabbit or anything else. An ability is not like a picture of a field of ducks or a field of rabbits, against which the duck-rabbit can be seen as a duck or a rabbit right now. If I were to describe ability as some sort of (as yet undetermined) arrangement of nerves in the brain and eyes that waits to be called into action, maybe it would seem more like a background. It would be always there, but only active when needed. For example, a spider sitting at the edge of its web feels nothing until some prospective prey gets trapped. The vibrations caused by the captured insect tell the spider where on the web it is. The web symbolizes the spider's ability to find its prey: always there, designed but dormant, until set to vibrate by the hapless bug. You might be more willing to think of an ability as being like background if it were akin to the spider's web.

And this may prove to be true in some cases. Someone with an ability, say, to serve a tennis ball at 120 miles per hour might possess a certain arrangement of nerves and muscles that, like the spider's web, could be called into play when needed. When I see the duck-rabbit as a duck, I call into play my ability to talk about ducks, and perhaps also my ability to remember them. The ability to do this was there all the time, like the web. It may even turn out that only those people with a certain ability have *this* arrangement of nerves and muscles and that all people with this arrangement have that certain ability. It might turn out that way.

Wittgenstein, however, would say that while such a discovery could be very interesting, it is only a hypothesis. It would not tell us what the concept of *being able to do* or *having an ability* or being *master of a technique* in fact is. We would never refer to brains, nerves, or muscles to teach someone what having an ability is. We never mistake what might be the cause for what *is* the ability. Rather, we say of someone that he can do something, or has a certain technique under his belt, when he can do what is called for in the appropriate situation. He need not be acting a certain way all the time, but he will act that way when those actions are called for. While having an ability is in some sense always there, like a background, it is not always announcing itself. It is always there in the sense that we say of someone that he knows English even when he is silent, or speaking another language. He is master of English even when asleep. It may be that, through training and environment and genetics, his brain is "wired" in such a way that he will speak English when called upon. If it was discovered, however, that his brain was organized differently (say exclusively in the "French-speaking style") yet he could speak only English, we would still say that he was a master of English. And this is enough to prove that the ability to speak English is simply not equivalent to any state of the brain and nervous system.

So what about our suggestion that when we see the duck-rabbit first as a duck, then as a rabbit, we supply a sort of background or context in thought? Well, whatever we supply, it's not a background in the ordinary sense. Our ability to do things with words allows us to say of ourselves and others that we experience a change of aspect. The concept of *ability* shares something with the concept of *background* or *context*, but there are important differences, as well. As long as we remind ourselves of both, we'll run less risk of confusing the two. For now, we can say that, in a sense, knowing a language is something like providing a background or context for ambiguous figures and maybe other kinds of aspects.

The importance of this discussion lies in the role of the imagination in our experience of a change of aspect. If we say that we provide a context with which to surround an ambiguous figure like the duck-rabbit, this context could be said to be imagined. Wittgenstein puts it this way in talking about "some arbitrary cipher":[2] "And here I can see it in various aspects, according to the fiction I surround it with" (*PI*, p. 210). This "surrounding with a fiction" is the work of the imagination. The imagination allows for an image to acquire *a meaning* when before it had none or to acquire additional meanings. We can say that, while not giving us information about the world, the imagination still lets us see parts of the world (especially pictures) as meaningful. It does so by providing the context in which they can be seen *as* one thing or another.

If my earlier argument holds and the imagination does not necessarily provide background or context in the form of a picture (as when we see the duck-rabbit in a field of rabbits), then what does it do? With what does it surround what I see? It might be clear by now what Wittgenstein would say. The imagination surrounds our perception with words. Our ability to use words brings about our seeing the aspects of things. The amalgam of seeing and thinking is prepared in the crucible of the imagination, where what I see and how I think are joined. The outcome is an experience, that of a change in aspect. Such an experience might surprise us, as when we suddenly recognize a face or see a similarity. How did we not see that before? It was there all the time. This is a genuine experience: it has content and it has duration.[3]

Why, however, would a conceptual investigation—which is what Wittgenstein and I have claimed to be making—take an interest in experiences? How does a certain experience fit into a world of concepts? "Pain is pain," you might object, "no matter what you call it, even if you can't call it anything at all. That's a real experience." This much is true: we experience pain even before we have learned to use a single word. But I do not get any clearer about what pain is by reflecting on my pain now. Nor do we come to understand the experience of a change of aspect by trying to capture what happens when the Necker cube flips for me or when I suddenly see the duck-rabbit go from duck to rabbit: "Do not try to analyze your own inner experience. . . . Do not ask yourself 'How does it work with *me*?'—Ask 'What do I know about someone else?'" (*PI*, pp. 204, 206). Experiencing a change of aspect of any kind is as genuine an experience as is that of pain, and as little subject to explication by observation of my own states. If it seems strange that the experience of seeing a change of aspect requires that we can say something, we need to remember that "the *concept* of seeing is modified here" (*PI*, p. 209). Wittgenstein does not mean to suggest that all seeing requires the mastery of language. Animals see, and so do infants. But seeing aspects, *seeing* something *as*, is not the same as seeing, though closely related to it.

We often come to see things as connected when we experience aspect changes or when we suddenly notice similarities or recognize an old friend. "These lines can be seen together. I never imagined that before." "Now I see how he looks like his grandfather. I'd never made that connection before." The imagination sometimes merely shifts the emphasis. Instead of looking at *these* together, look at these. The result is often an expression of surprise or wonder that these parts could go together at all and that I hadn't seen that relationship before. We think of the imagination as allowing flights of fancy. The imagination can create the most unrealistic alliances, which might bemuse or startle us without providing that experience of "Aha! This too is possible, this too *makes sense*." The new connections that are made when we see changes in aspects strike us as not fanciful, as not mere imagination, but rather the work of the imagination in its revelatory guise. I say "revelatory" because when we, for example, see a resemblance we hadn't before seen between two people, something real seems to strike us for the first time. (This is why aspect-seeing is like seeing.)

Imagination can also be thought of as the faculty of freedom. The imagination seems unrestricted by what is actually in front of us or what we have experienced in the past. Yet one of the recurring themes in Wittgenstein's account of the aspect experience is that certain words are "forced" from us when we describe these experiences or that they "feel right" in certain circumstances. For example, we describe the experience of an aspect change as seeing even though we know that nothing in the outside world has changed when the aspect changes. We don't attribute our visual experience of a change of aspect entirely to our imagination. And it seems right—it feels right—to call what happens a change from seeing one thing to seeing another, though this is a modified concept of seeing.[4] How can the imagination be both "free" and "forced"? From whence comes this force? We feel compelled to describe our experiences in certain ways. This suggests that the force comes from our language: "What fits . . . is the use of the word which forced on me the idea that I *see* this. What I have learned about the use of the word must be forcing me to use the word here" (*RPP II*, 370). We might put it this way: Imagination enables the possibilities inherent in our learned language to meet our eyes. The freedom of the imagination to provide new meanings for perception is a freedom derived from language, which is both ours and our inheritance from others. In that sense, the freedom of the imagination binds us to all other speakers. Only through this bondage can it act meaningfully, that is, freely. Am I saying that imagination is entirely a verbal faculty? Well, I don't know how far to go with this. But I am saying at least that without words we would not be able to imagine many things. Without words we also would be unable to see many things.

B. Aspect Blindness

If seeing aspects is a kind of seeing, then what would it be like to be aspect-blind? What is the world of the aspect-blind like? What might they lack that others have? Our concern is not a clinical one, though later in the chapter I'll offer some suggestions about how the concept of aspect blindness might help us talk about certain forms of aphasia and autism. Our interest continues to be with the conceptual. Can aspect blindness shed more light on the place of aspect-seeing among the concepts of experience? We'll then compare aspect-seeing with Wittgenstein's notion of "experiencing the meaning of a word."

Let's begin by asking: What is blindness simply? What is it for someone to be blind? How do we use words connected with blindness and how do we teach their use to others? We can begin by saying that blindness is the inability to see. Does this definition help us understand what blindness is? Well, do we yet know what seeing is? It seems we would need to if a definition or description of blindness in terms of seeing is to satisfy us. We emphasized in chapter two that seeing is not a phenomenon. That is, no one can observe seeing. It is not like walking or breathing or talking. They can be observed, measured in different ways, and altered at will within certain limits. Seeing is not like that. Seeing is more like thinking than it is like walking. The expressions of seeing, like those of thinking, are observable, measurable, and analyzable. Walking can be studied in detail and its abnormalities can be categorized through observation. We do not, however, come to understand better the concepts of *seeing* and *thinking* through experiments, notwithstanding the superficial similarity of the grammar of words like "seeing" and "walking." The surface grammar obscures the fact that neither I nor anyone else can observe my seeing.[5]

If seeing cannot be observed, then neither can blindness if we define it as an inability to see. This seems right. The characteristic phenomena of seeing, such as "looking at a landscape" or "turning away so as not to see something" (*RPP II*, 132), distinguish the sighted from the blind. The blind will not behave in these ways and will behave in other ways, such as walking cautiously when crossing a street, or turning an ear rather than the eyes toward the source of a sound. We distinguish the sighted and the blind by what they can and cannot do. To the blind, it might seem as if the sighted can touch things with their eyes.

Blindness is an abnormality: most people can see, but some cannot. (A clam is not blind, even though it cannot see.) Blindness is not something one has, like a tumor or a broken leg. These can be looked at, observed. We don't say of someone that he *has* blindness, but rather that he *is* blind. In a sense, his blindness defines him and affects all aspects of his life and behavior. To learn how it feels to be blind, it would not be enough to close one's eyes for a while. The blind lack abilities that the sighted person who shuts his eyes does not lack. Blindness is a *whole person* condition.[6] Lesser forms of blindness exist, as in a person who has some residual vision, but not enough to allow him or her to function normally without aid. Color blindness is the inability to perceive differences between some or all colors that other people can distinguish. A determination of color blindness is made by asking the person to do something, for example to respond to questions about what he or she sees on a test chart. "Change blindness" and the related "inattentional blindness" refer to

an inability to notice changes in a scene or to perceive even important events. They occur either when some visual disruption takes
place (a blink, a flash of light) or when subjects fail to attend to certain parts of a scene or event because they are concentrating on some
other part.

What we've said about blindness can be adapted to aspect blindness. Wittgenstein raises the possibility of aspect blindness by asking,
"Could there be human beings lacking in the capacity to see something *as something*—and what would that be like? What sort of consequences would it have?" (*PI*, p. 213). Since experiencing a change
of aspect is the most striking of aspect experiences, we should first
of all say that the aspect-blind will not see the aspects of something
change. The Necker cube will not flip for the aspect-blind individual,
though he might see it in one context as from above and in another
as from below. (Wittgenstein is uncertain about this.) That startling
experience we have when the cube instantaneously shifts, performs
its quantum leap without traversing the intermediate space: that
experience would not be available to the aspect-blind. While looking at the duck-rabbit, they will never have occasion to say—will not
have the ability to say—"Now it's a rabbit!" They will not have been
able to learn how to use these words, and unless they can, we cannot
say that they see the duck-rabbit changing from duck to rabbit.

While Wittgenstein wants to deny to the aspect-blind the experiences associated with changing aspects, he does not want to say
that the aspect-blind cannot see, for example, that the double cross
(fig. 23) contains both a black cross on a white background and a
white cross on a black background. (Wittgenstein allows the possibility that a child, even before it has learned to talk, could point
alternately to a white cross and a black [*PI*, p. 207].) "[The aspect-
blind] will simply not be supposed to say: 'Now it's a black cross on a
white ground!'" Here, the 'now' and '!' are telling. It also seems possible that if the aspect-blind person does not see the Necker cube
jump between aspects, he might not see the two-dimensional drawing as a cube at all. He might still "recognize it as a representation (a
working drawing, for example) of a cube" (*PI*, p. 213). He would also
be able to take it as a cube, as we might take a topological map for
a hilly terrain. When I read such a map I can tell where the slope of
the hill changes and by how much, where the summit is, and where

the valleys lie. I know my way around the map as a map, but I don't see the hilly land when I view the map. In like manner, we can imagine that the aspect-blind don't see the three-dimensional quality of the Necker cube. They can say which parts of the drawing represent which faces of the cube, perhaps even which represent views of the inside and which of the outside faces. But in a sense they cannot simply read it off from the drawing the way they could from a three-dimensional model of a cube. Their relationship to it might be akin to that of a beginning reader of a script entirely new to him. The reader must sound out each letter, and words don't look familiar. He will usually improve with practice, and he will eventually see the words differently. The truly aspect-blind person will never show such development because he is blind, not simply inexperienced or new to the task. (We don't say of a one-year-old child that she is illiterate, even though she can't read.)

Should we say that someone who is aspect-blind will fail to recognize the similarity between two faces? We will at least want to say that he won't suddenly recognize his old friend or suddenly see how the son looks like the father. Once again he will not be able to express any kind of "aha!" visual experience. He will not have the experience that something has changed but everything has remained the same. But because the aspect-blind ought to be able to learn language, we must allow them the ability to understand and obey requests like "Get me another one of *these*." If we don't allow this much, then it seems we would no longer be considering them as simply aspect-blind, but rather also as unable to understand language in a broad sense. (No one can be considered a fluent speaker if he is unable to use the same word for two different objects—that is, to acknowledge that these two things are similar.)

Recognition of the similarity of two faces, however, may require a different kind of seeing of resemblance than that of two objects. Psychologists categorize the inability to recognize faces as a special form of disability called *prosopagnosia*, or face blindness.[7] Prosopagnosia is a form of visual agnosia, the inability to recognize objects. The prosopagnosic can remember all sorts of things, such as books and music and how to get around a city. But he or she might be unable even to remember his or her own face enough to pick it out in a photograph. Prosopagnosics can compensate for their deficits, often so well that no one realizes that they simply cannot recognize faces. They look for cues, such as unique facial features that might mark a person as, say, his or her spouse. Tone of voice, gait, mannerisms all contribute to the strategy of the prosopagnosic. In the title case study of *The Man Who Mistook His Wife for a Hat*, Oliver Sacks recounts the story of Dr. P., who, perhaps because of a brain tumor, could recognize the face of his own brother only by focusing on specific features, "that square jaw, those big teeth—I would know Paul anywhere!"[8] In the full sense of "recognize," Dr. P. did not recognize his brother's face, but deduced it from particulars he did recognize. The face as a whole made no sense to him. This seems to be a striking case of aspect blindness. The aspect-blind can figure things out, can take something as something, but they cannot see what the normally sighted can.

Expressions on people's faces are aspects of their faces.[9] When we look at a face, even a schematic drawing of a face, we see that it has an expression. We might not immediately be able to give this expression a name, but we see that the face has some expression. The aspect-blind might not see this and might need to figure it out. "Oh, I see that his lips are tightly pursed and his forehead wrinkled. He must be annoyed." His relationship to the expression on a face might be like ours to an upside-down face, as in figure 29, based on an experiment first done by Peter Thompson in 1980.[10] With both faces inverted we tend to notice only that they differ, but not exactly what this difference means. What are the expressions on these two faces? We might be able to work this out by carefully observing the parts, but the expressions don't jump out at us. When the faces are turned right-side up, most of us are surprised, if not shocked, at what we see. We take in the whole and see at once not only the expression of the face on the right, but also the unnaturalness of that on the left. The aspect-blind will not have the sudden reaction that most of us have to the expression on a face viewed right side up.[11] A person who is aspect-blind would not suddenly see a change in what Wittgenstein calls the "internal relations" of things: "What I perceive in the dawning of an aspect is not a property of the object, but an internal relation between it and other objects" (*PI*, p. 212). In chapter two, we said that an internal relation was one that was essential to one or both of the things related, such as an arc of a circle to the center of

Figure 29. Face orientation.

that circle. When the duck aspect of the duck-rabbit dawns on me, I perceive an internal relation between the ambiguous drawing and a duck or a picture-duck. I could not see the duck aspect unless it had that relation to a duck or a picture-duck. The relation that I see needn't be one between two objects that both appear to me, but it is a relation that I perceive nonetheless. The aspect-blind would not see the duck-rabbit switch from duck to rabbit. They would not see that internal relation change. But is it not also imaginable that aspect blindness might take different forms, more or less extreme? There might be an extreme sense of aspect blindness about which we would say that the person could not see the drawing of the duck-rabbit at all as most of us do. He wouldn't see the duck-rabbit as a picture of the head of an animal, and therefore wouldn't see the change in aspect with which we are familiar.[12] His relationship to this picture would be very different from ours. He would be unable to make the same sorts of use of it as we do, such as to imagine it as an illustration in a book of ducks and rabbits. In general, aspect blindness would show itself as a different relationship to pictures in general. For example, in a painting that portrays a galloping horse or a runner in motion, the aspect-blind would not see the motion of the horse or the runner as a normally sighted person would. Wittgenstein puts it this way:

> Let's assume that someone cannot see the picture of a runner as a picture of motion: How would this come out? I'm assuming that he has *learned* that such a picture as this portrays a runner. Thus that he can say that it is a runner; how will this man differ from normal human beings? I shall assume that he will show absolutely no understanding that motion is being represented in a picture. And what would we call the signs of this defective understanding? (*RPP II*, 483)

If he could copy the picture of the runner or the horse exactly, we wouldn't say that his visual sense was defective. If he saw a real horse or person running, he'd have no trouble recognizing their motion. What is his relationship to pictures, and how is it abnormal? Our questions will not be answered by any discovery about the state of his eyes, brain, or nervous system of the kind we would expect from a psychologist or neurophysiologist. We are interested in the concept of aspect blindness because we have argued that seeing aspects is a form of seeing, and to know what seeing is requires that we know about the concept of seeing, not about eyes and brains.

For a start, we might say that a person who could not see this picture as one expressing running (though he knows that it is meant to represent running) would likely carry on a conversation about it differently from those who could see it that way. He might not talk about the power of the leg muscles, the forward motion of the runner or the galloping horse, perhaps not even the goal of the movement or how this movement affects others in the picture. He might be able to follow a discussion like this, though he'd likely be more comfortable talking about form and color than about motion and force. In one sense he can see what is there, but in another sense he is blind to what the picture means. A discussion that was couched in terms of motion would be difficult for him to follow, because he does not see the implications of motion in the picture, though given time he might figure some of them out. He reads the picture as we might learn to read an x-ray or a music score, by looking for cues that help him understand what is going on. With training, he might become proficient at this, just as a blind person might become good at making his way around unfamiliar places. In both cases, however, the blind and the aspect-blind do not see. They remain in the condition we are in when reading a map: we simply cannot see the terrain, though we can work out what it must be like and what path would be the best to take.

You might say that, if the aspect-blind act as I have described, they really do consciously what the rest of us do unconsciously. They take lines and shapes and colors on paper or canvas and through effort come to the conclusion that this picture must be meant to represent something in motion. After all, nothing is really in motion in the painting, is it? When we say we see a runner or a galloping horse in the picture, we're not strictly correct, are we? A running horse runs. Nothing in the picture runs, and my visual image of the horse or man certainly doesn't run either. Perhaps the aspect-blind see more readily what is right in front of us all and do not add to what they see, as the rest of us must be doing. Just as the color-blind may be less susceptible to camouflage, the aspect-blind may be less influenced by whatever it is that brings the rest of us to say—in some sense falsely—that the man in the picture is running.

There is something attractive about this way of viewing aspect blindness. Perhaps the aspect-blind don't see what isn't there, and so in a sense are more clear-sighted than the rest of us. We're reminded of Hume's view that the true contents of our mind are atom-like impressions and ideas that are joined together by custom and habit. The processes by which they are synthesized are as likely to lead us to falsehood as to truth. Nothing moves in that picture of the galloping horse. It's all as still as can be.

This sounds right—and it sounds very wrong. It's true that if I look at a picture and suddenly realize that it depicts a galloping horse, nothing has suddenly begun to gallop. There is no "And they're off!" marking a burst from the starting gate as at a race. At a race, I see something move. In the picture, nothing moves across the paper or canvas. If it did, it would not be part of the picture, but something extraneous to it. Yet we see a big difference between a picture of a horse running and one of a horse grazing, or between a man walking and a man standing still. Perhaps we ought to describe the difference between the moving and stationary figures simply in terms of the orientation of their limbs in space, the angle of their necks, the curve of their musculatures. But this would seem awkward and out of place. "Why do you say it so strangely? The one is moving, the other isn't." And that would be the right response. It would take effort on our part to describe the running and still figures in this "Cartesian" way, as if an equation of their shape would tell us something more immediate and true than simply saying that they are moving or still. When we look at the picture, we *see* the horse galloping; we don't deduce it, consciously or unconsciously, from the way its limbs are positioned. Nothing is moving and yet something is: this is the expression of seeing an aspect. And this is what the aspect-blind cannot do.[13]

To the aspect-blind, certain experiences are closed. They see everything other people see but cannot bring to bear on what they see the descriptions that would justify us in saying something like, "Yes, they see the horse galloping" or "Now they see the duck-rabbit as a rabbit." Experiences are closed to them because they cannot do certain things with words. As a result, their relationship to pictures is different from that of most people. They will construe pictures as a computer might, "by means of key features and schematic relationships" (Sacks 1987, 15).[14] The ambiguity of pictures—their potential to represent more than one thing—escapes the aspect-blind. We can admit, acknowledge, and enjoy the fact that a picture of a walking man is both in motion and not in motion. In fact, the possibility that both aspects of a picture are available to us heightens our interest in pictures. The low tolerance for ambiguity of the aspect-blind makes their relationship to pictures different. To the extent, however, that our own ability to see aspects and experience changes in aspect arises from the amalgam of language and perception, we might say that the deficiency of the aspect-blind is to be found in the imagination, where eyes and language come together. Their imagination does not regularly provide multiple descriptions of pictures. Recall that in chapter two we explored how Wittgenstein's suggestions about how we teach and learn language, and how the meaning of a word is its use, led us to conclude that aspect-seeing combines visual perception and language in a way that creates the possibility for certain experiences, such as sudden recognition and the flipping of the Necker cube. Since the aspect-blind have nothing wrong as such with their eyes—they can see in the non-aspectual sense as well as anyone else—their deficiency seems to be one either of language or of the amalgamation of language and sight in the imagination. Imagination normally has the power to provide more than one linguistic description for what we see. Sometimes we exert our imagination in order to see something as something else. We might, for example, need to make an effort to see a triangle as an overturned object (*PI*, p. 207). In the cases in which we have been most interested, those of seeing aspects and experiencing changes in aspect, the imagination provides descriptions. Our ability to do things with words keeps ready to hand multiple descriptions of the objects of perception. As we have seen, one does not precede the other. There is not first a perception and then a description of it, or first a description with the perception falling into place thereafter. Perception and description walk hand-in-hand. The aspect-blind lack this intimacy of sight and speech. And if it is through language that ambiguity enters our experience, the world of the aspect-blind must be a *literal* world, perhaps a prosaic one, in which everything is only what it is and nothing else besides. In the extreme case, their world must be devoid of wonder.

I have been speaking both as if aspect blindness interests us only because of its conceptual place amongst the concepts of seeing and also as if the aspect-blind were real people. Well, are they? Is aspect blindness a kind of pathology that ought to be noted in *The Merck Manual*? Wittgenstein's interest in the concept of aspect blindness lies in the possibility or imaginability of such a condition. To be able to imagine this form of visual disability clarifies the concept of aspect blindness itself and consequently that of seeing aspects and experiencing their changes. But while what is imaginable is not always actual, the reverse is true. What exists in reality must be possible. Examples of real people or recognized conditions that manifest forms of aspect blindness can aid the imagination: "Is scientific progress useful to philosophy? Certainly. The realities that are discovered lighten the philosopher's task, imagining possibilities" (*LWPP I*, 807).

We'll look very briefly at three kinds of examples. One important caveat: The disabilities I'll discuss are complex, yet I will present them as if they are simple. I have left unasked many questions that psychologists, cognitive neuroscientists, and physicians have asked and continue to ask. I have raked across and smoothed very uncertain ground, but I do not want you to get the impression that there are not other very interesting ways to look at these disabilities. My interest is to derive from these cases something that will help us in our conceptual journey.

a) *Dr. P.* Dr. P., the man who mistook his wife for a hat, suffers from agnosia and especially prosopagnosia, the inability to recognize objects and faces. Dr. P., a gifted musician and teacher of music, at first seemed normal to Sacks. When, however, at an instruction to put on his *shoe*, Dr. P. reached down and grabbed his *foot*, Sacks knew something was amiss. "Was he joking, was he mad, was he blind?" (Sacks 1987, 10). Sacks is sure that Dr. P. is neither joking nor mad, nor is he blind in the optical sense. When Sacks shows him some pictures from a copy of *National Geographic*, he notices that Dr. P.'s eyes would

> dart from one thing to another, picking up tiny features. . . . A striking brightness, a color, a shape would arrest his attention and elicit comment—but in no case did he get the scene as a whole. . . . He never entered into relation with the picture as a whole—never faced, so to speak, *its* physiognomy. He had no sense whatever of a landscape or scene." (pp. 10–11)

Later Sacks discovers that while Dr. P. easily recognizes the five regular solids of geometry (he can name them when shown models), he can give only a rather odd description of a glove that he holds in his hand. "'A continuous surface,' he announced at last, 'enfolded on itself. It appears to have'—he hesitated—'five outpouchings, if this is the word. . . . It could be a change purse, for example, for coins of five sizes'" (p. 14). Only later, when by accident he has put the glove on, does he exclaim, "My God, it's a glove!"[15]

Dr. P.'s behavior shows both a broad visual agnosia and a grossly diminished ability to see things as wholes, especially faces and pictures. Of his mistaking his foot for a shoe (as he later mistakes his wife for a hat) we might say that he can't see his shoe as a shoe. But does he see his foot as a shoe? While he reaches for his foot when told to put on his shoe, it's not clear that he has any idea how to put it (his foot) on. That is, can we say he is blind to the foot aspect of the thing at the end of his leg, or has he lost his ability to do things with certain words? Is his agnosia visual or verbal, or can these two perhaps not be separated? Does he understand what Sacks is asking him to do, but see the object wrong? Or does he misunderstand the request, but in fact do what he thinks he's being asked to do? I don't know how to separate the visual from the verbal in this case, and that may be because of the intimate link between visual and verbal that aspect perception reveals.

Dr. P.'s inability to take in whole pictures and faces suggests that he cannot see the *gestalt* of a scene. Wittgenstein considers this a form of aspect blindness: "Can we imagine people who never see anything *as anything*? . . . For the time being let us call such people 'gestalt-blind' or 'aspect-blind'" (*RPP II*, 478). It makes sense to think that the failure to see the parts as constituting a whole (or gestalt) is a form of aspect blindness. In a sense, the forms of colored ink on paper that make up the *National Geographic* picture are simply that: colored shapes on a page. To make them into a picture of something requires normal human eyes. The scene that is depicted is an aspect of the ink on paper, an aspect Dr. P. cannot see. We learn that he also cannot see the emotions expressed in faces in a movie shown on television.

Sacks offers some account of exactly what might be going on with Dr. P. Though he is well aware how puzzling and complicated Dr. P.'s actions are, Sacks believes that in Dr. P. "all power of representation and imagery, all sense of the concrete, all sense of reality, were being destroyed" (p. 17). Dr. P.'s wife shows Sacks a chronological series of paintings her husband did, moving from "naturalistic and realistic . . . finely detailed and concrete" to "more abstract, even geometrical and cubist" to finally "nonsense . . . mere chaotic lines and blotches of paint" (p. 17). Dr. P perceives the abstract but is no longer capable of perceiving particulars. So for Sacks, Dr. P.'s disability might be considered a degeneration of the sense of the concrete.

This might be the right way to think about what Dr. P.'s world has become and is continuing to become: more abstract. But in light of our discussion up to this point, we can put the matter more simply and directly: Whatever the cause might be, Dr. P. is becoming aspect-blind. He is losing his ability to *see* things *as*. It is not that his world is growing abstract, but rather the objects of the world no longer show him their many faces, their aspects, their possibilities. He reaches for his foot as if it were his shoe. It has not become abstract, but rather can be for him only one thing, related he knows in some way to a shoe. His paintings become less representational because he has lost the ability to *see* paint on canvas *as* a naturalistic scene. The abstract painting is unambiguous; it does not purport to represent. He can no longer make sense of representations because they demand the ability to see aspects. This degradation of his power to see goes hand-in-hand with the degradation of his power to understand words. What Sacks takes to be an erosion of his ability to visualize may be the flip side of his loss of verbal understanding.[16]

Dr. P.'s visual world undergoes profound change as he becomes aspect-blind. He does not, however, lose any of his musicality. In fact, most of the everyday actions that he can still perform with fluency he does to music. He shows no signs at all of becoming aspect-deaf. He remains able to speak intelligently about music, to appreciate its nuances and beauty, and to play it (when he does not need to rely on reading a score, which he can no longer do). But Dr. P. is losing his ability to do certain kinds of things with words. Any sense of *wonder* he might have had in the face of a great painting or novel or poem, provoked by the ambiguities inherent in experiencing these things through words, has been replaced by bewilderment. The delight that the normally sighted often take in running up against a new way of seeing things or a suggestion that things needn't be this way is absent to the aspect-blind, who might find the unfamiliarity of everyday things, pictures, and people merely paralyzing. When imagination fails, the world alters dramatically.[17]

b) *Aphasia.* More than half a million people suffer strokes in the United States every year. These "cerebrovascular accidents" (CVA) cause the destruction of brain tissue in one of two general ways: an occluded artery in the brain (thrombosis or embolism), or a burst blood vessel (hemorrhage). Depending on where the injury occurs, a variety of symptoms may be manifested. I do not want to minimize the complexity of the symptoms that can attend a stroke or the variety of rehabilitation techniques that are marshaled to help stroke victims achieve some measure of improvement. The account I am giving is simplified, but this does not mean the problems are simple ones. When a stroke damages the central speech area, the two most common forms of *aphasia* (simply, a disturbance of language function) are Broca's aphasia and Wernicke's aphasia.[18] People who suffer these disabilities have in common a difficulty repeating even short sentences without error. Those with Broca's aphasia retain relatively good ability to comprehend what is said to them, but their own speech is labored, agrammatical, and short. Those with Wernicke's aphasia speak fluently, but with *paraphasic* speech. That is, they often can't find the right word and so substitute a brief description in its place, like "the thing you sweep the floor with" for "broom." Often their fluent speech takes the form of mere double-talk, a kind of nonsense without direction or control.[19] Their comprehension of spoken language is severely impaired. It is often not clear that they can understand the command to repeat, so it is difficult to determine if they can repeat sentences.

The Broca's aphasic's speech is characterized by content words. These people tend to have a much easier time reacting appropriately to concrete words when they are in the presence of the objects named, but do much less well when the objects are absent. For example, Howard Gardner (*The Shattered Mind*, 1976, 66) tells of one of his patients who had great difficulty following the request to pretend to blow out a match when no match was present. But when shown a real lighted match and given the same command, he responded with normal, smooth, appropriate, and successful motions. We might speculate that among other problems they have, people who have suffered damage to Broca's area of the brain have diminished ability to provide a context that will allow the words they hear to have meaning. It's as if words for them are often out alone—contextless and hence stripped of meaning. This is another way of saying that these aphasics no longer can do certain things with words because without context, words lose their tool-like quality. The aphasic's failure to provide a spontaneous context for words makes him very much like the aspect-blind. The Wernicke's aphasic is in a way worse off because his fluent speech masks even to him that his words are contextless. While someone with Broca's aphasia labors in an effort to find the right word—that is, to clothe his words in a way that will let them be used appropriately—someone with Wernicke's aphasia seems less willing or less able to make such an effort. His speech is already effortless, but the context his imagination seems to be providing for it is a mere wind-egg.[20]

In their publications, writers and researchers on aphasia naturally tend to reveal their opinions on how language works. When they are not describing the location of a brain lesion or reporting how their patients responded on a series of aphasia tests, they often try to describe, in more general terms, what they think is going on in aphasia. It is worthwhile to look at a few examples of such descriptions, which rarely reflect the perspective on language that Wittgenstein has offered. In one case where a researcher has made use of Wittgenstein's views and has rethought how to describe the symptoms of aphasia, the clinical results have been remarkable.

Gardner says this about the consequences of damage to Wernicke's area of the brain:

> Wernicke's area appears crucial in two functions: relating incoming sounds to the representations (or "meanings") which allow understanding of discourse; selecting and arranging meaningful units for essential conversion into comprehensible, coherent speech. These functions are obviously essential for understanding and emitting language. According to this traditional model, reading and writing depend upon a preserved ability to extract meanings from linguistic materials and to encode ideas into meaningful units. (Gardner 1976, 69)[21]

Gardner offers a widely accepted description of how language works, though such descriptions have become more sophisticated in the years since this was published. In the cognitive neuropsychological model of language and its dysfunctions, the mind is considered to be composed of a number of *modules,* each functioning in essentially one way.[22] For example, one module recognizes phonemes (which are the theoretical representations of sounds) as they are spoken, while another module stores phonemes that are already formulated but as yet unspoken. An assessment for aphasia, such as PALPA (Psycholinguistic Assessments of Language Processing in Aphasia), consists of a battery of tests that examine particular modules to determine where impairment lies and what therapeutic steps might best be taken.[23]

Both Gardner's account and that of cognitive neuropsychologists can be thought of as based on forms of information processing. The mind-brain processes units or atoms in various ways, both to comprehend and to produce meaningful language. The processing takes place inside the individual. Clearly, certain atomic linguistic facts pertain to what is outside the individual, but the heart of what it means to be fluent in language is to be found inside, in the phonemes, the meanings, and how they are all synthesized and analyzed. This view of speaking and understanding leads to certain ways of describing the deterioration of language skills. Aphasics may lose the ability to "retrieve" words with ease, or to "find" the right words for their wordless thoughts.

Wittgenstein, however, issues this warning:

> Have "Help!" and "I need help" different senses; is it merely a crudity in our conception that we regard them as equivalent? Does it always mean something to say "Strictly speaking, what I meant was not 'Help!' but 'I need help.'"
>
> The worst enemy of our understanding is here the idea, the picture, of a 'sense' of what we say, in our mind. (*RPP I*, 498)

According to Wittgenstein's view of how language works, there are no atoms of meaning in the mind that we communicate by finding appropriate words. *Meanings* and *words* are not *processed* because meanings are uses. They are not structures or units or linguistic thought-atoms present in the mind's modules. Rather than looking inward to find out what meaningful speech is, Wittgenstein has emphasized that we ought to look outward, to the settings and contexts in which we do things with words. *Meanings in the mind* is a conceptual dead end. To the extent that psychologists, neuropsychologists, and physicians think of language in this way, they will interpret the symptoms of aphasia in like terms and prescribe therapies accordingly.

In his work on aphasia, one researcher, Charles Goodwin at UCLA, seriously considers Wittgenstein's understanding of how language works (Goodwin 2003). His results are striking. Goodwin writes about a successful lawyer, "Chil," who suffered a left hemi-sphere stroke, probably in Broca's area of the brain, which left his right side partially paralyzed and his ability to talk severely compro-mised. He was able to understand what was said to him and he could gesture with his unparalyzed left hand. His neurosurgeons "insisted that since nothing could be done to repair his brain he would spend the rest of his life in bed in a vegetative state." But against this advice, his family sent him to a rehabilitation institute, where he learned to walk with a brace and to say three words, "yes," "no," and "and": "Note that all three presuppose links to other talk. . . . This vocabu-lary set presupposes that its user is embedded within a community of other speakers. His talk does not stand alone as a self-contained entity, but emerges from, and is situated within, the talk of others, to which it is inextricably linked" (p. 91). Goodwin proposes that Chil might be able to engage in "complicated language games" by relying on the verbal and contextual resources provided by others even if he cannot provide these for himself. Although Chil has lost the ability to provide context for his own words from imagination—and hence is to some extent aspect-blind—he nevertheless can make use of con-text provided by others, including the language that they produce, which he can still understand.

Goodwin wants to argue—and Wittgenstein has made sim-ilar arguments—that "rather than being instantiated in autono-mous cognitive structures, the crafting of meaning is intrinsically an interactive process, something that people do in collaboration with each other" (p. 95). Meaning is not internal, as cognitive neu-ropsychologists and others assume, but external, part of a language-game which we play with others.[24] Goodwin alludes to section 7 of *Philosophical Investigations* when he says that meaning arises only through a word's being part of a language-game. Goodwin recog-nizes that the meaning of a word is its use in a language and not a mental state, process, or object. The gestures Chil uses, along with his three words, are not merely the outward expression of a mental process, but activities meant to engage the attention of and encour-age responses from those around him. Chil can let his family know his complex wishes and communicate far more than one might expect with just three words. The meaning of a word is not some-thing carried around with the word. (This is the Augustinian view with which Wittgenstein begins *Philosophical Investigations*.) Rather it is "mastery of the practices required to use that sign competently within a relevant language-game" (p. 105). Chil is able to communicate beyond the expectations of his neurologists because meaning resides not in him as an individual—not in a brain or a mind—but in those language-games that link him to those who share his life. By adopting Wittgenstein's view of language and language-games, Goodwin succeeded in helping Chil regain a higher degree of communication skill than his physicians expected.

c) *Autistic Spectrum Disorder (ASD)*. Autistic spectrum disorder is characterized by a triad of impairments: qualitative impairment in social behavior, communication deficits (both verbal and nonverbal), and deficiencies in imagination (including impairment of pretend play). A widely accepted theory locates the major symptoms of autism in a deficiency in the neuro-cognitive mechanism that allows for the normal ability to develop a "theory of mind" (Frith and Happé 1999, 1–22). A *theory of mind* usually means the ability to attribute mental states to others and tailor one's behavior accordingly. (The story about the ice-cream man, described in chapter two, tests for development of a theory of mind.) Psychologists tend to talk as if people *have* mental states, like intentions and beliefs, and that a developed theory of mind allows us to judge and attribute those states correctly.[25] Some argue for a theory-building theory of mind theory (whew!), in which we learn to think inside the other's head, as it were, and propose to ourselves in what state she is likely to be. Others claim that there must be a hard-wired neural mechanism for the ability to attribute mental states to others. In either case, many psychologists view beliefs, hopes, and intentions as states, like being cold, being in pain, and being sleepy, except that the former are mental while the latter are primarily physical. It is the sign of a more advanced form of mental development to be able to infer mental states in addition to physical ones.

Children with ASD, including those with Asperger's syndrome, have difficulty making these attributions. They do significantly less well than normal children on theory of mind tests and tasks.[26] They can have a hard time distinguishing "John thought that Emily was in the park" from "Emily was in the park." Representations of the physical world ("in the park") cannot easily be kept separate from those of the mental world ("John thought"). Among mental states, psychologists include beliefs, feelings, knowledge, desires, hopes, fears: all must be represented in some way in our minds in order for us correctly to attribute such states to others.[27] At least that's what some psychologists say. Children with ASD might mistake a joke for a lie or find it hard to distinguish sarcasm from deception. While normal children seem to show an effortless development in ability to recognize what others mean, those with ASD struggle to do so.

We might say that children and adults with ASD manifest some of the symptoms of being aspect-blind. They have difficulty perceiving ambiguities. They may learn what facial expressions mean only by painstakingly piecing together cues from parts of the face and from context. They have an associated resistance to changes in routine and an insistence on sameness. Children with ASD also show a marked difference from normal children in their perception of ambiguous figures. A study I cited earlier showed that among the general population of typically developing children, the ability to perceive aspect changes spontaneously (as in seeing the duck-rabbit first as a duck then as a rabbit without any prompting) correlates with success on theory of mind tasks, such as the ice-cream test (Rock, Gopnik, and Hall 1994). A more recent study looks at how well children with ASD are able to reverse ambiguous figures spontaneously (Sobel, Capps, and Gopnik 2005). Because children with ASD tend to do less well on theory of mind tests than normally developing children, it comes as no surprise that they also spontaneously reverse ambiguous figures significantly less frequently. Theory of mind tests, however, generally measure a child's ability to attribute mental states to other people. Why would performance on such a test also predict their ability to experience aspect changes? These researchers suggest that perhaps "a single cognitive ability" enables us to experience aspect changes spontaneously and to perform well on theory of mind tasks. This makes sense. What this single source ability might be, however, is not clear. Following Wittgenstein we might suggest that it is primarily verbal in nature. To be able to recognize (or even infer) the mental states of others is not like being able to see what kinds of clothes they are wearing or how they are walking. To know what a person believes, for example, is not to know something about either his brain or his mind, but rather to know what he has said and done, and would say and do, in certain circumstances. We would no more look inside a person to determine that he is in a state of anxiety than we would to determine that he is in the state of Maryland. To be able to say what mental state another is in— or what mental state I am in myself—requires an ability to do things with mental state words. Perhaps it is the case that children with ASD have not been able to learn to play the language-games associated with mental states. Perhaps they cannot *see* a face *as* expressing a mental state because, for reasons yet unknown, their imaginations cannot provide multiple descriptions for what they perceive. A human face to them is not also an expressive face, as it is for most of us. Psychologists might do well to explore this deficit from the linguistic point of view rather than the representational point of view. Doing so might help tie together conceptually the autistic child's relationship to ambiguous figures and his difficulty perceiving the mental states of others, which is crucial for appropriate social behavior. Children with ASD also seem less susceptible to certain kinds of optical illusions, such as impossible figures like the "Penrose triangle" and the "devil's fork" (Mitchell and Ropar 2004).[28] They show less inclination to wonder about these otherwise perplexing figures. In a picture in which an ellipse is meant to represent a circle, they copy the ellipse much more like an ellipse than do normally developing children, who tend to copy it as more circular. We might say that the children with ASD don't *see* the figure *as* a standard circle; they are blind to one of its aspects.

The study of ASD is complex and ongoing, and I don't mean to suggest that there is any simple way to understand the data of all kinds that have been gathered over the last fifteen years. I am interested in the conceptual, not the clinical. I have looked at a few cases of real human deficit in order to suggest that diagnosing certain kinds of human inability as aspect blindness might help us see Dr. P, Chil, and the autistic child a bit differently. They share qualities that make them more like one another than we might have thought. We can deepen our understanding of them by looking at Wittgenstein's remarks on experiencing the meaning of a word.

C. Fat Wednesday

Wittgenstein tells us that the meaning of a word is its use. A meaning is not a thought or an object or a brain state or an experience. Words, like tools, are what they do, and what they allow us to do with them. We use words in various contexts, and their meanings differ in different contexts. As we saw in chapter two, these contexts, or language-games, encompass virtually all human activities in which language plays any role at all. They are rule-governed and public, neither random nor private, and they provide the frameworks within which we can do things with words.

It comes then as something of a surprise to learn that Wittgenstein wants us to think about "experiencing the meaning of a word" (*PI*, p. 182). At the conclusion of his discussion of aspect blindness in *Philosophical Investigations*, he writes:

> The importance of this concept [aspect blindness] lies in the connection between the concepts of "seeing an aspect" and "experiencing the meaning of a word." For we want to ask "What would you be missing if you did not *experience* the meaning of a word?"
>
> What would you be missing, for instance, if you did not understand the request to pronounce the word "till" and to mean it as a verb—or if you did not feel that a word lost its meaning and became a mere sound if it was repeated ten times over? (*PI*, p. 182)

Three reasons come to mind as to why these initial remarks might strike us as cryptic and unexpected. First, if the meaning of a word is its use in the language, what exactly do I experience when I "experience a meaning"? Does it make sense to say that I experience a use? *All* the uses of a word in its various employments and language-games? Second, Wittgenstein has warned us against taking "what goes on in me" when I say something meaningful as illuminating the concept of meaning.[29] Isn't the experience of meaning an issue that should be left to psychologists to explore? Third, even if we can in certain circumstances be said to have experiences of word meanings, what would their significance be? The meanings of the words are still their uses. Regardless of what I may experience, I will be understood on the basis of what I say and in what circumstances I say it. The concept of meaning as use—the central concept of meaning on which Wittgenstein has based most of his arguments—remains untouched by these peculiar experiences. Why should we take an interest in them?

I seem to have my hands full. Not only do I need to address Wittgenstein's own question about what someone who didn't have these "experiences of meaning" would be missing. I must also try to get clearer about the importance of the concept of "experiencing the meaning of a word." I faced a similar challenge when I tried to explain the concept of experiencing a change of aspect. How are the two kinds of experience related? Would I be justified in calling those who fail to experience the meaning of a word "meaning-blind"?

Let's begin by laying out a bit more exactly what "experiencing the meaning of a word" is. Try this experiment. Say the word "bank" all by itself, without a sentence to provide context, and mean a financial institution. Now say the same word and mean the bank of a river. (There are more possibilities for this word.) Do you understand what I'm asking you to do? That is, does the request to say "bank" and mean it in different ways make sense to you? If it does—and it won't to everyone—can you say what you do when you mean "bank" first one way and then the other way? It's easy to imagine contexts in which the word "bank" would quite naturally mean one or the other. "I need to get some money, so I'm going to the bank." "I tied up my boat down by the bank." In these sentences the ambiguity of "bank" is not noticed because the sentence in which it is found prevents the word from even having two meanings. (We might be able to imagine a joke or pun that turned on this very ambiguity.) The analogy with the duck-rabbit should be clear. Against a field of ducks, we see a duck, while among rabbits, a rabbit. The context disambiguates both the duck-rabbit and the word "bank."

The experiment I had you perform, however, asked that you imagine "bank" out alone, with no support at all from surrounding words in a sentence. (This is not unlike looking at the duck-rabbit all by itself.) The experiment does not ask, "What does the word mean when said this way?" but, "Can *you* mean by it first one thing then another?" (This seems similar to asking you to see the duck-rabbit alone first as a duck, then as a rabbit.) In the sense of *meaning* as use, it doesn't really sound right to ask someone to *mean* something by an isolated word, a word that is idling and not doing work. I might certainly ask, "What did you mean by that?" when the situation for such a question is right. It might be a request for your intention in saying something. Words, however, require context in order to express intentions. An expression of intention is not a description of a mental act or state or feeling. The difference between an act done with intention and the same act done without it does not lie in something that accompanies the former and is absent from the latter. It lies rather in the circumstances in which the act is done. These include what comes before and after, what I would say if asked, and so forth. So to mean by "bank" a financial institution, if I say this word utterly alone and devoid of all context, is not to express an intention when I say it.

Well, then, what could it mean to mean something by a word alone? Pronounce "bark" and mean it as a verb. I can try to tell you what goes on in me when I do this, but that would only give you one individual's personal experience, not an insight into this mysterious mutation of the concept of meaning. It is important to think about the fact that I understand this request. I think most (but not all) of you do, too. To understand it means that it has a place in our language. We know how to use it.[30] When we pronounce "bark" and mean it as a verb, perhaps our speech is accompanied by facial expressions, a certain tone of voice, or a gesture. These all constitute part of "the stream of thought and life" (*RPP I*, 504) in which words have meaning and in which I can mean one or the other of the aspects of "bark".[31] These accompaniments to what I say, however, are not themselves the experience of meaning. Not every meaning need be accompanied by something to be an experience. By "bank" I can mean a money bank without making any type of gesture at all. Where gesture can distinguish between ways in which I mean a word, then the gesture is not the experience because it cannot be separated from the word. An analogue might be a passage in a piece of music that gives us a "special feeling":

> We sing it to ourselves, and make a certain movement, and also perhaps have some special sensation. But in a different context one should not recognize these accompaniments—the movements, the sensations— at all. They are quite empty except just when we are singing this pas-

sage. . . . . The experience is this passage played like *this* (that is, as I am doing it, for instance; a description could only hint at it). (*PI*, sec. 156)

Similarly, the experience of the meaning of the word "bank" as a verb might be this word said like *this*. While we can have the experience without the accompaniment, we cannot have it without the word. Here there is a range—a family—of possibilities for what we mean by "experiencing the meaning of a word."

Our reaction to puns is another indication that words alone carry meaning in some sense, and that we can experience these meanings. If you didn't *experience* the meaning of the words, then how could you laugh at puns? Wittgenstein has this one in particular in mind:

> What is the difference between a hairdresser and a sculptor?—A hairdresser curls up and dyes while a sculptor makes faces and busts.

No context sets the stage for this joke, and no gestures, tones of voice, or intonation are available to prejudice the interpretation one way or the other. (Still, I can imagine telling even this one badly. Can you?) Wittgenstein says that "We do laugh at such puns: and to that extent we could say . . . that we experience their meaning."[32] Our laughter expresses our experiencing two different meanings either simultaneously or in close succession. This pun is especially fruitful because it is layered: each word or phrase of the punch line has two meanings, each pair of words has two, and there are two ways to answer the initial question. We don't figure all this out and conclude that the joke is funny or clever. Just as the duck-rabbit and Necker cube surprise us when they suddenly change aspects and as the figure of the man hidden in the chaos suddenly appears, so too, are we surprised by our own sudden realization of the multiple meanings of the words and phrases of this joke. We laugh spontaneously and at once, if we laugh at all. The existence of puns in the language depends on ambiguity. We laugh at them because we experience the meanings of words out of context and away from their ordinary employment. Some people recognize puns but don't find them funny. They don't laugh as if they were suddenly taken aback or surprised. I'm sure you know people like that.

We can approach this phenomenon of experiencing a meaning from another direction. Try this experiment. Say a word, "book," for example, over and over again. After a while does it become a meaningless sound, a nonsense syllable? It does for me, as do most words, including names, even my own name. The meaning of "book" seems to erode as I repeat it. Psychologists might explain the cause of this experience. Wittgenstein, however, wants to suggest that this is further indication that words out alone still have meaning, because they can lose their meaning when mistreated in this way. The degradation of meaning would not be possible unless meaning were present in the word to be degraded. If you don't have this experience when you repeat a word, it is unlikely you can experience the meaning of a word.

That we do experience both a word's meaning and its loss of meaning does not suggest that we ordinarily experience meanings while we talk, listen, read, or write. If someone says to me, "I'm going to the bank," and I ask him which bank he means, the money bank or the river bank, he'll tell me, and what he tells me will be what he meant. But he won't tell me on the basis of any experience of meaning he had, for he had none. Just as only in special circumstances do we talk about the aspects of a picture, or *seeing* something *as*, so too, only in certain circumstances does it make sense to talk about a *meaning experience*.

You object: "Look, you've told me again and again that the meaning of a word is how the word is used, the purposes for which we use it, and the language-games in which we use it. After you just about convinced me of this, you now want to tell me that there is a sense of meaning that a word can have when it is unemployed, idle, on the dole. But if meaning is the work a word does, how can a word out of a job mean anything? Why not call this other meaning, this isolated meaning, the one that vanishes when I repeat a word too many times, by a different name? Why call it *meaning*?"

This is a good objection. Wittgenstein seems to want the best of both worlds, one in which meaning is use and the other in which it is something of which a word can be full and which can be taken from it. These seem incompatible. He wants, however, for us to acknowledge that the inclination is there to call both of these *meanings*, just as we were inclined to call what happens when we experience a change in aspect-*seeing*, even though we knew that nothing outside had changed and so in some sense we couldn't be seeing the change in aspect at all:

> When I pronounce a word while reading with expression it is completely filled with its meaning.—"How can this be if meaning is the use of the word?" Well, what I said was intended figuratively. Not that I chose the figure: it forced itself on me.—But the figurative employment of the word can't get into conflict with the original one. (*PI*, p. 214)

Wittgenstein says something similar about seeing a picture of an animal pierced by an arrow: "'To me it is an animal pierced by an arrow.' That is what I treat it as; this is my *attitude* to the figure. This is one meaning in calling it a case of 'seeing'" (*PI*, p. 205). This is not a case of knowing, where one might ask, "How do you know it is an animal pierced by an arrow?" "Here it is *difficult* to see that what is at issue is the fixing of concepts. A *concept* forces itself on one. (This is what you must not forget.)" (*PI*, p. 174). Just as the concept of *seeing* forces itself on us, Wittgenstein believes that the concept of *meaning* forces itself on him—and maybe on most of us—when we experience the meaning of a word:

> But if a sentence can strike one as like a painting in words, and the very individual word in the sentence as like a picture, then it is no such marvel that a word uttered in isolation and without purpose can seem to carry a particular meaning in itself. (*PI*, p. 215)

Can we hope to get clearer about what he means by such expressions as, "the figure forced itself on me," "a sentence can strike me," and "a word can seem to carry a particular meaning"? All these expressions suggest that something happens outside our control—assuming, of course, that we acknowledge similar inclinations and experiences in ourselves. We seem to be at a moment in the discussion where reasoning things through is giving way to inclinations and forces.

Wittgenstein offers a "special kind of illusion" that he thinks will help:

> I go for a walk in the environs of a city with a friend. As we talk it comes out that I am imagining the city to lie on our right. Not only have I *no*

conscious reason for this assumption, but some quite simple consideration was enough to make me realize that the city lay rather to the left ahead of us. I can at first give no answer *why* I imagine the city in *this* direction. I had *no reason* to think it. But though I see no reason still I seem to see certain psychological causes for it. In particular certain associations and memories. For example, we walked along a canal, and once before in similar circumstances I had followed a canal and that time the city lay on our right. (*PI*, p. 215)

In this somewhat odd example, the illusion is *experienced*. Wittgenstein has not figured out (erroneously) that the city lies to the right. That would not be an experience, but a calculation or inference. He simply feels, as it were, the city to the right. I know that I've had similar experiences, especially while driving, when I was sure my destination was *this* way, but of course it was *that* way. In some of those cases, but not all, I had articulable reasons for thinking what I did. (My wife would certainly want to know my reasons, especially if she disagreed with me about the right direction.) In the example Wittgenstein gives, there are no reasons to be given, except perhaps associations from the past of which he is not conscious and which would have no practical bearing on the present walk anyway.

We might say that without obvious reason, a way of talking was forced on Wittgenstein the walker. It simply seemed right to say that the city lay over there. That he was wrong is important to the example because it excludes the possibility that he might have calculated (even subconsciously) where the city was and that his feeling could have arisen from his calculation. In fact if he'd paid a bit of attention, he'd have known not to trust his feeling. Well, when I want to say that I can experience the meaning of a word in isolation, even though a word's meaning in the primary sense is its use, I am in a situation like the walker. I have no other way of expressing my experience but to say that it comes from the meaning of the word out alone. I can't provide reasons that would connect the two meanings of "meaning," and thereby justify my inclination to call the object of my experience a "meaning." But the inclination is there and that says something.

If I were the only one to be so inclined, the only one to be "forced" in this way, then while this might be of interest to my therapist, it would not be of much value to an investigation of the concept of meaning. Wittgenstein, however, is pretty sure that most people will understand what he describes. They will understand it because this extended or modified concept of meaning fits into the larger framework of how we talk about meaning. It is not a *primary* experience: "'But what is this odd experience?'—Of course it is no odder than any other; it simply differs in kind from those experiences we regard as the most fundamental ones, our sense impressions for instance" (*PI*, p. 215). The experience of the city's lying on the right, of saying "March" as a command, and of feeling "as if the name 'Schubert' fitted Schubert's works and Schubert's face" (*PI*, p. 215), while not fundamental, are important throughout human life, especially in art, music, poetry, and elsewhere, as we'll later see.

The concept of an isolated word's having a meaning, and of my being able to experience that meaning or experience its loss, are not essential to the primary sense of meaning as use. Just as aspect-seeing is called "seeing" by extension, and the aspect-blind are not optically blind, similarly a word that has lost its meaning for me may not be taken as empty by my listener:

> If I say "Mr. Scot is not a Scot," I mean the first "Scot" as a proper name, the second one as a common name. . . . Try to mean the first "Scot" as a common name and the second one as a proper name. . . . When I say the sentence with this exchange of meanings I feel that its sense disintegrates.—Well, I feel it, but the person I am saying it to does not. So what harm is done? (*PI*, sec. 150)

Of course, if I switch meanings in my mind while speaking, it might result in a funny ring to what I'm saying: "[O]ne might tell someone: if you want to pronounce the salutation 'Hail!' expressively, you had better not think of hailstones as you say it" (*PI*, sec. 149).[33]

Some words hit the mark. When we finally find the right word after searching, we may not be able to tell why it is right. "It fits, it works, it sounds good." Sometimes these reasons are all that is needed; others agree with us that this word works best. Sometimes it takes some talking about the fit, not necessarily making arguments for and against it, but testing the word out as one might test a car or a new baseball glove. This experience of finding the right word acquires real significance in aesthetic talk—about painting, music, and literature—where fine differences can be the start of long discussions.

> That is to say, the first utterance is of course merely "*This* word fits, *this* one does not" or the like; but then there may be discussion of all the widely ramified connections made by each of these words. That is to say, it is *not* all over once that first judgment has been made; rather what it depends on is the *field* of each word. (*RPP I*, 357)

Finding the word with the right fit is not like finding the solution to a mathematical problem. I can explain why this is the solution to the problem, whereas the best I might be able to do to help you see that the word fits is to tell a story or propose an analogy. Just as seeing aspects and experiencing the meaning of a word are related to seeing and word-use respectively, so the right word might be related to grammar in the broad sense. There is no technique for finding the fitting word, just as there is none for bringing someone to see a change in aspect or to experience an isolated word's meaning. He has to get it, using as a springboard the techniques he has mastered. "If you want to improve your chess game, you must learn to strengthen your position in the center of the board." Some get it, others don't.

When a word becomes empty of meaning for us, it becomes a mere sound.[34] Out alone, cut off from all context in which it could be at home by the constant sounding of only itself, it is no longer even a word. But as long as I can surround it with a fiction, like an arbitrary cipher whose aspects appear along with the fictions I create, even an isolated word can remain alive and meaningful.[35] This suggests that perhaps when I can still experience its meaning, the word out of context is like a fish out of water: still alive until it is either thrown back in or dies on land. To take a less graphic example: a piece of household furniture moved outside begins to lose the character of furniture. By removing it from the environment in which it performed its usual function, I convert it almost into something other. I would paint a picture of it differently now. (The odd look of a bed or refrigerator sitting by the curb arrests us.) We still recognize the piece, even though it cannot perform its usual job in this new place. Eventually, it degrades and loses this attachment to what it was. It becomes *junk*.

If we don't want to be left with two senses of "meaning," use-meaning and the meaning of an isolated word that I can experience, we need to address a few basic questions. How do I learn to use the various expressions connected with isolated meanings? How do I teach their use to others, and how do I know when to correct the mistakes others make and to applaud their successes? What comes of my using these expressions, what consequences do they have? These are the very sorts of questions we asked about what it meant to experience a change of aspect. We learned that unless one could do certain things, including saying certain things, it would not be right to say that one had seen an aspect-change. Teaching and learning require public consequences so that a teacher can guide the learner toward speaking correctly about seeing aspects. There are people who can't learn to talk in the right way about these experiences. We cannot meaningfully say that they nonetheless have these experiences. Earlier we toyed with the notion that in some sense I provide a context for seeing an aspect, and I provide a change in context for my experience of a change in aspect. This context, however, turned out to be a technique, namely, my ability to use language. Without this ability, I could not be said to *see* because without it I could not be taught what the experience of aspect-changing is.

The situation we face when we experience a word's meaning requires that we ask the same kinds of questions. This might help us understand how the second, "emergent," sense of meaning ties in with the fundamental sense of meaning—the uses to which a word is put in its various language-games. These questions are not easy to answer:

> The difficulty is to know one's way about among the concepts of "psychological phenomena."
> To move about them without repeatedly running up against an obstacle.
> That is to say: one has got to *master* the kinships and differences of the concepts. As someone is master of the transition from any key to any other one, modulates from one to the other. (*RPP I*, 1054)

Our problem then is how the language-game played with the word "meaning" in its primary sense of use-meaning is related to the one played with the word "meaning" in its emergent sense, as when I say, "I just now said 'bark' in its meaning as a verb."

Wittgenstein puts the problem this way:

> How did you learn to speak it in *that* meaning?
>
> If anyone says, "Just now I spoke the word in isolation in *that* meaning," he is playing a totally different language-game from someone who tells me he meant *this* by this word in that report or order.
>
> And so now it is either essential, or inessential, that he also uses the word "to mean" in the first case. If it is essential, then this first language-game is a reflection of the second one. (*RPP I*, 1055)

Take as an example the relationship between a chess game played on a board and a game of mental chess, played by two people in their heads. People learn how to play chess by being taught in the usual ways. The board is visible to both teacher and pupil. The names, positions, and powers of each piece are demonstrated, the rules gone over, and so forth. When they play a game, they both look at the same board with the same arrangement of pieces. If questions arise, they are likely to be about the rules of the game, not about whether or not they are both *seeing* the same arrangement on the board. Mental chess is different but related. We learn to play it by first learning to play chess in the usual way. We may or may not have an image of a chessboard in our minds as we play. If we do, it is not the sort of thing we can look at, because a mental image is not a picture, though it is related to pictures. If the players disagree about what the arrangement of the board is after several moves, they can't consult a common board-image, nor can they each look to their own board-images for help, since they disagree precisely about *them*. In these and other ways mental chess is not like chess on a board. But if both parties can agree on who won, can agree after the game as to what exactly the moves were, can write them down, show them to others on a board, then they will have successfully played a game of mental chess.[36] The way they later *express* what took place in the game is just like the way they might have *described* a chess game on a real board. The expression of what they did in their minds can be the same as the description of a game of board-chess, but they cannot *describe* their game of mental chess.[37] A description is the sort of thing that can be corrected by comparing it to the real item. Mental chess is a different game from board chess, but we wouldn't be wrong to call it chess. I needn't even say that the word "chess" is "forced" on me here when I name this mental game. No forcing seems necessary. But it is still not chess. After all, there is no board, there are no pieces, and move after move nothing changes. Just as I am ready to say that I see something different when I experience a change of aspect even though nothing has changed, so, too, when I move a mental chess piece on a mental board, something is different, but nothing has really changed.

Another example of a similar relationship is calculating versus calculating in the head. We often do simple arithmetic in our minds and act with confidence on the basis of our results. We might even be able to explain later how we arrived at our results. But this does not imply that the language-game of calculating is the same as that of calculating in the head: "Only after you have learned to calculate—on paper or out loud—can you be made to grasp, by means of this concept, what calculating in the head is" (*PI*, p. 220). When one learns to calculate in the primary sense, there are criteria for one's being able to do it. Your teacher looks at your work on paper and corrects your errors. The reason calculating in the head cannot come first is because there is no such public criterion for what the learner has done. He might say that he has calculated, but what if I said that perhaps it simply strikes him that he calculated? As with a disagreement in mental chess, there is no way to settle this pseudo-dispute and hence no way to teach a child what calculating in the head is before he or she learns to calculate in the ordinary way. Once I learn to calculate on paper and then to calculate in my head, the expression of what I do in my head can be the same as the description of what I do on paper. Once again, however, I cannot describe what I do in my head:

> Is calculating in the imagination in some sense less real than calculating on paper? It is *real*—calculating-in-the-head.—Is it like calculating on paper?—I don't know whether to call it like. Is a bit of white paper with black lines on it like a human body? (*PI*, sec. 364)

Other examples of concepts related to one another in this and similar ways include: looking at pictures and having a mental image;

talking and thinking; waking experiences and dream experiences;[38] seeing and seeing aspects. It is also true that "meaning" in its primary use bears a similar relation to the *meaning* that an isolated word can have. For example, in giving a report I might be asked what a certain word means. I can explain its meaning in that context—that is, in that language-game. Or when I read a poem expressively I might pronounce a certain word in such a way as to emphasize its meaning in that poem. Its meaning seems to come forth, to stand out from the words around it. Or in giving a speech, I might at a certain moment make a gesture, point to my heart for example, thereby drawing out the meaning of a particular word. These are all instances of words in context standing out, being made to show their meanings. Of course, these meanings are use-meanings, that is, meanings in the primary sense. The words have meaning at all only because they are being used in a context, for a purpose. Without their place in the whole language, they would be just noise.

Now we remove the context, the whole environment that gives the individual words their meanings in use. We certainly cannot play the same language-games with them, but what can we do with them? What is their new status? Imagine that while playing a game of chess the board and pieces are taken away. You and your friend carry on the game mentally. The board and pieces are gone, and along with them certain sorts of things you might have done with them, like settling disputes, instructing onlookers, and so forth. But something remains that is enough like chess to cause us to call it by the same name, with the disclaimer "mental" added. We have some idea of the relationship between the two.

Now imagine that you're looking at a picture which is then taken away. You are left with your mental image of it. You might say you have a picture in your mind. Your mental picture, however, is not a picture. There's nothing wrong with calling it a "mental picture," if we keep in mind that the adjective "mental" is not like, say, the adjective "large." A large picture is a picture. A mental picture is not a picture, but is related to a picture. The words "mental picture" and "picture" have different grammars but are closely related: we can express our mental picture in the same way that we might describe a real picture. In a sense, something of the picture remains in your mind after the picture is taken away, though that something is not a picture or even part of a picture.

Well, maybe we can say that the same kind of thing happens when I experience the meaning of an isolated word. Something remains of the word's usual embedded meaning, but this is not a meaning in the primary sense. Only after we have learned the meaning in its primary sense—the *use* of a word—can we be helped to understand the meaning of an isolated word, its emergent meaning. Only then will we be able to use expressions like "this word is full of its meaning," or to react when repetition erodes the meaning of a word. If we want to say that the isolated word is not truly isolated, but carries its original language-games along with it, we will not be very wrong. Just as the rules of mental chess are very much like the rules of board chess, so we might say that contextual meaning and isolated meaning bear something in common. The latter derives from the former but no longer has the same use. (The "meaning" of a completely disintegrated word is a limiting case: it has no use at all.) I can try, by means of ordinary use-meaning, to teach another what this extended or secondary or emergent meaning is. And I will know that he understands me by what he can do with this concept. I know when someone has understood what mental chess is when he can succeed in carrying out a game and perhaps review it with real pieces on a chess board. I know someone has calculated in his head not merely by his arriving at the correct answer but also by his being able to show me how he got that answer. I'll know that someone has grasped what experiencing the meaning of a word is if he can laugh at puns, suggest novel juxtapositions of words, or find the right tone of voice to distinguish between two isolated meanings.

Wittgenstein raises a further related question:

> Given the two ideas "fat" and "lean," would you be rather inclined to say that Wednesday was fat and Tuesday lean, or the other way around. (I incline to choose the former.) Now have "fat" and "lean" some different meaning here from their usual one?—They have a different use.—So ought I really to have used different words? Certainly not that.—I want to use *these* words (with their familiar meanings) *here*. (*PI*, p. 216)

Wittgenstein remains uninterested in the causes of his inclination, which may be associations from childhood. It is the *inclination* that matters:

> Asked "What do you really mean here by 'fat' and 'lean'?"—I could only explain the meanings in the usual way. I could *not* point to the examples of Tuesday and Wednesday. (*PI*, p. 216)

The primary meanings of "fat" and "lean" apply mainly to people and animals. These words can also be used metaphorically, as in someone's having a fat bank account, or in his running a lean business. The metaphorical meanings can be explained by reference to the primary meanings. The metaphors can be stated in other ways in light of the primary meanings. A fat bank account is a large one, with lots of money in it. A lean business has little waste, little excess over what it needs to operate.

"Fat" in "fat Wednesday" and "lean" in "lean Tuesday" are, however, *not* metaphors. They cannot be explained by describing the relation between "fat" and "Wednesday":

> The secondary sense is not a "metaphorical" sense. If I say, "For me the vowel *e* is yellow" I do not mean: "yellow" in a metaphorical sense,—for I could not express what I want to say in any other way than by means of the idea "yellow." (*PI*, p. 216)

Does this notion of a secondary, non-metaphorical meaning of a word make sense to you? If the idea of the meaning of an isolated word makes sense, then this ought to also. If "fat" can have a meaning related to—but not the same kind as—its usual use-meaning, then perhaps that meaning is at work in this context. The contextless word out alone, which possesses a derivative meaning, might yet serve a function when placed in a new context. In fact, if the only sense of meaning that we had was use-meaning, could we imagine that "fat Wednesday" was anything but nonsense? (Maybe you think it *is* nonsense. Perhaps it is.) A metaphorical use of "fat" relies on some commonality between words. Something fat is big in bulk. A bank account can be big, too, in quantity. So a fat bank account makes sense. Language-games cross here in a fairly obvious way. But no such obviousness strikes us in "fat Wednesday."[39] In fact most of us are surprised not just by the juxtaposition of "fat" and "Wednesday," but also by their sounding right together.[40] We can't explain the fit, but we experience it. It is as if a new gesture has been created. "When a theme, a phrase, suddenly says something to you, you don't have to be able to explain it to yourself. Suddenly *this* gesture too is accessible to you" (*RPP I*, 660). A word that I learned to use with a particular meaning I now use in a new way, spontaneously, like *this*. Wittgenstein also mentions "the feeling of the unreality of one's surroundings" as an experience of the same kind (*RPP I*, 125). Why use precisely that word ("unreality") for this feeling? He chooses it *because* of its usual meaning, which has nothing to do with a feeling. I give it a new use, in part simply by saying that I have a "feeling of unreality." Others may understand this, and if they do, perhaps the aptness of the expression arises from something deep in our common linguistic activity. I don't know where it comes from or why it sounds right, but like a gesture, it appears spontaneously and no other way expresses better what I feel.

Not everyone who reads what I've written about secondary meanings and experiencing the meaning of a word will be able to match up his or her own experiences with the descriptions here. Maybe "fat Wednesday" sounds silly, or if not, then you think that at least there should be a way to explain what it means. Maybe the meaning of a word doesn't degenerate for you when you repeat it many times. There may be people who are meaning-blind. They're able to *use* words in their usual ways, but unable to make much sense of an experience of meaning or loss of meaning. Just as we wondered what relationship the aspect-blind would have to pictures, now we might ask: what stance would a meaning-blind person take to words?

A word has a physiognomy. Our familiar words almost look like what they are. Misspellings jar us, as do mispronunciations. We notice this especially while we are trying to learn a new language in its own country. The words of the foreign language haven't yet acquired the feel that will allow us to hear and speak them comfortably. In our minds, we still translate the unfamiliar to the familiar. Gradually, the new language takes shape for us. It begins to look and sound right. We begin to choose and value the words of our new language as we do the words of our old. The physiognomy of a word is first and foremost that of a word in context, in use. Our familiar words seem to look at us as if they were familiar faces: "But a face in a *painting* looks at us, too" (*PI*, p. 181). As the blobs of paint become a face that looks in the context of the painting, so too the physiognomy of a word arises from the language. That is why the words of our new language begin to look different, and our relationship to them changes as we grow more familiar with how to do things with them.

We also value names. We frame signatures. We think that a great person's name seems to fit his accomplishments and works:

> It is as if the name together with these works, formed a solid whole. If we see the name, the works come to mind, and if we think of the works, so does the name. . . . The name turns into a gesture. (*RPP I*, 341)

Someone who didn't understand this might be thought of as meaning-blind. Our relationship to *numbers* might be something like his to words. Except for perhaps some of the smaller numbers, we generally don't take the same interest in individual numbers as we do in words, and especially names. Numbers seem not to carry personality, except perhaps to a few people.[41] Think of the dehumanizing effect of replacing a person's name with a number. The number seems to offer less of a handle on who the person is. It seems not to fit a human being the way a name does. Words resonate for us, they call up images, other words, memories. Numbers seem to require our working through them to figure out their relationships. The meaning-blind man, however, "would not feel that names, when heard or seen, are distinguished by an imponderable Something" (*RPP I*, 243). He might not feel strongly the loss attendant on replacing a name with a number. On the lighter side, considerations such as these help explain why you are amused by the story of the four comedians at the comedians' convention (if you are amused). Three were seasoned veterans, the fourth a novice. All of them knew all the jokes so well that they could simply refer to them by number. The four were standing around together, when one said: "How about 15?" at which they all laughed. Another joined in, "15's okay, but what about 63?" This really broke them up. Then the new comedian offered his. "Hey, guys, get a load of 59." Dead silence, not even a grin. The fourth comedian piped up: "I guess some people just can't tell a joke."

Just as the aspect-blind could not carry out the request to "*see* this triangle *as* a mountain," the meaning-blind would have trouble knowing how to *hear* the word "bark" *as* a noun, or how to *say* it *as* a verb. He wouldn't understand what he was being asked to do, though he'd have no trouble using the word in context. He could obey the command to *use* the word "bank" first as a verb and then as a noun, but not to *say* it alone with those meanings. We might call someone who doesn't understand these sorts of things—doesn't understand what it means to say that Abraham Lincoln's signature seems to fit the man—"prosaic" (*RPP I*, 342). His imagination fails to carry him beyond the usual. We can also compare him with someone who lacks a musical ear. When teaching music we might instruct a pupil to "*hear* these measures *as* a march, then you will play them correctly." For many students, this will be enough to get them to do the right thing, but not for someone who doesn't have a musical ear. He might want more specific instructions, such as exactly where to place the stresses. He plays all the notes right, but something is missing. The teacher may be able to provide what the student asks for, but that is not what was meant by the original instruction. This student cannot make his way around. A meaning-blind person will be like this toward words. He will want to know why "fat" and "Wednesday" can be juxtaposed. He will insist that "fat Wednesday" must be a metaphor and he will want to understand how the two words with their ordinary meanings fit together. But as we've seen, "fat Wednesday" is not a metaphor. It can no more be unpacked than can the director's instruction to his actor to "make a crafty face" be translated into facial geometry. Either you get it or you don't.

We laugh at puns because we have our footing in our language. In Abbott and Costello's esteemed "Who's on First" baseball routine, there is a sequence in which Abbott repeats "who" three times, and we laugh each time, because the meaning-blind Costello can't hear "who" as both an interrogative pronoun and a proper name, as we can. Abbott has introduced the players: the first baseman's name is "Who." This is not so clear to Costello.

C: You know the fellows' names?
A: Yes.
C: Well, then, who's playin' first?

A: Yes.
C: I mean the fellow's name on first base.
A: Who.
C: The fellow playin' first base for St. Louis.
A: Who.
C: The guy on first base.
A: Who is on first.
C: Well what are you askin' me for?
A: I'm not asking you—I'm telling you: Who is on first.

On the other side, consider what Virginia Woolf says about our relationship to ancient Greek. Let's assume that we've studied it a lot and made ourselves as aware as we can of the culture and history of Greece:

> Where are we to laugh in reading Greek? There is a passage in the Odyssey where laughter begins to steal upon us, but if Homer were looking we should probably think it better to control our merriment. To laugh instantly it is almost necessary . . . to laugh in English. . . . The French, the Italians, the Americans . . . pause, as we pause in reading Homer, to make sure that they are laughing in the right place, and the pause is fatal. Thus humor is the first of the gifts to perish in a foreign tongue, and when we turn from Greek to English literature it seems, after a long silence, as if our great age were ushered in by a burst of laughter. (Woolf 1984, 36–37)

That fatal pause can afflict the meaning-blind as they attempt to figure out what might be funny about a pun or joke. They might be able to understand it, but they can't hear it. For them riddles become puzzles. In the face of ancient Greek, we are all meaning-blind, aren't we?

Wittgenstein calls an aspect "an echo of a thought in sight" (*PI*, p. 212). Thought makes its presence felt in our eyes from time to time through the various phenomena related to seeing aspects. It doesn't seem right to draw a strict analogy in the case of meaning, because thought is almost always manifest in our speech. It doesn't appear only occasionally. Yet the meaning-blind person is missing something. Wittgenstein gives this image:

> If I compare the coming of the *meaning* into one's mind to a dream, then our talk is ordinarily dreamless.
> The "meaning-blind" man would then be one who would always talk dreamlessly. (*RPP I*, 232)

Dreamless sleep doesn't sound so bad, does it? Sometimes we describe our best nights' sleep as dreamless. Maybe there's an upside to being meaning-blind. Maybe sometimes it's better that meaning doesn't make itself known. What would be lost if we never dreamed? Does our experience of dreaming shed any light on our dreamless sleep? Does dreaming make us aware of dreamless sleep—an awareness we might never attain without this contrast? Wittgenstein at least wants us to see that the meaning-blind never have an experience we sometimes have. The experience is secondary: we can't dream unless we sleep, but we can sleep without dreaming. So, too, we can't experience the meaning of a word unless words are usually used by us with their non-experienced use-meanings.[42]

Perhaps these experiences are echoes of another kind, from deep within the shared inheritance that is our common language. Its depths can be sounded in many ways, but we must attune ourselves to what messages they send back. Words out of context or in radically new contexts can be a kind of sounding device, as we test what might sound right. We ourselves judge this and it behooves us to cultivate not only our skills with words, but our experience with how others have dared use them. Words have the power to stir the imagination, and the imagination in return can unlock what might be hidden in language or be possible for it: "We react with certain words, and we react *to* them" (*RPP I*, 1). So much greater then is the loss of the ability to do things with words suffered by people like Dr. P. and Chil. Others, such as those with ASD, haven't experienced loss, because they never had those powers to begin with.

In the next chapter, we'll try to apply some of what we've learned about aspects and meanings in particular, and about language in general. How do we begin to talk about a painting, a piece of music, a poem? How might seeing aspects and experiencing meaning be a part of that discussion? We are interested in what can broadly be called "aesthetic experience," not in evaluating paintings or symphonies to see what makes one better than another. Nor are we interested in why we *like* certain works of art. We will concentrate on experience, because aspects are directly connected to experiences, as are the emergent meanings of words. And like the experience of a change in aspect, aesthetic experiences involve both perception and intellect, amalgamated in the crucible of the imagination. We'll begin the next chapter, then, with experience. Our exploration will be brief, narrow, and necessarily unsatisfying. But it will be a start.

CHAPTER FOUR

Aspects and Art

I may draw you a face. Then at another time I draw another
face. You say: "That's not the same face."—but you can't
say whether the eyes are closer together, or mouth longer,
or anything of this sort. "It looks different somehow."
This is enormously important for all philosophy. (*LA*, 31)

A. Experience

When the duck-rabbit morphs from rabbit to duck, when the Necker
cube flips, when I recognize my old friend or pick a face out in what
was a picture of chaos—in all these cases I experience something.
Something happens, often suddenly and unexpectedly, without
any easily describable thought or deliberation or effort on my part.
Like all experiences, these are temporal. The Necker cube reversal
seems to be instantaneous: one moment the cube is pointing down
to the right, the next moment it's pointing up to the left. Recognizing my long-lost friend might be punctuated with small revelations,
doubts and uncertainties, half-recognitions, until I finally see him.
When Homer's Odysseus returns home incognito after a twenty-year
absence, Argos, a dog that was only a puppy when Odysseus left for
the Trojan war, recognizes him at once. (Perhaps dogs are hard to
fool because they do not speak.) Telemachus, Odysseus's son, takes
longer to see him, even after Odysseus removes his disguise. It's not
even correct to say he "recognizes" his father, since Odysseus left
when Telemachus was barely an infant. Although Telemachus has
been told how much he resembles his father, it is a marvel that he sees
Odysseus at all in the man standing in front of him.

Experiences occupy time. They also occupy me. Some experiences—say, the experience of pain—can occupy me completely. Pain
can keep all other experiences at bay and even prevent me from
thinking about anything else. Such experiences involve the senses
in a broad and consuming way, and their expressions often seem just
to come from me, without any hesitation. I find myself crying out
"Ouch!" or "Ah!" without reflection or formulation; these are hardly

157

words at all. Even something like "That really hurts!" doesn't *describe* my pain; it *expresses* it.

Both humans and animals have such experiences. We are animals, after all, but we also have other, more distinctively human experiences that shape our lives and define us both as individuals and as members of a species. Seeing and other forms of perception that can be said to be accompanied by thought or connected to thinking are closely related both to aspects and to our experiences of art and music. Later we'll look in more depth at the connection between seeing aspects and "experiencing the meaning of a word." This will help us understand how good descriptions of art works can enhance our aesthetic experiences and even create new ones. That is why we need first to spend some time exploring how thought informs visual experience.

While all visual experiences are perceptions, not all perceptions are visual experiences: "If you are looking at an object, you need not think of it" (*PI*, p. 197). This sort of looking without thinking is what Wittgenstein means by perception simply. This is certainly what we do much of the time when we see and hear. Such seeing is thoughtless, but not necessarily stupid or careless. It is simply seeing, devoid of an obvious or conscious connection with language. Perhaps I see this way when I drive a car or when I appreciate the beauty of a natural scene, wordlessly soaking it all in, uninterrupted by questions posed by others or by myself.

Architects and builders looking at a blueprint might have a more mindful perception. They don't simply *see* the building in the blueprint—they *read* it. When we look at a paragraph of text in our native language or a topographical map of rugged terrain, we cannot instantly see what it means; we must read it. So, too, the architect sees by deliberately figuring out the blueprint. He can tell you what the lines and numbers mean, but he does not immediately *see* their meaning. (A skilled musician reading a score is in a similar condition.) Should the architect's looking be interrupted by the question "What do you see?" his answer would be that he sees a plan, a drawing. He does not *see* a room or a building, though he might *imagine* one. In a sense, he sees what is in front of him but must figure out what it means. Surely, the experienced architect's or builder's relationship to a blueprint will differ from mine. He will be more at home with it and in it. But he will still see a plan, not a house.

So, first we have that virtually mindless seeing that we do so much of the time while walking, driving, or paying attention to a conversation and not to our surroundings. Much of what I see at such times lies on the periphery of consciousness, barely present even when right in front of me. This kind of seeing cannot be underestimated, but it cannot be called an experience. It does not occupy me, even though I am doing it. Second, we have the architect who looks at a plan and reads it. He is occupied while doing this, but his need to interpret what he sees through what he knows about the conventions of such drawings indicates that he does not *see* the building in the plan. Rather, he works out what the building looks like. His perceptual experience is of the drawing, not what the drawing means, though he might be thinking about what it means. A third mode of seeing, the most relevant and significant for us in this chapter on art and music, is both a perception and a visual experience. These experiences can be described:

> I look at an animal and am asked: "What do you see?" I answer: "A rabbit."—I see a landscape; suddenly a rabbit runs past. I exclaim "A rabbit!"
>
> Both things, both the report and the exclamation, are expressions of perception and of visual experience. But the exclamation is so in a different sense from the report: it is forced from us.—It is related to the experience as a cry is to pain. (*PI*, p. 197)

When asked, I say that I am seeing a rabbit. When one runs across my field of vision, I exclaim, "A rabbit!" In both cases, as Wittgenstein says, my ability to describe what I see shows that thought is involved in the perception itself. Thought is mixed in; it makes an amalgam with the purely visual.

Aspect-seeing is a visual experience that can be described. It may come upon us suddenly or gradually. Or it may be that the aspect I see has become a permanent part of my perception, as when, after recognizing the face in the puzzle-picture, I can no longer see anything but the face in it. To this characterization of aspect-seeing I want to add the way in which the description is *forced* from me or simply *seems right* to me. It can be forced when suddenly I exclaim that something new has come on the scene, though nothing has changed outside to make me say so. I see something I hadn't seen before. The "aha!" moment of a change of aspect is akin to the sudden darting of an animal across my visual field or the sudden swerving of a car in traffic. It attracts me, it occupies me, and I see it all at once without needing to figure out *what* I am seeing. I might be able to give myself these visual experiences, as I can get the Necker cube to flip almost at will or the duck-rabbit to waffle back and forth between duck and rabbit. I do not need to be taken by surprise in order to experience a change of aspect, nor have a visual experience at all, though I would not be inclined to *exclaim* something like "Now it's a duck!" if I had brought on the change of perception myself. What distinguishes the visual experience of a change in aspect from that of the darting rabbit is that there is no change in the world that corresponds to my former experience. The aspect change causes the same forced exclamation as the real animal but without the animal. If you were with me when the rabbit darted by, you too might have exclaimed, but not so when the aspect changed to a rabbit for me.

What makes a perception into an experience is my becoming able to describe what I see, even if I don't actually do so. When I suddenly recognize my friend in a crowd, I needn't say his name either out loud or to myself in order to have the visual experience of recognizing him. But if, when asked, I could not say who it was that I saw, I would not be justified in claiming either that I recognized him or that I had had a visual experience. The possibility of these experiences is bound up with our ability to describe what we see. If I cannot tell you what I see, then I cannot tell myself either. I would then have no right to say even that I was having a visual experience. If I am the only one who can know, then not even I can know. The public, social nature of language and language learning requires that my visual experiences must in principle be shareable.

This feature of how language works relates in important ways to what we see when we look at paintings and what we hear when we listen to music. I explained in chapter three that Wittgenstein believes that the phenomena of experiencing a change in aspect are important, in part, because they shed light on experiencing the meaning of a word. Both these experiences and their correlative absences (in the aspect-blind and the meaning-deaf) can be explained and understood only on the foundation of language as a learned skill that helps us do things. Let's now turn to our experiences of viewing works of art, especially paintings. About this complex subject we'll be able to explore only a few small suggestions, and we will rely on what others have said about aspects and art to guide us.

B. Seeing a Painting

> The duck-rabbit. One asks oneself: how can the eye—this *dot*—be looking in a direction?—*"See, it is looking!"* (And one "looks" oneself as one says this.) (*PI*, p. 205)

Why do we hang pictures on our walls? Why do we visit museums and galleries full of all kinds of paintings? Why do we return to look at the same paintings again and again? We also listen to the same music over and over, no matter how familiar it becomes to us. Often this very familiarity attracts us. Is it so very obvious why paintings and pieces of music give us pleasure, beckon to us, and why we also want to see new paintings and hear new music? It would be naïve for us to think there might be just one explanation for our enchantment by paintings and music. There are no doubt countless reasons, which extend to other forms of visual art such as sculpture. We can't uncover all the possible ends served in human life by paintings and music, but we can focus on the role played by aspect-seeing and aspect-hearing in our relationship to some of them. To make this modest start, we need to look at some paintings and listen to some music. How do we describe our experiences with paintings and music? What does it mean to understand a painting, and how can such understanding be conveyed to others? Can we get others to see and understand what we do in a painting? Over what sorts of things is aesthetic disagreement possible, and is it important at all that we agree or disagree about art? Can people be hopelessly blind to what is of interest in a painting or a sonata? Underlying these questions sits an enormous one: Why does art matter? What is its point? A lot of questions, all worth exploring from many sides. But my job is not to address every question, even if I could. I want to explore how the connection between aspect-seeing and language, which includes what Wittgenstein has called the "secondary meanings" of words— which I have called "emergent meanings"—can help us better understand our aesthetic experiences and how we talk about them and about works of art.

Aristotle is a good thinker to turn to at the start of any inquiry about art. He suggests that one reason we enjoy looking at pictures and sculptures and going to the theater is that we delight in recognizing similarities and differences between the art works and things or events from real life. Through the eyes, we come to know that this painting in front of us looks like an alpine scene as I either once saw it or imagine it would look. But over here, on the gallery wall, this amateurish portrait, by contrast, fails to capture its subject. The proportions are wrong, the skin too pale, the smile forced. Similarities and differences catch our attention. We can pass preliminary judgment on these paintings, at least from the point of view of their success at representing their subjects. This simplification of Aristotle's more complex and subtle developed position serves as a first step in supplying a possible explanation for why we are attracted to pictures— at least representational ones. (Other problems arise when we turn to abstract art or installation art or performance art. Even Impressionist paintings offer their own challenge to considering resemblance to be the magnetic core of art.)

Most paintings we look at, however, are not about people we know or places we have been. Many are fictional, growing almost entirely from the artist's imagination. Their appeal for us can't be because they look like people, places, and objects that we know or because we detect that they are accurate representations of what we have seen in life. Still, we can see in them possible people, places, events—and sometimes even impossible ones that strike us by their contrast to what is and what can be. Take as an example the portrait of the French philosopher, René Descartes, by the Dutch painter Franz Hals (1580–1666) (fig. 30). Now, I don't know if this looks like Descartes, but if I compare it with other portraits said to be of Descartes by Jan Baptiste Weenix (1621–1660) and Sebastein Bourdon (1640–1670), I can be somewhat confident that this portrait is of Descartes and that in some important way it looks like him. At least it looks like the other two paintings. The very least I can say is that the

Figure 30. *Portrait of Descartes* by Franz Hals.

artists intended for us to see Descartes in these paintings. It is the peculiar characteristic of our relationship to pictures that we see into them the very objects that they depict. We regard the picture, the drawing, the photograph as we do the object itself, and so in a sense we see what is there and what is not there simultaneously. In these pictures we see Descartes.

And yet, in a substantial way, Hals's painting of Descartes does not resemble Descartes. We also see in the picture lines and shapes, paints and colors. If we had the actual painting in front of us, we would notice brushstrokes and varying thicknesses of paint. This is, after all, paint on canvas, not a human being. Descartes's dog might have found more in common between the painting and an old painter's palette than between it and his master. But our natural description of this canvas—at least what first comes to mind—is: a portrait of Descartes. This natural description will involve things not belonging to the description of the picture as a merely physical object. It is not just a physical object of a certain size and weight, useful merely to cover a wall or display our wealth. Those dabs of paint—Descartes's eyes—look out at us; we can study the expression on his face and wonder what it reveals about this man and the way Hals saw him. In this paint-covered canvas we see a human being. That one can see into a picture the very thing of which it is a picture is one of the reasons we hang pictures on our walls. We don't mistake the portrait for the person, yet we look at it and it looks back at us almost as if it were a person. We are simultaneously aware of its dual nature, its two aspects: It is paint on canvas. It is Descartes. The physical object is a representation. Someone else might see it as something in need of transporting, another as an investment. Perhaps neither would take the time to ponder the character of the man portrayed.

It might be better to say that, though I see the painting as a portrait of Descartes, I can *regard* it as a painted canvas, a heavy object, or an investment. The aspects of the painting are more properly the ways we see Descartes's face and what it expresses. Do we see an arrogant face? A pious one? An inquiring one? If I tell different stories from Descartes's life, might we see different aspects in this face? And yet these concepts—that is, how we use the words "seeing" and "regarding"—lie very close to one another. If I stand near the portrait, perhaps all I see is colors, brushstrokes, and paint. Part of the power of a painting as a representation comes from just this awareness that what we see both is and is not what we see. We never mistake the portrait for the real article, the painting for the man, as we might an artfully executed *trompe l'oeil* column in a Roman church.[1] Critics will talk about both the character of a portrait and its brushstrokes. Describing a self-portrait by Tintoretto, Andrew Butterfield writes: "[T]he picture presents a young man of smoldering intensity. . . . The brushwork is evident and animate, flickering with highlights and shadow across the surface of the skin" (Butterfield 2007, 10). Part of our attraction to paintings is their dual nature. But even when we forget the physical aspect of a good painting, we are left with ambiguity of *meaning*, and this is perhaps at the root of why representational art (and, later, nonrepresentational by contrast) draws us in. Something about art speaks to what we might call the ambiguity of human nature. We are all Proteus, whether we like it or not.

Similar questions about music challenge us. Why do we write, perform, and listen to music at all? Why do we return to the same pieces again and again, finding that they continue to give us pleasure? Think of those things we experience just once, such as newspaper articles. They are consumed. Similarly, what objects do we not hang on walls that we could? Wittgenstein remarks that while we sometimes place "pieces of text" on the wall, we do not in like manner hang "theorems of mechanics" (*PI*, p. 205). Music is especially interesting and difficult to bring under the umbrella of the concept of aspects because music is not generally intended to be representational. While some of Beethoven's sonatas have been given nicknames, such as "Pathetique" and "Moonlight," this is not because they sound like pathos or moonlight, which do not sound at all. And yet when a name or a description of a sonata sounds right, mustn't there be a reason for its striking us as appropriate? I'm inclined to say yes, and I suspect that the reasons have something to do with resemblance to patterns of human life, such as the rhythm of our walk and speech, modulations of our voice, and in general the gestures that comprise a large part of human communication, expression, and activity. But whatever hypotheses are proposed to account for those names, the fact that they seem appropriate (and others might, too) is where I begin. Without speculation, much can be learned simply from these beginnings. After first considering visual art, I'll return later to music and to the ways that aspects can help us understand its place in our lives.

Let's look for a while at a famous painting by the Italian Baroque painter Caravaggio (1571–1610), *The Calling of St. Matthew* (see fig. 31 facing p. 208). All we have in front of us is a small reproduction, flat and lacking the textures of the original. The original was painted around 1600 and hangs in a small corner chapel in the Church of San Luigi dei Francesi in Rome. On the other two walls of the chapel hang two other depictions of scenes from the life of St. Matthew, *The Martyrdom of St. Matthew*, directly across from *The Calling*, and *The Inspiration of St. Matthew*, between the two.[2] All three can be seen in the photograph of the chapel in figure 32. A gate prevents visitors from entering the chapel, so it is impossible to view *The Calling of St. Matthew* head-on. Most people, therefore, see it an angle from the right. Even without knowing about the painting's setting in a church, I think I can see that it is a religious painting. Without trying to say exactly what it means for this painting to be religious, I want to say that this description fits the painting. Perhaps the title helps me, or I know the gospel story of Levi's conversion and subsequent change of name to Matthew. I don't know what goes into my seeing it as religious, and I'm not sure everyone would agree with me that the paint-

Figure 32. Contarelli Chapel, Church of St. Louis of the French, Rome.

ing expresses a religious moment or religious feeling. Describing it as religious opens up the larger question of what we need to know about a painting, an artist, or a culture in order to see it this way. I won't be able to address this question, although it is both important and complex.

One way of confronting this object is to consider it as a physical thing. It is a large (about eleven foot square), heavy composition of canvas, wood, and paint. Someone responsible for moving the painting would want to know something about its aspects as a physical object and might even see it simply as such. It poses certain kinds of problems for the mover that have nothing to do with its subject matter. If we look closely at the canvas, we can see that the paint has been applied thinly. Only a few colors have been used. We might even be able to make out the brushstrokes. Someone with a trained eye could detect different brush sizes and perhaps even the haste or care with which the paints were applied to different parts of the painting. When I consider the geometrical aspect of the painting, I see that it is divided into roughly two parts. The standing figures on the right form a vertical rectangle; those gathered around the table on the left a horizontal block, or perhaps a triangle. The two groups are separated by a vertical void, bridged by the pointing hand. There is a kind of grid pattern of verticals and horizontals that serves to knit the picture together: the window, the table, the finger of the bearded man sitting at the table, a stool, a line running up the wall in the upper left. The contrast of light and shadow serves to guide my eye subtly across the painting from right to left.

Most interesting to me and what attracts me to the painting first is its aspect as a representation. To most viewers, *The Calling of St. Matthew* is not simply a heavy physical object or paint on canvas or a geometrical pattern of vertical and horizontal lights and darks. It is a picture that recounts a moment. As we know from its title and from Scripture, the painting represents a turning or conversion. Levi becomes Matthew, and his world changes. Before, he was a tax collector for the Roman emperor; afterwards, he is a follower of a charismatic teacher. He sees what he had not seen before. Caravaggio's painting attempts to express this moment of conversion, or what I might call a sudden change of aspect in Matthew's life. The setting seems ordinary, everyday, perhaps a room in a tavern. Yet, even if it did not hang in a church, most people would still recognize the painting's religious character. Is it the languid, pointing hand of the tall figure on the right, whose posture seems to command without hesitation and without instilling fear, and which seems to claim its authority from no merely human origin? The light streaming in from the right over the head of Jesus draws our attention to his face and hand. There is also an urgency and dignity about the painting that suggests there is other, more important work to be done than counting money. Some people might come to see this as a religious painting only with help from cues—for example, the halo over the head of Jesus. Others will recognize this aspect right away. They will see whatever it is that makes the painting religious without needing to figure it out. Does one need to have had religious experience in order to be able to *see* this painting as religious and not merely to *know* that it is? I don't know, nor do I know how much one needs to know of history, traditions, and myths to see the painting this way. It is certain that if I don't know what paint is—if, say, I was raised in a society in which paint was unknown—I will not be able to see this object in front of me as *paint* on a canvas, just as the duck-rabbit could never be seen as a duck by someone who had no experience with ducks.

One way of looking at the content of this painting that has become standard, and to which I shall offer a competing suggestion, is something like the following: The bearded tax-gatherer, Levi, is seated at a table at the center of a corolla consisting of himself and four others, perhaps his assistants. Coins litter the table, and the hunched-over figure on the left appears to be counting some of them. The group is lighted by a source at the upper right. Jesus, his eyes veiled in shadow, with the halo hinting at his divinity, enters with Peter. A gesture of his right hand summons Levi, who is surprised by the intrusion of these barefoot men, and perhaps dazzled by the sudden light from a just-opened door. Levi draws back and gestures towards himself, as if to ask, "Who, me?" while his right hand remains pressed onto some coins. The two figures to the left are so concerned with counting money that they are oblivious to the arrival of Christ, and so symbolically deprive themselves of the opportunity he offers for salvation. The two boys in the center do respond, the younger one drawing back as if to seek Levi's protection, while the older, with his sword hung conspicuously, leans forward somewhat menacingly towards Peter, who seems to freeze him in place with a finger. For the moment captured in the picture, no one does anything. In another second, Matthew will rise up and follow Jesus, and his world will be forever different. The painting captures the very moment of Matthew's turning.[3]

This description of what we are seeing when we look at Caravaggio's painting is both revealing and compelling. The central character in the painting is illuminated by a light that seems to point directly to him. The surprised expression on his face, coupled with his pointing index finger, shows that he is responding to the arrival of Jesus and Peter. This would be consonant with what critics take to be the artistic standards of the time, with the most important figure in the center, looking more prominent than the surrounding persons. For critics who accept that Caravaggio is painting in the traditional way—albeit with new, marvelous techniques, especially his use of dark and light—there is no question about who in the painting is Matthew. This is what I *see*, at least at first look. It is also how the painting is interpreted, that is, how knowledge I have (or think I have) of the story of Matthew, the traditions of painting, and maybe even of the life of Caravaggio, can lead me to *reason* that the figure in the center is Matthew. Thinking about the painting, however, and drawing conclusions from my thoughts, is not exactly seeing, though what I believe can influence what I see in different ways. I'll have another look at the painting and try to defend myself from the temptation of the obvious.

I might be helped by returning to the accounts of Matthew's calling that are given in three of the Gospels. I can't be sure if Caravaggio wants to stay true to these accounts or deviate from them, so I can't simply say that they ought to guide me in how I try to see the painting. But I can begin with them anyway, since Caravaggio fully expects his viewers to be familiar with them:

> As Jesus passed on from there, he saw a man called Matthew sitting at the tax office; and he said to him, "Follow me." And he rose and followed him. (Matt. 9:9)

> And as he passed on, he saw Levi the son of Alphaeus sitting at the tax office, and he said to him, "Follow me." And he rose and followed him. (Mark 2:14)

> After this he went out, and saw a tax collector, named Levi, sitting at the tax office; and he said to him, "Follow me." And he left everything, and rose and followed him. (Luke 5:27–28)[4]

The accounts are bare and simple, merely hints of what might have taken place within Matthew and those around him. What strikes me, however, is what the stories do *not* say. No account suggests that Matthew hesitated or questioned before leaving his collection table when summoned by Jesus or that Jesus expected to need to persuade Matthew. Of course, as I said earlier, Caravaggio's understanding of the story may be that we ought to expect a human being to doubt and question and ask in a situation such as this, where one is about to surrender one's livelihood and life at the behest of a stranger. Caravaggio may fully agree with those who have taken for granted that the bearded central figure is the evangelist. But if I allow myself to break loose of this idea, who then would be Matthew? What does the silence of the Gospel account let me *see* in the painting that I otherwise might have missed? Jesus does not seem to think that he'll need to stay long to answer questions, because his foot, seen in the lower right, is already turned, as if he is about to leave as soon as he has arrived. We see it as a foot about to move, not one planted on the floor awaiting a hesitant response. Further, is it perfectly clear at whom Jesus is looking and pointing? The dabs of paint that are the eyes of Christ are looking, but they are not looking at the illuminated central figure. Isn't the arc of his finger met by the hunched-over young man, whose back curves up and toward Jesus as if he is about to rise? Do I see him rising up, perhaps even see the curled fingers of his left hand beginning to push on the tabletop? His eyes are the only ones among those of the five figures at the table that are not illuminated by the bright light streaming in from the right. Both his eyes and those of Jesus are in shadow, and I am drawn to both pairs of shadowed eyes not because they are focal points of lines of light or because they are centrally placed or because the Gospel story tells us something about them. The paint has created human eyes in shadow, and they beckon me because I want to know whose eyes they are and what they mean. The young man's eyes do not question or wonder. They seem almost entranced, not even seeing the coins in front of him on the table. The eyes of Jesus send out their power just under the line of illumination, guided by his hand and outstretched index finger, which also remain surrounded by the dark background of the unilluminated wall. Even the pointing finger of the bearded man now seems to take up the same direction and is no longer point-ing at himself, but rather away from himself toward the young man. Can you see the painting this way?

The long-standing traditional interpretation tells us that the man in the center must be Matthew because he is wearing a hat appro-priate to the office of tax collector. He is old enough to fill a respon-sible position and to employ young men as his helpers. His startled, puzzled eyes look directly at Jesus, as if he at least thinks that the words "Follow me" may be intended for him. Critics also argue that if we consider the historical context of the time in which Caravag-gio painted and measure the picture against that set of standards, then Caravaggio must be representing the subject of the picture as central and prominently lighted, looking more important than those around him. The danger in relying on such historical information is that one does not know if the artist is painting within the tradition or attempting to move outside it. This is why we need to rely on what we *see* first and foremost, and leave historical facts aside, as a kind of hypothesis but not a real seeing. Hypotheses may prove untrue, but what I see cannot. What I see may change as I study the painting. It may change as I hear others talk about it. It may even change as I learn more facts about the painter and his work. But my seeing is not an interpretation. To get clearer on why this is so and why it's important, I'll go back to the duck-rabbit.

When the drawing of the duck-rabbit looks to me only like a duck—perhaps because I am seeing it against a background of duck drawings—I simply see a picture of a duck. I don't need to figure out that it's a duck by hints or cues. I take it in whole, a duck. Now if I look at it not against any duck background, but simply as is, I will sometimes see it as a duck, sometimes as a rabbit. That is the way this ambiguous picture presents itself to us. Even when the rabbit aspect dawns on me, I do not *interpret* the picture to be that of a rabbit. Nothing has changed in the picture and so I cannot use any new hints or cues to determine that in fact the picture is now that of a rabbit. There were no duck marks, and there are now no rabbit marks that tell me that in fact this must be a duck or this must be a rabbit. I simply see in each case. I do not figure anything out, as I might when I try to read a blueprint or analyze a painting. Interpretations can be wrong; further information can lead me to change my interpretation.

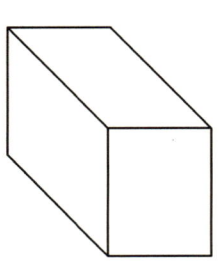

Figure 33.
Rectangular prism.

But I cannot be wrong about seeing the duck-rabbit as a duck or a rabbit. What I see will not change if I'm told that this is not actually a picture of a duck-rabbit, but is rather something else. Given this information, I might see something more in addition, but the duck and the rabbit cannot be taken away from me. Wittgenstein gives an example of a drawing of a rectangular solid, which can stand for any one of a number of things (fig. 33). You could imagine such an illustration

appearing in several places in a book, a text-book for instance. In the relevant text something different is in question every time: here a glass cube, there an inverted open box, there a wire frame of that shape, there three boards forming a solid angle. Each time the text supplies the interpretation of the illustration. (*PI*, p. 193)

I must do something when I interpret the picture. That I am interpreting the picture a certain way is shown not only by my saying so but also by how I use the picture or how it helps me to understand what the text is saying. Interpreting a picture in this way does not necessarily involve seeing the picture *as* what I interpret it to be. Rather, what I say tells my listener that I am interpreting without seeing. I might, for example, say that if this is a wire frame, then I can hang it from the ceiling by hooking something around one of its corners. I might even draw a second picture to illustrate this or the textbook might provide one in the course of its discussion. But I do not see the lines as wire. Nor would I see the rectangles in the drawing as wood if it were intended to illustrate "three boards forming a solid angle." I can *treat* the rectangles as wood, I can imagine what would happen to them in different circumstances, but this is not the same as seeing them as wood. While I do not see the figure as any of these, the interpretation of it as one of them helps me make sense of other suggestions in the text. The interpretation works or doesn't work according to how it helps me understand.

Wittgenstein, however, goes on in the same passage we just quoted to say, "But we can also see the illustration now as one thing now as another.—So we interpret it, and *see* it as we *interpret* it" (*PI*, p. 193). In these cases I seem to do something along with seeing, though this may not be the best way to put it. I interpret with the help of, say, the textbook in which the figure is an illustration. I also see what I have interpreted. For example, I might be able not only to interpret, but also to see, this figure as a closed box. I see the figure as it is *used* in the text. It might seem easier to me to see it that way than as one of the other interpretations Wittgenstein offers. I'm not sure. (I can't *see* it as a red box or a wooden box, for instance, though I can interpret it to be one, if the text asks me to do so. I can't see the *stuff* it's made of or its color, though I can imagine it.) In another case, Wittgenstein asks us to consider the "aspects of a triangle," such as the one in figure 34.

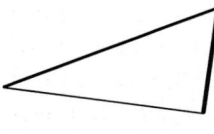

Figure 34. Triangle.

This triangle can be seen as a triangular hole, as a solid, as a geometrical drawing; as standing on its base, as hanging from its apex; as a
mountain, as a wedge, as an arrow or pointer, as an overturned object
which is meant to stand on the shorter side of the right angle, as a half
parallelogram, and as various other things. (*PI*, p. 200)

As in the drawing of the box, the triangle can be seen as any one
of a number of things when the interpretation calls on us to use it in
a certain way. The use to which the figure is to be put helps determine how we see it. Interpretation, while not exactly a figuring out
as in reading a blueprint, is not yet fully seeing. When I turn to the
duck-rabbit, however, the situation is different. I needn't do anything at all—or at least not anything I can articulate—when I see
the duck-rabbit first as a duck then as a rabbit. (I don't *do* anything
either when I see, for example, an ordinary spoon in ordinary circumstances.) Seeing the duck-rabbit as a duck is more like seeing a
real duck than interpreting the 3-D box drawing as a wire frame is
like seeing a real wire frame. (There are gradations of seeing-as. It is
a complex concept, as Wittgenstein often reminds us.)

When we look at a painting, we engage all three of the kinds of
seeing I have just articulated. There is straightforward seeing, as
when I see a picture in front of me. There is what we can call interpretive seeing, which involves figuring out or some other kind of
more conscious exercise of the imagination. Finally there is aspect-
seeing, when I feel that I am not doing any interpreting at all, yet I
am not simply seeing something like a spoon. Seeing the two orientations of the Necker cube is an example.

Consider *Woman Holding a Balance* by Jan Vermeer (1632–1675)
(see fig. 35 facing p. 208) as an example of a painting that needs to
be figured out, as many of Vermeer's paintings ask to be. It is overtly
allegorical, which means that in order to understand it, in order even
to *see* it, the viewer needs to know to what the various elements of
the painting refer. A young woman stands before a table, gazing at
a balance, which she holds delicately in her right hand, while her
left hand rests gently on the table. Is she waiting for the swinging of
the balance to cease? Has she been, or is she, weighing something?
To describe her dress, I might need to know something about how
Dutch women in the mid-seventeenth century dressed, though I can

at least say that her jacket seems to be bordered in fur, and she is wearing a loosely tied white cap, which acts to frame her face. I am drawn to her face and her right hand by both the light entering from the window and the line of sight that seems to flow from her eyes to the balance. Vermeer uses these structures to tell my eyes what to do and thereby suggests where the locus of meaning in the painting lies. I might marvel at the exquisite technical mastery he shows, how he balances vertical and horizontal lines throughout the painting and how the light that fills the room seems to be diffuse and warm— achievements that are central to my recognition of Vermeer's accomplishments as a painter. But the realm of seeing and meaning is my focus, technical mastery less so, however remarkable it might be. I am concerned less with *how* Vermeer painted the woman's eyes than in the fact that they are *gazing* at the balance.

Once I have said what I can see in the painting, I must then begin to study it. I seem to be drawn into this painting in order to interpret it, to figure out how its meaningful parts cohere. This kind of interpretation may not result in my seeing differently, as I might have come to see the hand of the young man in Caravaggio's *Calling of St. Matthew* pressing against the table. The interpretation I must undertake to become better acquainted with Vermeer's painting is something like figuring out the roles played by its dominant parts. (Technique might help me determine which parts are dominant.) I can get a feel for what parts are important from the form, though I then need to think about the significance of these parts. Arthur Wheelock, who teaches art history at the University of Maryland and serves as curator of northern Baroque painting at the National Gallery of Art, says this about the painting:

> Behind the woman looms an awesome painting of the Last Judgment. . . . Its dark rectangular shape, with its horizontal and vertical emphasis, establishes a quiet, stable framework against which Vermeer juxtaposes the figure of the woman. The visual association of the woman and the Last Judgment is reinforced by thematic parallels: to judge is to weigh. Christ, his arms and hands raised, sits in majesty on the Day of Judgment. His gesture, with both arms raised, mirrors the opposing direction of the woman's balance. His judgments are eternal; hers are temporal. Nevertheless, the woman's pensive response to the balance she holds suggests that her act of judgment, although different

in consequence, is as conscientiously considered as that of the Christ behind her. (Wheelock 1981, 106)

Wheelock's remarks help to establish for me one of the painting's themes, perhaps the main theme. He picks out moments in the painting for us to consider, such as Christ's upturned arms and their inverted image in the balance. The mind carries this connection beyond mere coincidence of form towards the suggestion that judgment and justice are at the heart of both the final day and this day on which the woman weighs and considers. I continue along with Wheelock to spin out more, perhaps deeper, understanding:

> Most interpretations of this painting contrast the eternal values represented by the Last Judgment and the material concerns of the woman. The painting is thus interpreted as a Vanitas theme. The woman has been called the personification of Vanitas. These theories, however, are based on the assumption that the pans of the balance contain precious objects, generally identified as gold or pearls. Recent microscopic examinations of the painting reveal that the pans contain neither gold nor pearls, but are empty. (Wheelock 1981, 106)

My unaided eyes cannot even see, according to Wheelock, what is or is not in the pans. And yet my interpretation of the picture depends on this. A very close look, "microscopic examination," in fact, can change my understanding of the role of the woman from the personification of vanity to that of a person who accepts her "responsibility to weigh and balance her own actions. The mirror on the wall opposite her refers to the search for self-knowledge" (Wheelock 1981, 106). I now interpret the balance as empty, not being used to weigh gold or pearls or other marks of vanity. And I then *see* the balance as empty: I see it as I interpret it, as Wittgenstein puts it.

I can go further. While pointing out the influence that the Last Judgment and the emptiness of the pans have on an interpretation of the painting, Wheelock is also leading me to understand the mood and thoughts of the main figure, the woman holding the balance. "The woman does not appear tempted by the jewels that lie on the table before her: she concentrates on the balance in her hand. Her attitude is one of inner peace and serenity" (Wheelock 1981, 106). Is it possible that I now also *see* the expression on her face differently?

Has it changed for me, not perhaps with the suddenness and completeness of the duck-rabbit, but more subtly, from a face expressive of vanity and self-centeredness to one of equilibrium and balance? Has my reinterpretation of the role of other elements of the painting opened up to my eyes a different facial expression, a different woman?

In a sense the reinterpretation has almost created a new painting. It has certainly made me consider whether the meaning of the painting might be other than what it had been accepted as being. But it has also helped me to see the woman's face differently. One might say that I have been brought to interpret the expression on her face differently, but that the expression is the same as it was, much as a word in a new context might take on new meaning but remain the very same word. The question arises, then, when we recognize a face as expressing, say, vanity or self-awareness, whether we *see* that quality in the face or *interpret* what we see? In the striking cases we looked at in chapter one, I think it is clear that we *see* something we didn't see before, even though nothing changes in the pictures. This is the heart of seeing aspects. In Vermeer's painting, we have an intermediate situation. Some of the features of the painting, such as the Last Judgment, alter their function but not how they look. I interpret them differently and use them differently in my description of the painting. The pans of the balance change their meaning once I allow close examination to convince me that they are empty. (Would even closer examination reverse this?) Their look has changed in a way because my looking has changed. I would, however, like to suggest that when I look at the woman's face and consider its expression, I don't interpret what I see, though my interpretation of other things might influence my seeing. I see her face and its expression. We learned in chapter three that Dr. P., Oliver Sacks's man who mistook his wife for a hat, needed to figure out faces from cues. Often people with ASD have trouble seeing facial expressions for what they are. Generally, however, we do not interpret a face. This ought to strike us as marvelous.

Many paintings can be termed allegorical: the viewer needs to know or figure out the meaning of various elements in order to understand the import of the whole. Some paintings are even explicitly titled to reveal their allegorical intent.[5] Some of the paintings of

William Hogarth might interest us because he, too, placed emphasis on reading his paintings while at the same time portraying facial expressions with mastery:

His work . . . is less about visceral enjoyment than decipherment. The experience is more literary than visual. . . . His engravings are composed of little visual signs that ask to be given literary meanings in order to create a narrative—such as when a table is overturned, a person has particular skin blemishes, a certain statue is on the mantelpiece, a harlot has a type of hat near her bed, a man has his hand in his pocket in a suggestive way, or a spaniel is sleeping or awake. (Schwartz 2007)

The viewer can take a kind of Aristotelian delight in deciphering such works. That is, she comes to know something, to recognize what this particular object signifies and how it fits into the narrative that is the whole picture. Sometimes this figuring can result in new seeing, as in the Vermeer painting. But it need not, and this in itself would not diminish the value of the work, though it would make it less interesting for my discussion of aspects and language.

In trying to understand what is involved in seeing a painting or listening to a piece of music, I am interested in only a sliver of what might be considered important. I have no doubt that great works of art achieve their status for many reasons, including innovation, depth of expression, use of images, execution, scale, and chance. My concern is in some ways small: what do we see when we look at a painting, and how is this seeing related to what we might say or what someone like an art critic might say to us?

Leonardo da Vinci (1452–1519) painted *The Last Supper* (*Il Cenacolo*) (fig. 36) between 1495 and 1497 over dry plaster on the north wall of the refectory of Santa Maria delle Grazie in Milan. It was recognized as a masterpiece of originality and energy from the moment of its unveiling, and different from any previous image of the Last Supper. "In most earlier paintings, Christ and the Apostles are lined up along the table and appear relatively inert and inexpressive. Their gestures are restrained, their faces impassive; there is little sign of communication between them" (Butterfield 2002, 17). A good example is the version of the scene painted in 1486 by Ghirlandaio (1449–1494) (fig. 37). One of the main differences between

Figure 36. *The Last Supper* by Leonardo da Vinci.

Figure 37. *The Last Supper* by Domenico Ghirlandaio.

it and Leonardo's version is the intensity of emotional expression in Leonardo's depiction of the disciples. Their faces, their hands and arms, their very posture all seem to suggest—in fact, shout out—that something extraordinary has just happened or is happening. A long tradition holds that Jesus has just announced to his disciples that someone among them is about to betray him.[6] Their very human response to this disclosure seems almost to overwhelm any attempt to frame the scene in theological or supernatural terms. The painting captures one very emotional moment for the group of followers, who had considered themselves bound by their love and devotion to Jesus and have now been told that there is a traitor among them. Not long after the painting was completed, artists began to paint, sculpt, and draw versions of it in which they changed details but retained the distinctive gestural forms and facial expressions of the original. Leo Steinberg tells us that Goethe, in a famous essay on the painting, helped perpetuate the admiration for it "as a supreme realization of instantaneity" (Steinberg 1973, 300). It was long felt that clarity of expression and unity of meaning were hallmarks of the best art. Leonardo's painting achieves both to a high degree because it captures the complex emotional condition of a group of individuals at a moment of extreme tension. Under a guiding light such as this, there seems to be little room for the possibility of new aspects revealing themselves in the painting. Steinberg, however, develops an argument that places ambiguity at the core of Leonardo's masterpiece. He claims that the painting is simultaneously both secular and religious. It is secular because it represents the betrayal of someone by one of his own followers. It is religious because it represents the establishment of the Eucharist and the disciples' reactions to Christ's words, "This is my body, this is my blood" (Steinberg 1973, 300).[7] The reactions of the followers can be seen as a response to this extraordinary event as well.

Steinberg argues that shortly after *The Last Supper* was completed, when artists realized its extraordinary quality and began copying it, there was already some disagreement about what the painting represented. He says that this disagreement manifested itself in those copies: what artists retained of the original, what they eliminated, and what they actually changed. The essence of the picture was seen to lie in the "distinctive pattern of gesture, expression, and motion made by Christ and the Apostles" (Butterfield 2002, 17). Differences in interpretation were reflected in differences in details. Two striking examples are the copies made by Rembrandt (1606–1669) and Rubens (1577–1640).

Steinberg suggests that Rembrandt's version (fig. 38) is "wholly secular," because it emphasizes the capture of momentary human emotion. In this copy—or rather this adaptation—of the painting, there is no indication of the institution of the Eucharist: no bread

Figure 38. Rembrandt's version of Leonardo's painting.

or wine is prominently figured. According to Steinberg, Rembrandt brings out what he takes to be the theme of the painting by leaving out some things. Betrayal does not in its own right carry religious implications. Leonardo's painting, therefore, is seen as a triumph of Renaissance humanism, a significant move away from theological requirements that influenced most painting up to that time. This, at least, is how the argument goes.

Steinberg, however, thinks there is more to be said—and more to be seen in Leonardo's *Last Supper.* "Our task," writes Steinberg, "is to declare how the work of art looks to an age that no longer insists on seeing the Renaissance as a movement of triumphant secularism" (Steinberg 1973, 298). He thinks that there has long been a "deep-rooted prejudice against multiple functions" in a work of art, a prejudice that considers ambiguity in a painting to be an imperfection, especially in works prior to the twentieth century. This view seems to tie art to knowledge and the belief that knowledge, too, must be unambiguous and be expressed in unambiguous terms. In the end, the rational approach insists that everything be figured out and that rightness and wrongness apply as well to art as to science. But to Steinberg, disagreements among scholars and artists about what the *Last Supper* depicts are not indicators that the truth about the painting has yet to be determined. Rather, Steinberg sees these disagreements as hints that Leonardo is doing more than one thing at a time. Even early on, there was little agreement about what exact moment of the betrayal narrative the painting depicted. Are the disciples responding to Jesus' saying that someone will betray him, or to his statement that he who dips the bread along with him is the betrayer? Steinberg wonders, if the moment depicted can be "stretched out" to encompass both important remarks, which are separated in the gospel accounts, why should we not think that the moment extends still further, to the institution of the Eucharist? The prominent placement of the bread and chalice in Rubens's version (fig. 39)—actually by Pieter Soutman (1580–1657) with the blessing of Rubens—suggests that there was disagreement even back then over what moment Leonardo's painting captured: betrayal or Eucharist, secular or sacred. One might say that the moments of betrayal and Eucharist are emotionally incompatible, and so the same facial expressions and bodily gestures could not serve to convey the response to both: "[V]iolent shock, revulsion, dismay at the announcement of the betrayal; mute reverence in approaching Communion" (Steinberg 1973, 310). But wouldn't the command to eat the flesh and drink the blood of another human being be met with shock, horror and disgust? When John the Apostle writes in a different context about Jesus' command to "eat my flesh and drink my blood," he says that "many of his disciples, when they heard it, said, 'This is a hard saying. Who can listen to it?' . . . After this many of his disciples drew back and no longer went about with him" (John 6:60, 66).

Figure 39. Rubens's version of Leonardo's painting.

Yet we needn't try to imagine that the reactions of the apostles in Leonardo's *Last Supper* must be the same under the painting's two aspects, secular and sacred. Can the apostles' gestures and expressions be seen in more than one way? When I see the duck-rabbit as a duck and then as a rabbit, must I say that the duck looks like a rabbit? In fact what we learned about seeing aspects earlier, in the simpler case of the duck-rabbit, is just this: that what characterizes a change in aspect most fully is the realization both that something has changed and that nothing has changed. When the duck-rabbit switches from duck to rabbit, I know both that I had been seeing a duck, and now am seeing a rabbit and that nothing in the picture itself has changed. In the more complex case of the gestures and expressions in Leonardo's *Last Supper*, I can say something similar if I want to support Steinberg's view that the painting is inherently ambiguous and yet do not want to equate the disciples' emotions upon hearing about the impending betrayal of Jesus with their feelings at the institution of the Eucharist. My effort as observer of the painting must be to *see* it first *as* a representation of response to betrayal, and then to *see* it *as* a representation of the first communion. Steinberg urges us to "ask *how* the uproar at the announcement of treason *becomes interpretable as also* a dramatization of the momentous 'take, eat, this is my body'" (p. 312). My answer is that I come to *see* the very same things, especially the gestures and faces of the men in the painting, *as* expressive of different emotional conditions. Of course there are other elements in the picture that might lead me to do this, other hints that might help me provide for myself the mental context in which I can see differently. Steinberg directs our attention to the hands of Jesus. Goethe saw these hands as outstretched with "divine resignation" while Jesus sits in silence after having asked the fateful question, Which one of you will betray me? (Goethe 1986, 40). Steinberg, however, says they are pointing to the bread and wine. Jesus is still speaking in this account. This suggestion might lead us to begin to consider, with our minds and with our eyes, that the scene represented is—also—that of the institution of the Eucharist. Aren't Judas's betrayal and the institution of the Eucharist *theologically* united as well? Steinberg also suggests that we can view Christ in the picture as reaching for, or at least pointing at, the loaf of bread near his open left hand.

The significance of the loaf at Christ's open hand is attested again by its syntactic relation to the nearest Apostle. In the "secular" interpretation of the event, the pose of St. James (with outstretched arms) [immediately to Christ's left] is understood *as an expression of shock* over the announcement of the betrayal. In the Eucharistic interpretation it *becomes the wonderstruck reflex* to an unsearchable mystery. . . . Taken in isolation the gesture may indeed lack definition, but it is not a solo performance. (p. 330)

In a similar way, we can also look at the hands of Thaddeus, second from the far right. Goethe sees Thaddeus's right hand coming down sharply into his left, a gesture of something like "Didn't I tell you! I knew it!" (Goethe 1986, 42). Steinberg asks us to consider how the picture might change for us if we take that hand as coming down slowly, as in a ritual form of communion-taking, cupping the hands to receive the bread-body. Do we then see Thaddeus's emotional state as reverent, expectant? I would like to say *yes*. But how do we come to see those hands as moving slowly? How do we see James's arms not as an expression of shock, but of wonder? (How do we see the duck-rabbit as first a duck, then a rabbit?) I don't know. Sometimes (and I think looking at the *Last Supper* is one of those times), I simply read or hear what someone like Goethe or Steinberg suggests, open my eyes, and see.

All well and good, you say, even if you aren't fully convinced that the aspects of Leonardo's painting are seen, rather than interpreted and understood. But you wonder, don't you—I know I do—whether Leonardo intended his great painting to be an ambiguous representation of two events, secular and religious. Certainly we can bring arguments to bear on both sides, and a resolution of the problem might even be worked out. Again, I don't know. Much like the ongoing debate on how to understand the United States Constitution—either through an appreciation of the intent of the Founding Fathers or through our own contemporary usage and and practices—I think an answer is not to be taken as the truth, but as an interpretation. Let's say that Leonardo intended his painting to represent only the moment of betrayal and the apostles' immediate reaction to it. While some questions might be left unanswered under this interpretation, the painting as whole would still exhibit a unity that would repay careful attention and continue to give aesthetic pleasure. But even if Leonardo intended the painting to be clear and unambiguous, presenting to us either something secular (treason) or something sacred (Eucharist), but not both, there remain to us at least two further possibilities to take seriously. Both cut to the heart of what a work of visual art is—in particular a painting—and how the artist stands in relation to it. (Clearly there may be more than one such stance and more than one answer to what a work of art is. I don't mean to imply that matters are as simple as I seem to be making them. They definitely are not.)

First, a painting throws questions at us and we at it. Some paintings seem to challenge us with their thematic material, with their opacity, or with their expression of technical mastery. We confront paintings by asking what they are about, how the parts cohere, why this subject is important or of interest. Steinberg claims that an old painting, one that has been viewed and reviewed, written about and analyzed, still can offer something new to later generations. "The novelty of the subject is the whole of the work responding to different questions" (Steinberg 1973, 298). These questions need not be the ones that the artist had in mind when creating the work. The artist may have had no questions in mind at all. But if a good painting can be made to respond differently to different questions, might it not be considered almost limitless in its potential to be seen differently? New viewers unleash new aspects over time when they break free of old ways of seeing and thinking. With some of the greatest paintings, like Leonardo's *Last Supper*, this might be particularly difficult to do because of strong and persistent opinions over time. For Steinberg this painting, like a visual paradox, continuously shifts back and forth between its multiple possibilities, refusing ever to settle on only one (Butterfield 2002, 17). This shifting can take place for one viewer or can occur over generations, for different viewers at different times.

You object. "This is mere imposition of current ways of thinking onto a work that arose in a very different aesthetic climate. Further, relying on the essential ambiguity of art only 'provides the critic with an excuse when his evidence is weak or contradictory' (Butterfield 2002, 17). You may be far from Leonardo's own intent, which may very well have been simplicity and clarity. What you seem to be urging is that the *Last Supper* is some kind of glorified duck-rabbit. Get real!"

Okay, Leonardo may not have intended his painting to be ambiguous, and if Steinberg insists on that, then we can part company with him. But this is because I'm not at all certain about the importance of the artist's intent to our experience of a painting as a visual object. I do mean to raise here the question of the artist's intent versus his inspiration, of the artist's conscious awareness of what he is trying to do as compared with his seeing that what he has done feels right. There might be more to a painting than meets even the artist's eye. If we imagine that the creative act is participation in something about which the creator is perhaps only vaguely aware—such as the resonances between shapes and colors on a canvas or words in his native language—then why not say that he might remain unaware of some of the aspects of his own work? Is this just another way to weasel out of making an argument for what a painting is about? I don't know, but I believe that there may be reason to think that a great painting is in a deep way irrational and also inaccessible to one person or one age. What may be most important about a painting is its describability (Steinberg 1973, 302). And how someone—a critic, an art historian, a friend, ourselves—describes a painting can get us to *see* the painting differently. We may notice things we hadn't before, even though they were right in front of us. Or we may see connections we hadn't seen and thereby allow the painting to fall together differently. When a new way of looking at the painting becomes dominant in our minds (and in our eyes), we find it almost impossible to go back to an earlier way of seeing. When the puzzle-picture in chapter one finally becomes a human face for you, it is almost impossible for it ever again to look the way it did before. Such a dominant seeing can become the right way or the right interpretation simply because we just can't see anything differently—or anything different. But a painting that lends itself to ever-new ways of being described can help break us and our eyes of the habit of thinking and seeing in only one way, the habit of believing that the main point in art is to discover what is there.

Steinberg makes another juxtaposition that is at first surprising but that, on further reflection, makes sense when considered in the context of seeing aspects in paintings. He draws our attention to the early twentieth-century movement in art known as cubism, of which Pablo Picasso (1881–1973), Georges Braque (1882–1963) and Juan Gris (1887–1927) were the primary exponents in painting. While there are several ways to describe cubism, I can say that it at least involves the "mixing of the successive and the simultaneous," as the Cubist painter Jean Metzinger said in 1910 (Steinberg 1973, 156). Objects, people, and scenes are broken up and re-assembled in a new way, in an effort to portray multiple aspects of the subject matter at the same time. Cubism as an extended development in art is more complex than this; it extends to literature and even architecture.[8] Consider Picasso's *Women of Algiers (Version O)* (fig. 40), a Cubist painting from late in Picasso's career. The incompatible perspectives of the women's bodies threaten to contort the picture beyond recognition and meaning. Bodies pose at unnatural angles. All this would simply be a fantastical mess if we didn't imagine that the artist is displaying to us several physical aspects of these women simultaneously, aspects which might in reality only be visible over time as the figures turned or a viewer walked around them. Yet Picasso has managed to weave them into a coherent, vibrant whole, which pulsates within its borders. Hasn't Leonardo accomplished something similar, perhaps unconsciously? *Il Cenacolo* captures a moment in time with uncanny detail and complexity. About this few people would disagree. Rather than decide which moment—the secular one of betrayal or the religious one of transubstantiation—we ought to say that Leonardo portrays both moments simultaneously. Unlike

Figure 40. *Women of Algiers (Version O)* by Pablo Picasso.

Picasso's Cubist painting, however, which presents incompatible *physical* aspects all at once, Leonardo succeeds in depicting incompatible *emotional* aspects in the same pictorial space and time. Each painting achieves a unity that consists in the reconciliation of contraries. Picasso seems to achieve this through form and color while Leonardo asks us to see the painting first one way then another.

The juxtaposition of Leonardo's painting with cubism makes sense from the point of view of aspect-seeing. Both Leonardo's and Picasso's pictures can be seen as displaying multiple aspects of their subject matters on one canvas, the latter intentionally, the former perhaps inspirationally. Like the duck-rabbit, these paintings contain more than meets the eye, because in meeting the eye the painting also meets the mind and therefore meets language, the source of all ambiguity. Like most good paintings, these open themselves up to continued discussion about what they are. In talking about them, we allow them to reveal ever more possibilities inherent not only in the painting, but also in language. The work of art and the ways it is described fuse in intelligent viewers and carry them along in ways that may prove unpredictable and highly fruitful—or they may run into dead ends. They won't know unless they try, and keep trying, to describe what they see. There may be more than thirteen ways of looking at the *Last Supper*.

We can hear aspects when we listen to music. Wittgenstein scatters remarks about music throughout his writings, but nowhere concentrates at any length on how hearing the aspects of music might help us make sense of what we are listening to, or how we might lead others to hear what we do and thereby heighten their appreciation of music. Wittgenstein came from a very musical family,[9] and he was said to be an extraordinarily good whistler.[10] I, of course, am not particularly interested in these anecdotal bits of his life, but rather in what he said about music. Can the vocabulary of aspects help us experience music in a new way?

C. Musical Aspects

Understanding a sentence is much more akin to understanding a theme in music than one may think. What I mean is that understanding a sentence lies nearer than one thinks to what is ordinarily called understanding a musical theme. Why is just *this* the pattern of variation in loudness and tempo? One would like to say "Because I know what it's all about." But what is it all about? I should not be able to say. In order to 'explain' I could only compare it with something else which has the same rhythm (I mean the same pattern). (One says "Don't you see, this is as if a conclusion were being drawn" or "This is as it were a parenthesis," etc. How does one justify such comparisons?—There are very different kinds of justification here.) (*PI*, sec. 527)

Unlike the paintings we have looked at, a piece of instrumental music such as a Beethoven sonata or a Brahms symphony is not in any obvious sense representational. While all sorts of noises fill our lives every day, few of them sound much like music. From time to time a composer attempts to mimic or represent sounds from other contexts, such as nature or battle. For example, near the end of the second movement of Beethoven's sixth symphony (suggestively called the *Pastoral*), a flute, an oboe, and a clarinet join to create sounds that remind the listener of a nightingale, a quail, and a cuckoo, respectively. To my ear, the clarinet really does sound like the bird—or the clock. How you hear it might influence how you understand the rest of the movement, or what picture you paint in your mind about the scene this programmatic piece portrays. Beethoven writes of this movement that it is a "scene by a brook," and of the symphony as a whole he says that it consists of "recollections of country life." Tchaikovsky's *1812 Overture* calls for cannons to be fired representing—cannon fire. And Leroy Anderson's *The Typewriter Song* introduces the sounds of the office—with a typewriter.

To see the duck-rabbit in its different aspects takes both thinking and perceiving. We perceive and think, not sequentially, one following the other, but as Wittgenstein says, as an amalgam. The union is seamless and complete, yet it does not create an entirely new thing, such as a chemical compound with properties that may be entirely different from the elements that constitute it. It also requires imagination to hear one musical theme as a variation of another. Such hearing is not a hypothesis or based on a hypothesis. It does not involve beliefs that may prove to be wrong. It is direct and immediate hearing: I hear this theme as a variation of that one.[11] While it does not make sense for me to ask you to try to hear this sound as louder or see the grass as red (because these are *sensations*), it does make sense for me to ask you to try to hear this melody as a variation of another or to see this red as a drop of blood (because these are *perceptions*). It makes sense, then, to say that the imagination is involved in this kind of hearing as it is in aspect-seeing. Hearing *x* as *y* is part simple perception (of sound) and part engagement of the intellect or imagination.

Consider the first four measures of a simple melody, "Twinkle, Twinkle Little Star." Figure 41 shows them in the key of C-major:

Figure 41. "Twinkle, Twinkle Little Star" in C-major.

How does this melody differ from mere *noise*, from the sounds we hear around us all day? One difference is that the melody does not sound complete until it returns to C on the word "are." The notes seem to be pulled in the direction of C, the tonic, almost as a declarative sentence is pulled toward the period at its end. Played all by itself fourteen times, the tone C does not sound like it's "going anywhere." It would be drained of whatever force it had in it to begin with, just as a word repeated many times loses its meaning. The tonic needs to be surrounded by other notes in order to sound like a tonic, or a *center*. To convince yourself of this, listen to the same melody in the key of G-major (fig. 42), where G begins and ends the melody. Listen to how C sounds in this version. It is the very same note. A "sound-frequency detector" would detect the same number for the frequency of C in both versions. But in the second one, in G-major, the tone C does not sound like a stopping point. It hasn't the feel of a period at the end of sentence, or even of a comma or semicolon, which D in the second measure has.

Figure 42. "Twinkle, Twinkle Little Star" in G-major.

How we hear C in these two cases is analogous to how we see the duck-rabbit against different backgrounds. In a field of picture-ducks, it's seen as a duck, just as in the field of C-major we hear C as the tonic. Against a field of picture-rabbits, the duck-rabbit is a rabbit, just as C sounds like something other than the tonic when surrounded by G-major. (Musicians call C in the key of G-major the "sub-dominant," which is the same role that F plays in the first example in the key of C-major.) The tone C, which doesn't change in a physical sense, displays two of its aspects in these two examples. Our ears *hear* this, just as our eyes *see* the duck or the rabbit in the duck-rabbit.

Musical tones differ from noise because they have *meaning*. Their place or function in a key (which is their context) determines their meaning, much as a word's use is its meaning. When we hear the same tone differently in different contexts, we're hearing different aspects of it. When a piece of music modulates, that is, changes from one key to another, all the tones take on different meanings. They play different roles in the new key from those they played in the old. We need to hear a tone *in a key*, not out alone, or in a jumble of noise, for it to be part of the force field of a melody.

What happens when someone first hears a melody as a variation on another one? Let's consider a specific example, the theme from the first movement of Mozart's A-major piano sonata (K. 331). Figure 43 shows the first four measures of the main theme. Focus on the treble only, since that carries the melody.

Figure 43. Mozart Piano Sonata in A-major (K. 331), First Movement, Main Theme.

Figures 44 and 45 show the first four measures of two of the variations Mozart gives of this melody. He labels them variations, so we know that is how he intended them to be heard.

If we attend only to those notes that occur on the heavy beats of each measure, we'll see something interesting. (The heavy beats are the first and fourth in each measure of 6/8 time [fig. 44], and the first and third in 4/4 or common time [fig. 45].) All three excerpts begin at C-sharp or C, move up to E, down to B, up to D, down to A, up to B and C, and finally rest on B. (The third measure of Varia-

Figure 44. Mozart Sonata, Variation III (Minor).

Figure 45. Mozart Sonata, Variation VI.

tion III stretches out the move from A to B by interposing a phrase beginning on G-sharp which doesn't touch down on B until the start of measure four.) So we can reason our way through to seeing how these last two melodies are variations on the first: they have something in common. (Perhaps we'd consider them all variations on one another, except that the main theme seems to present the skeletal melody in clearest form.) But do we *hear* these as variations? How do I describe my experience of first coming to hear the last two melodies as variations of the first one? A psychologist or neuroscientist might ask about what goes on in my brain when I recognize a variation, but I are not interested in this, or rather I think that this way of approaching the question misses the point. What I want to know is conceptual, not causal, because without first knowing what it is we are talking about, any discoveries about brain activity will only seem to pass by the central questions. That is, unless we first become clear about what hearing a variation is—which involves understanding how and when we use words like "variation"—accumulating quantitative information about the brain will not tell us what such hearing amounts to.

So we return to the question, What happens when we first *hear* Variation III or Variation VI *as* a variation on the main theme of Mozart's sonata? The experience might be something like when I first see the human face in the chaos of figure 22 in chapter one. Or it may be akin to recognizing my old friend after a long separation, seeing his young face in this older one. When I ask myself what happens when I suddenly recognize the original theme in this new one, when I hear the connection between them and hear how the variation comes from the original, I'm not sure what to say. Once again, as with the duck-rabbit and the other aspect-changing visual perceptions I've looked at, nothing has changed in the "objective" perception. If I'd listened to either variation before hearing them as variations, then in a sense what I now hear when I hear them *as* variations is the same. But just as when I suddenly see a resemblance between two people, here too I make a connection that creates a new experience for me. The experience, however, can be described only by making reference to the melodies I've been hearing. That is, hearing a melody as a variation on another is not an experience that can be separated from the very melodies around which the experience takes place. And when I describe to someone as I would to myself what it is that I now hear that I didn't hear before, I might say things like (of Version III, which is written in A minor): "This is the pensive version of the more stately original, more brooding and moody than it." Or of Version VI: "This version, with its allegro tempo and 4/4 time, is more playful, almost like some kind of quick, impatient dance, and the whole melodic idea seems to be let out more rapidly than in the original." At least these are the sorts of things that come to my mind when I try to say what it is that allows me to connect the melodies to the original theme. An experienced musician might find other ways to describe what she hears, but we are most interested here in the "aha!" moment of recognizing through the ears the relation of theme and variation that we hadn't heard before.[12]

Have I described my experience of coming to hear something new in what I'd been listening to? Well, how would I teach someone else what it means to hear a theme as a variation? How would I determine that she had learned to hear the variation? These questions turn the aspect-hearing experience from a first-person experience to a third-person experience, as we have done with aspect-seeing. Rather than introspect and expect to find experience inside, I ask how we would know of another that *she* is hearing a new aspect of a melody. I would not look into her mind or brain, even if I could. (The psychologist or neuroscientist might want to.) I would want to find out what she could do with the original melody and variations, which includes what she would now be able to *say* about them. She might show that she now hears the variation by being able to continue to explain how the rest of the variation (beyond the first few measures) is like the opening, how it, too, carries through the same relationship with the main theme of which it is a variation. She might also show that she now hears the variation by playing it differently on the piano, bringing out by her phrasing, tempo, and emphases its connection with the main melody. So even though she might not be able to say what it is that makes this melody a variation of that one, she might have learned a new gesture, as shown by her playing, or by how she judges the playing of others. The description of her experience of now hearing the variation may *be* the description of an action, such as playing the piece a new way or saying something.

We may tend to think of having an experience—such as seeing the Necker cube flip or first hearing Variation III as a variation on the main theme—as the *cause* of our subsequent behavior. We play the piece this new way because we now hear it as a variation. You may be tempted to say that, at least in your own case, you know that first you hear the variation and then you say something or you play the piece or you make a gesture. You're tempted to view the experience and the subsequent action as two different things. The former could have taken place without the latter, you want to say. Experience here, its consequences there. However, this way of looking at experiences, especially aesthetic experiences and aspect changes generally, is precisely what Wittgenstein has been trying to tell us leads us astray. These experiences have more than a contingent connection with verbal and other expressions. If someone insisted that he did hear the melody as a variation but could do no more than say this—could not play the piece differently or help another hear what he does— we would not be justified in saying that he heard the variation. You cannot simply say, "Well, he ought to know. It's his experience." He is in no better position than you are to say that he has had this particular experience, because he has no way to show even himself that "variation on the main theme" is the correct way to describe what he hears. The correct description of what he hears requires the possibility of confirmation from others. It demands that even one's own experience—and this may once again sound odd—is not and cannot be radically private. (This is Wittgenstein's argument against private language applied to aesthetic experiences.)[13] When I describe to myself my experience of hearing a melody as a variation or hearing a modulation from one key to another, I need not convince myself that I am right. But I must be able to *do something* with my new experience that can justify others in saying that I indeed hear. Because such aspect experiences involve both perception and thought, there is one sense in which I can be wrong about what I hear and another sense in which I cannot be wrong.

This is not to say that when I hear an aspect change I depend on the authority of others and take on faith what they say about me and my own experiences. It's not that simple. I might accept on belief someone's claim that a painting I have not yet seen is dominated by the color red or that a piece of music I have not yet heard is full of crashing cymbals and loud trumpets. This sort of non-aspectual description does not imply that my imagination will be called on when I come to see or hear the things themselves. But I cannot similarly take on faith that the painting is awash in blood or that the music is full of pathos and triumph. These aspects of the works I must see and hear for myself, just as I must see and hear for myself whether they are beautiful. I might believe a musician who told me that the first movement of the Mozart sonata consisted of a theme and variations. I might even be convinced of this by being shown the score and having certain salient features pointed out to me. But such belief and conviction do not amount to experience, for which I must *hear* the themes *as* variations on the original. Someone can tell me to listen to the oboe in a Beethoven symphony, and if I know what an oboe sounds like, I will have no trouble doing so. But if he asks me to listen to the oboe's lament, he is asking me to engage my imagination, and I may or may not be able to do this. I may not hear the lament at all, even though I hear the oboe perfectly well. The lament is not drowned out by other instruments because it is not itself a sound that can be overwhelmed in that way. I may just not hear it, and so while I have the experience of hearing the oboe, I do not have the experience of hearing its lament. And this is shown not only by what I say, but by what I subsequently do. My musician friend may not be able to get me to hear it, just as some people never see Jesus in the chaotic drawing.[14] I cannot be said to understand the role of the oboe in the symphony or the variations in the sonata if I do not have the experience of hearing the lament or the variations: "Only when knowledge of a work of art alters one's experience does it become part of one's understanding" (Scruton 1997, 187).

When—"click!"—I finally hear the variation or the lament or a false cadence or an atonal twelve-tone row as an integral whole, I might be able to explain what has happened only in the sense that I can point out other things in the music that I could not before. This new ability of mine is a criterion for my experience. That is, if I could not do or say anything new, it would not be correct for anyone else to say I'd had the experience. And if it is not right for them to say it of me, it is not right for me to say it of myself.[15]

D. Emergent Meaning and Wine

> The concept of the "appropriate" will lie at the heart of all aesthetic judgment. (Scruton 1997, 140)

> Sometimes the word [that occurs to me] *is* the feeling of similarity. *Take note* that certain words occur to us, certain ways of expression. If this sounds something like psychoanalysis, maybe it is related. Do not always assume that behind every experience lurks a cause, which is the real thing. (*PE*, 10, first italics added)

> . . . for is what is linguistic not an experience? (*PI*, sec. 629)

If it is true that what we see and what we say are closely connected, then we stand to learn something about looking at works of art by paying attention to what we, and others more attuned than we are, say and are inclined to say about it. The way we learn and subsequently use words is central to many of our perceptual experiences. I want to propose that words are at the heart of all aesthetic experiences—at least all those that are more than merely expressions of taste.

Wittgenstein's interest in aspects leads him to consider the emergent meanings of words. These meanings play an important role in descriptions of works of art, in reviews by critics, in hints that music teachers give pupils and composers give performers, and in the way we generally talk to ourselves about art. They can provide us with new aesthetic experiences or deepen and enrich those we already have. As I discussed in chapter three, Wittgenstein connects emergent meanings with aspect-seeing through the concept of aspect blindness. He first raises the question of what we would be missing if we did not "*experience* the meaning of a word." He likens this to what one would be missing if someone did not see the aspects of a drawing or painting, or did not see the Necker cube flip from one orientation to another. In a similar way, someone who did not *feel* that a word was drained of its meaning by being repeated over and over would have a different relation to words from the rest of us. Most of us sense that a word grows meaningless when it is repeated too much. It becomes mere sound, as does a single tone played repeatedly on a piano. It feels emptied, but of what? Well, its meaning, what else? "But if meaning is use, as Wittgenstein and you have been eager to assert, how can the word lose its meaning? You've been telling us that meaning is not something a word carries around with it like a backpack. It can't just throw it off." And this is true. Wittgenstein, however, is interested in exploring a whole family of experiences that don't at first seem to fit with his overarching concept of meaning as *use*. For example, words can be pronounced so that we hear that they are "full of their meaning." They might be so spoken in the reading of a poem, but also in ordinary speech. Also some words just seem to fit certain descriptions. Their appropriateness might be explained in some way, but the experience of appropriateness, of fitting, is simply given, no matter what sort of account of it is proposed:

> When I pronounce this word while reading with expression it is completely filled with its meaning.—"How can this be, if meaning is the use of the word?" Well, what I said was intended figuratively (*bildlich*). Not that I chose the figure: it forced itself on me.—But the figurative employment of the word can't get into conflict with the original one.
>
> Perhaps it could be explained why precisely *this* picture suggests itself to me. (Just think of the expression, and the meaning of the expression: 'the word that hits it off.') (*PI*, p. 215)

Wittgenstein is more interested in the experience than in any hypothetical account because we teach and learn and use such expressions as "a word full of meaning" or "this word has lost its meaning" without any reference at all to possible explanations:

[I]f a sentence can strike me as like a painting in words, and the very individual word in the sentence as like a picture, then it is no such marvel that a word uttered in isolation and without purpose can seem to carry a particular meaning in itself. (*PI*, p. 215)

Most important for our purposes is that this meaning is connected to the usual meanings of the word. It is not something new, something different, but the very same meanings experienced in a novel context or out of context entirely. The example he gives from which the title of this book derives is "fat Wednesday." "Fat" in "fat Wednesday" is the usual, ordinary "fat" with which we are all too familiar. The use of it here, however, is not one of its ordinary uses. While its emergent meaning arises from its ordinary use or uses, and the language-games in which it is ordinarily used, "fat" here plays a role in a different game. The rules of this game cannot be articulated, or if they were to be, they would simply be those of the language-games in which "fat" is at home. Are there games with rules that are necessarily implicit and that would change if the rules could be codified? Wittgenstein never says so, and I'm not sure he would be comfortable with the notion of a language-game to explain emergent meaning. There needn't be a way to bring another to see the aspects I see or to recognize similarities I do. And yet it's right to call aspect-seeing "seeing." So, too, there may be no way to make explicit the rules of language-games centered on emergent meaning, and yet it might be right to call this "meaning" anyway. The meaning of "fat" in "fat Wednesday" is decidedly not metaphorical. A metaphorical use could be explained in other ways, such as when Thomas Aquinas calls God the sun. There he means that as the sun casts light on the earth, so too, God casts spiritual light on man's soul. The reasons we use the sun as an image of God can be expressed. "Fat Wednesday," however, you either get or don't get. Wednesday is not fat in any ordinary sense, because days simply can't be fat, nor can they have colors. Yet in this expression "fat" is used in its ordinary way; it's not a metaphor or an implied analogy or a muted allusion to something else. Metaphors can be paraphrased, but emergent meanings cannot be. It is crucial to aesthetic descriptions that words used in them retain their ordinary meanings. The word "fat" carries its meaning in some way along with it outside of any of its usual contexts, and when it is plopped down next to "Wednesday," *voila!*, something happens. Or perhaps for you nothing happens. Because we know our way around a language, these meanings can emerge for us. This experience and its absence are at the heart of descriptions of paintings, pieces of music, poetry, and therefore, of our aesthetic life. Something inexplicable—and essentially inexplicable—grounds Wittgenstein's sense of how we speak about art. This is not to say that talk about art is irrational or arbitrary or subjective. Arguments in aesthetics, however, are likely to be of a very different kind from those, say, in mathematics. They will consist more in putting things next to each other and in asking others to consider together elements that they might not have so considered before. To see how this plays out, we need to look at descriptions of works of art.

Let's begin, however, with descriptions that are definitely not about art. The descriptions that experienced wine tasters give of wines can be complex and somewhat intimidating to those of us who have neither the nose nor the vocabulary to appreciate them. Nose and vocabulary go together, of course, so that to develop one is to develop the other. Some people can learn this language-game, others cannot, and many others fall in between. (I, for example, can certainly tell a red wine from a white wine, especially if I'm allowed to look!) Similar descriptions can be found for beer, coffee, chocolate, olive oil, and perfume. Unless you're told which is being described, it's sometimes not easy to figure it out. Take for example this description and say whether it is of wine, chocolate, olive oil, or perfume: "Layers of cedar and raspberry strike a sharp upfront note, while clove and creamy notes add body while contributing an exotic, sumptuous character that conveys luxury in its essence. Might there also be a trace of rubber, though?" (Lanchester 2008). Maybe I'll tell you later. Or you can read the full article.

Here are some notes from winetastings conducted by *Wine Spectator* magazine. I picked them more or less at random. (That is, I didn't go hunting for just those descriptions that fit what I wanted to say.) All are of red wines:

> Piercing aromas of violet, iron and blueberry fruit are followed by a
> massively rich yet amazingly pure and precise palate of boysenberry

and blackberry flavors. The riveting finish is loaded with minerality and dark, velvety fruit. This is still young, with loads in reserve.

Really packed but supersilky, with a gorgeous beam of raspberry ganache gliding over super fine-grained tannins, while notes of incense, blackberry preserve, bittersweet chocolate truffle and black tea fill in the background. Seamless and very long.

Mineral, pebble, dried herb, currant and tobacco flavors are taut and a bit grainy. Though intense and compact, this is still rough-hewn, with chewy, cedary oak.[16]

These winetasting notes contain at least three kinds of descriptions of the wines under review. I like to think of the first kind as properties of taste and smell that I could detect myself or could learn to detect without too much trouble. The combined smell of violet, iron, and blueberry, while not something I'm likely to encounter in nature, contains components with which I am more or less familiar. This is not to say that I would without a pause detect these odors in the first wine. It might be at least as difficult as figuring out what colors have blended to produce some particular shade that I see. Still, the smell of violets, of iron, and of blueberries are all familiar to me taken separately, if not when mixed together. In a similar way, I think I might detect blackberry preserve in the second wine, though I wonder how that differs from plain old blackberry. As for notes of incense and black tea—well, I'd like to ask what kind of incense and what kind of black tea. But maybe I shouldn't be picky, since I think it's likely I would not do a very good job detecting these anyway. The third description focuses on tastes, though taste and smell are difficult to separate in general. (In fact much of taste beyond salty, sweet, bitter and sour might be due almost entirely to smell.[17]) Mineral and currant I might taste, maybe even tobacco. As for herb, I'd again ask which one, but that only shows that I haven't yet got the hang of wine descriptions. Still, these sorts of descriptions seem to involve ordinary words used in their ordinary way. I feel on familiar ground with them and think that I can begin to make an attempt at my own descriptions.

The second class of descriptive words contains some that I'd call technical, such as "tannins." These are also words whose use for describing wine could be learned. They have a clear connection to other experiences, such as "a loaded finish," or "fill in the background." Maybe even "grainy" fits into this class. With help from someone who knew how to use these words, I might be able to begin to use them correctly, too. "Grainy" is a bit difficult because one would hope that there are not really grains of anything in your wine—if there are, the wine should have been decanted to remove them. Still I'm willing to believe John Lanchester on this one. In a *New Yorker* article, he says he was incredulous that a "liquid could be called 'grainy.'"

> Then, a few nights ago, I opened a bottle of wine I'd been given, a Languedoc red called Le Pigeonnier, from the European heat-wave year of 2003, and, without concentrating very hard, took a sip, noticed something odd about the mouthfeel of the wine, and suddenly realized—*bam!*—that it was grainy. I'd found the famous grainy tannins, and the term actually made sense, because the wine definitely had a particulate, almost sandlike texture, not unpleasant, but distinctive. . . . Now I knew what grainy tannins were. (Lanchester 2008)

Lanchester's account of his revelation includes an explanation I can understand, because he can explain why the word "grainy" makes sense in this context. It does so because the wine really does produce a kind of grainy feeling on the tongue. That says enough, though it might take someone a while to learn to detect this—longer than it might take to detect real grains of something (like sand) in the wine. But once he's linked the word with the experience, he has it for good. Technical wine terms like "balance," "length," and "structure" can also be learned. They begin as metaphors, and their appropriateness can be explained. (This might even help a student learn how to use the words.) After a while, the wine culture absorbs them and they are no longer even metaphors, though it helps to pay attention to their origins outside of wines.

The third group of descriptive words is the one I'm most interested in, because they involve emergent meanings. They are neither literal descriptions nor metaphors that can be explained. ("Grainy" might have first struck Lanchester as a metaphor he just didn't get. But the description of his "aha!" moment suggests that he recognized an experience so much like that of feeling real grains in the mouth that he no longer thought of the quality of grainy as metaphorical.) The words I have in mind are those like "velvety," "supersilky," "chewy," and perhaps "taut." What could it mean for a wine to be velvety? A friend of mine suggested that a velvety wine tasted on the tongue the way velvet would. I found this account to be rather discouraging. I really don't want to run my tongue along velvet or even silk for that matter. And I know I don't want my wine to give me that kind of sensation. So I thought she was looking for something like what Lanchester sought in his account of "grainy": it feels like the real thing. This might work for "grainy," but it doesn't for "velvety," "silky," or "lush." One might say of the velvety wine that it feels (or tastes?) to the tongue the way velvet feels to the skin. And how exactly is that? Well, if I could explain the comparison then I wouldn't need to make it. More scientific-minded tasters, who are striving to develop a nomenclature that avoids terms too rich in what they consider to be romantic comparisons, would say that if I can't explain what I mean by silky, then I don't mean anything by it and I shouldn't use it. They are trying to taste and evaluate wines "according to verifiable, quantifiable criteria."[18] And this is okay, except that descriptions such as "velvety" can make sense, even if that sense cannot be articulated in any other way. It might be possible to replace it with a number, say, if experts agreed that this something was found in a wine. Then students would learn the number, or would learn some other more direct way of describing what they smell or taste. The link with the original term would eventually be lost simply because it could not be explained, the way "blueberry" or "acidic" can be.

These "wilder" expressions for wines (or just about anything else you can taste or smell), however, use emergent meanings of words—meanings that either click or don't. These words are not metaphors or similes, because they cannot be explained in any other way. The words have not taken on new meaning when applied to wines, like "massively rich," "seamless," and "rough-hewn" in the examples. These are words that have ordinary meanings and now in the context of wine have acquired new meanings, which can be related to their original meanings. When words are used with emergent meanings, however, they mean what they always have meant in their usual context or contexts. "Velvety" doesn't take on a new meaning when said of a wine, any more than "fat" does when it describes "Wednesday." In fact, that these words mean exactly the same thing in their new environment is very important not only for wines but also for aesthetics. They have carried meaning with them, in a sense, even though their primary meaning for Wittgenstein is their use. The web of a word's use reaches out in many directions and in many ways. We are often simply not aware which words might click in a given description until we hear them and they sound right to us. We might attempt to explain why they do, but often those attempts seem feeble and contrived. The fact remains that, for whatever reason, some words sometimes seem right, not just to me or you, but to others, too. And this experience of finding the right word or hearing the right word from another has an *inclusive* effect. It brings together in a common experience people who can make sense of an old word in a new surrounding. Such people can now use such words in conversing with each other. If I do not get it right away when I'm told the wine I am drinking is silky, I might be led by another to the point where I, too, could apply that word. This would be the criterion for determining that I understood the word and that I had had the experience the word reflects. How would the teacher get me there? Well, if it were a case of detecting the taste of something I wasn't familiar with or couldn't quite recall with sufficient precision, say boysenberry, then he might have me taste a boysenberry. If it were a matter of my not being familiar with certain technical terms, such as "tannins," he could give me some other things that were high in tannin and take it from there. If, however, we're stuck because I just can't get how a wine can be chewy or vibrant, he might resort to other things, which could best be called "hints."[19] My situation might be something like the person who is given a number series and asked to continue it just as it is, but at a certain point fails to see the right way to go (though he continues in some way). After trying for a while to learn how to use a word like "velvety" correctly—that is, to carry on conversations about wine with people who can use that word—if I still don't get it, well then, I don't get it. Learning comes to an end (*PI*, sec. 143). If I fail, it is not because there is something wrong with my nose or tongue (though that may be the case) any more than there is something wrong with my eyes if I fail to see the Necker cube flip or fail to see the Jesus figure in the puzzle picture or can't see the fingers of the young man in Caravaggio's *The Calling of St. Matthew* as pushing. I'm inclined to say that there is something wrong with my words, with my ability to use them. There are language-games I cannot learn to play well, and the language-game of wine description might be one of them. But if the hints of my teacher strike a chord with me, if they click in just the way that allows me to go on, I can better make my way in the world of wine tasting and describing. Others who know something about wines will be able to say of me that I have cultivated a nose or tongue for wine.

This may be of only moderate interest when it comes to describing wines, because wines lack meaning, and so do not affect us the way paintings, music, poetry, and other art forms can. This is not to say that winemaking is not an art. There is an art to winemaking, and it is a serious one, even if we would be wrong to rank it with painting and music and poetry. The physical pleasure we derive from wines can certainly be more intense and rich than that we feel in the presence of works of art. But aesthetic sensations are almost always weak. It is not for the tingles that we go back to Caravaggio, to Shakespeare, and to Schubert.

E. Talk About Paintings

To see is to prevail against the emptiness of formal argument.
—Hans-Georg Gadamer, *Truth and Method*, 345

It is *essential* [to art] that a painting can change its aspect for me.
—Wittgenstein, *RPP II*, 634

Teachers and critics of art share some similarities with enologists. Their differences are also striking. Both deal in matters that seem objective and subjective simultaneously. Wines can taste different at different times or in different circumstances, as when paired with different foods. Yet descriptions given by careful and experienced wine tasters strive to transcend these passing differences, in search of what we might say is the taste of the wine in itself. We think they may not always succeed because we believe that the same wine can taste different to different (normal) people, even under the same controlled circumstances. To what extent this is true, or to what extent it even makes sense, depends in part on how we learn to use the words associated with wine descriptions. One person may like the taste of blackberries, another dislike it. But that is far from saying that they taste something different when they sample a wine that both describe as having the taste of blackberries. That they agree on the description is the objective part; how they react to it is the subjective part. In a like manner, observers of paintings agree on the colors and shapes, the brushstrokes and paint quality in the paintings they observe together. This is the objective part. But they might disagree on what they see, which is to say that they can disagree about the meaning of the painting. Often they disagree about the aspects they see in the painting, not about whether they like this certain color or grouping of subjects in it. In this way the art critic differs from her enologist counterpart, because the wine critic does not treat wine as having aspects that might change or that might quite naturally and correctly be tasted differently by different people. Experienced wine tasters tend to agree on what the wine is, while experienced critics often disagree about the very nature of the painting at which they both are looking. In fact, it is essential to art that such disagreement be not only possible, but the norm. Both wine tasters and art critics acknowledge the importance of small differences to an appreciation of their particular subject. This is why both wine tasters and art critics ask for time to taste and look, conditions that encourage both, and much talk with other people about their subject. With wines, this talk is sometimes promoted by the use of words with emergent meanings like "velvety," which require not only a keen tongue and palate, but also an imaginative mind to create and appreciate such descriptions. So, too, in talk about art. The striking difference between them, however, is that wine talk can and should come to an end, but talk about a good painting can and must continue. The small distinctions we begin to notice, the ways we express visual and auditory experiences, and the ever-present possibility of seeing new aspects keep the conversation about paintings (and music and poems) alive and surprising. If a wine is re-tasted some years after a first tasting and the description of the taster's experience is different, he will of necessity attribute that to a change in the wine, in its development, its structure, its aging. But apart from something like the fading of colors over long periods of time, a painting does not change in itself. New descriptions reflect new ways of seeing the painting, just as the description of the duck-rabbit can change while we know the drawing we see on the page does not change. This is the essence of seeing aspects, and it is an essential part of our experience of art.

Now "duck" and "rabbit" are ordinary words, and when I see the duck-rabbit first as one then as the other, I do not rely on any sort of emergent meaning of the words to bring me to see what I might not have seen before. At important junctures, good critics and good teachers of art use words in emergent ways. That is, these words, full of their ordinary meanings (like "silky," "fat," "sad"), will be used in new ways while retaining their old meanings. These "new meanings" depend on the old, and cannot be expressed in any other way. "Fat" in "fat Wednesday" means—fat! And "sad" in "a sad painting" or "a sad piece of music" means sad in the usual sense. Of course both "fat" and "sad" cannot in any ordinary way be said to be qualities of days or paintings. We won't counsel Wednesday to go on a diet or try to comfort a sad painting. Nor is a painting called sad because it makes the viewer sad. Such descriptions express new experiences, if we understand them. They are in a real sense the new experiences themselves. If we "get it," we can go on and say and see things in a painting that we could not say or see before. In this way, such descriptions are related to aspects. They allow us to do new things with words, to play language-games that we heretofore could not play. Even wine descriptions enable us to experience and appreciate wines more by giving us words that can constitute the experiences.

All this depends on our getting it—on having such words click for us. We needn't be able to explain to another exactly why such words with their emergent meanings are appropriate. In fact, we cannot explain this. If we could, then we'd be treating these words as metaphors, in which ordinary words take on different meanings in new contexts—meanings that can be clarified and whose rules for use can be made clear (or at least clearer). No, emergent meanings are not explicable, just as we cannot get someone to *see* an aspect if he or she is blind to it. We can say things, provide hints, tell stories. But if my friend does not see the man in the moon, even though he sees the moon, I cannot get him to see it by any method. Words with emergent meanings are not hiding meanings or trying to be clever. They are appropriate, and in talk about art, the concept of the appropriate is central.

Art criticism serves many different purposes for students, art lovers, historians, and philosophers. In this chapter on the place of aspects in art and emergent meaning in talk about art, the focus must remain limited. That is, I'm not interested so much in art history as I am in the immediate experience of seeing artworks. This is not at all to suggest that an artist's life story or the historical or social context in which a work was produced is neither interesting nor valuable to our appreciation of paintings and pieces of music and poems. Rather, I want to remain as close as possible to the immediate experience (if I can fairly call it that) of viewing a painting or hearing a work of music. This experience might very well be altered by my learning about the circumstances under which the artist worked, the people who influenced him both professionally and personally, and the context in which he worked. Still, because all history, all facts about a painter, are in some sense hypotheses—that is, not present right in front of me and not subject to the kind of revision this red swatch of paint is—I shall continue to attend primarily to what I see and how critics talk about what they see. Any critic worth reading will quite naturally and correctly attempt to place the artist he is considering into a context. The critic will also tell us something about the technical achievements of the artist, for example the spectacular brushwork of Tintoretto, or Turner's ability to capture myriad ephemeral impressions of light.[20] These can be fantastically interesting to notice in a painting, as can other kinds of awe-inspiring accomplishments. Still, they are not my main concern, except to the extent that noticing them helps me see the painting more completely, more coherently, and differently.

Several short examples of critical writing on painting will illustrate the role that the language of aspects and emergent meaning plays in describing works of art. Consider the painting *Mrs. Salter* (1741) (see fig. 46 facing p. 211) by William Hogarth (1697–1764), which currently hangs in the Tate Gallery in London, along with several other Hogarth portraits. Sanford Schwartz writes that this painting

> presents one of Hogarth's most memorable faces, that of a plain, unguarded, slightly perspiry and fleshy person—and is a powerful portrait as well. The raw, candid way Elizabeth Salter looks at us, the billowing

pumpkin-colored dress she wears, and the picture's breathing, powdery-yet-oily surface are somehow inseparable elements. (Schwartz 2007)

This description illustrates in a marvelously lucid way how a talented and insightful critic can use several different ways of talking to bring to life the aspects of a painting while suggesting that all belong together in a unified whole. Recall the wine descriptions we looked at a few pages ago, in which we found three sorts of descriptive words, including those with emergent meaning. In Schwartz's brief word portrait of Hogarth's *Mrs. Salter,* I also find several uses of words. Perhaps the most literal word in the entire description is "oily," to describe the painting's surface as paint, not as a representation of a person. The reproduction we are looking at here certainly cannot capture the oiliness of the surface, but we have all probably seen enough paintings to know what it would look like. It would have a shiny, slippery look, a sheen that covers all parts of the painting, the look of dried oil paint or varnish. He also calls the surface "powdery," although there is no powder as such visible. The painting's surface may have the look of having had powder thrown on it, or mixed into the paints, though no real powder is present (unlike the oil that makes for the oily look). Mrs. Salter's dress is called "pumpkin-colored," and while one might use a word with fewer associations than "pumpkin," it does seem to describe the color pretty well. It also, however, has the effect of calling to mind the plainness and—how shall I say it?—decency of the humble pumpkin. Still, this is a color we are talking about, and as such it is part of the painting's existence as a purely physical object. It is, we may say, the physical aspect of the painting that is being described by words like "oily," "powdery," and "pumpkin-colored."

The description of Mrs. Salter's face as that of a "slightly perspiry and fleshy person" is of a different aspect of the painting, for now we are focusing on how paint has become the representation of a human face with specific attributes. We can actually see most of these in the painting at once, though we may not have noticed that her face is "perspiry." When we hear the word, we take note of a feature that was in front of us all along, but which we may not have seen. The critic's description is also for us a way to come to see what we'd not seen before, but which hadn't been hidden from us either. We may begin to wonder about why she is perspiring ever so slightly. Do we get a sense of the temperature in the room where the portrait was painted, or the closeness of the air? Or maybe we don't really *see* the perspiration. (After all, she's not sweaty as if she'd just come in from a jog in the hot sun.) Maybe we question the critic's eye, because we don't see for ourselves what he sees. Can he get us to see it if we do not? Well, he can suggest this description to us and if it fits, if it seems appropriate to us, then he has in a real sense gotten us to see what he sees, even though nothing has been revealed to us that had been hidden in any ordinary sense of "hidden."

He also suggests that Elizabeth Salter looks at us in a raw and candid way. I have remarked before how striking it should be that dabs of paint can look at us. Those eyes are made up entirely of paint. This look, however, is also characterized as raw and candid. Do we see that? If so, what do we see? Might we see something else if the description were altered, if instead of "raw and candid," he said that her look was "confident and comfortable"? Would these descriptions serve as well? What about "naive and simple-minded"? This last doesn't do it for me. It doesn't click at all, and if anyone said it did for him, I would think he was missing something in the portrait. I might try to get him to see this by pointing to certain features in the picture, such as how Mrs. Salter holds herself, and how her eyes seem to have a gentle sparkle to them. But if I failed to convince him with this that "naive and simple-minded" didn't go, there's not much more I could do. It would not be like trying to get someone to see the dress as pumpkin-colored. If he didn't see that, I would think that he didn't know what the word "pumpkin" meant. I would show him a pumpkin. But in the other case I assume that he does know what "naive and simple-minded," "raw and candid," "confident and comfortable," and "complacent and self-assured" all mean. It's not that he doesn't get these words. It's that he doesn't see something, or he sees something I see differently enough for me to want to say that he is missing out.

There is more to Schwartz's description. He uses several words with what I have been calling their emergent meanings. Once again, the meanings of these words have not changed from their ordinary ones, nor are the words used metaphorically or in any way other than their usual way. When, however, they are placed in new and

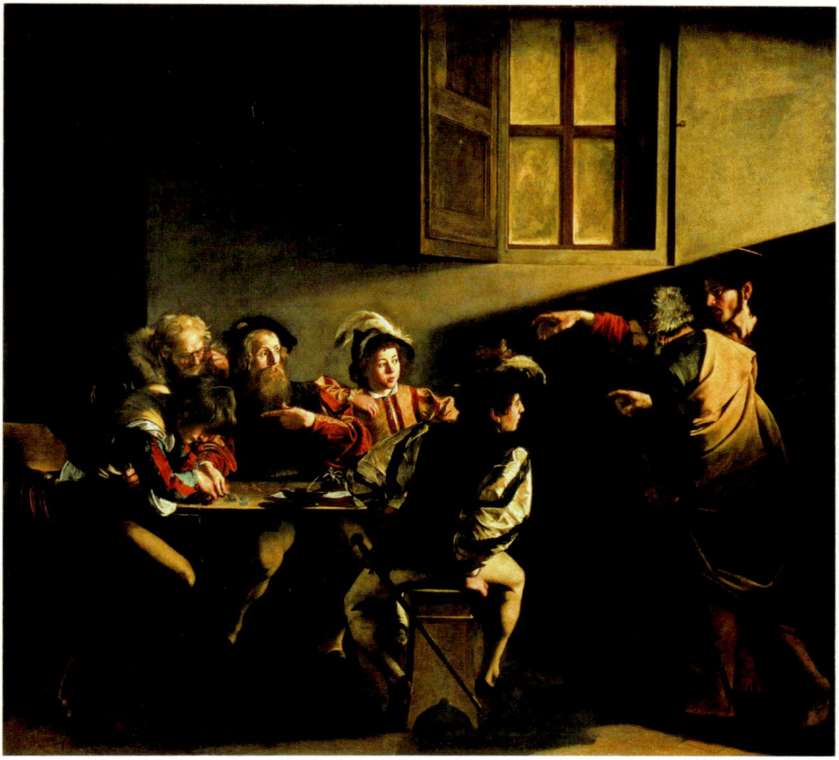

ABOVE:

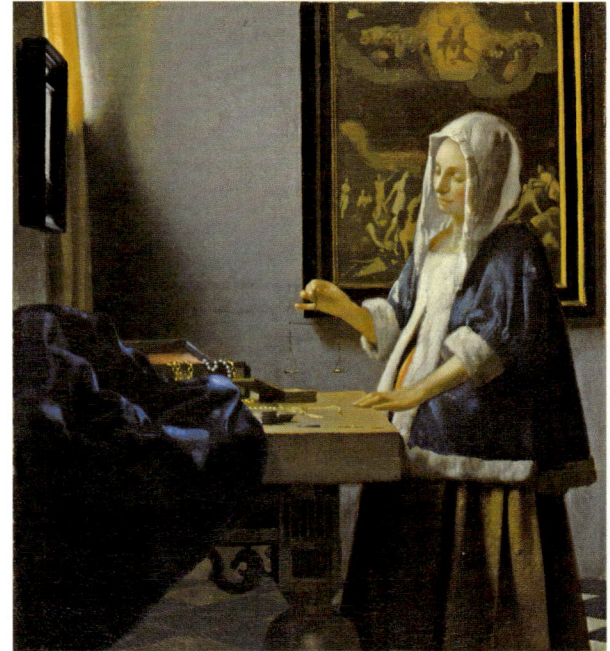

Figure 31. *The Calling of St. Matthew* by Caravaggio.

RIGHT:

Figure 35. *Woman Holding a Balance* by Jan Vermeer.

Figure 46.
Mrs. Salter
by William Hogarth.

Figure 48.
Adele Bloch-Bauer I
by Gustav Klimt.

strange (to them) contexts, something happens. This "something" is essential to aesthetic descriptions. Elizabeth Salter's look is called "raw," which in this case may mean unadorned or not covered up in any way, unprepared. Then we might say it has a metaphorical use in this context: as raw food is to cooked food so is her face to decorated or made-up faces. "Raw" can also mean something like "made raw or sensitive by the wind or cold." Rosy cheeks might seem raw in this way because cheeks exposed to the cold become rosy. I think her cheeks don't look very raw in this sense, and such a description might not create a happy union with "perspiry." There are other metaphorical possibilities for "raw," but perhaps its use here simply has to click with us. For it to click doesn't necessarily mean that we must agree with the description, but if we were to disagree we would need to counter with another word of our own, such as "flushed" or "blushing." What happens when "raw" clicks? Do we see something in the painting we didn't see before? Well, we may be able to say things now that we couldn't have said before, and there are things we certainly would not say because they would not seem to fit with "raw." (Perhaps "openness" would harmonize with "raw," while "devious" might not.) Words used with emergent meaning go or don't go with other words, even if we cannot say exactly what they mean, or how they relate to other words. That we can't make explicit the meaning of a word in an aesthetic context other than to give its usual meanings is of the first importance for understanding descriptions in aesthetics. Just as one cannot say how the duck differs from the rabbit in the duck-rabbit—yet they do differ—so, too, I cannot say why "raw" works while "flushed" does not. That the picture's surface is "breathing" is surely another instance of emergent use. We all know what breathing is, and we all know some metaphorical meanings for it. It is important that in this particular use, "breathing" means what it usually means, but it is being applied in a foreign context. If it clicks with you, then you have come to understand the painting better and can carry the conversation about the painting further than if you are simply stumped by what Schwartz is getting at by "breathing."

And so just as in a description of a wine by an experienced taster, here too, in the description of Hogarth's *Mrs. Salter*, we find mixed together at least three different uses of words. There is the straightforward description of appearance, as in color ("pumpkin") and texture ("oily")—just as a wine may be described as containing hints of raspberry or chocolate, or being of a certain color. There are also those parts of the painting's description that refer to the aspects of the painting as a representation. Mrs. Salter's dress is "billowing," and we see it so, even though nothing on the surface of the canvas billows. We see her face as "plain," her look as "candid," and we immediately know what this means. We may disagree or not see the face in these ways, but we know what it means to *see* faces as expressive of character, and not to *deduce* character from the look of the face. (There is no comparable description about wines, because wines do not display aspects and aspect changes. They have no meaning. But there are learnable, technical terms, such as "tannins," that are used in wine descriptions.)

Finally, words with emergent meanings are found both in Schwartz's description of Hogarth's painting and in the wine descriptions we looked at earlier. These words, such as "silky" (for a wine) and "raw" (for a painted face), take us beyond the ordinary meanings of words, beyond their ordinary uses, without creating new uses for them. The critic's use of such words derives its force from the interconnectedness of words in our language. These words touch a string that resonates throughout our ability to use words, and it is this resonance that gives their emergent meaning real value to us, even though we cannot explain from where or in what way these meanings emerged for us. Nothing changes about the ordinary meaning or meanings of these words, just as nothing changes in the Necker cube or duck-rabbit. But their use in new contexts fits, and this *fitting* helps us make sense of works of art. We would be foolish and would be missing the point of emergent meaning to insist that there must be some explanation for the power of these words. We would also be foolish to dismiss them as too vague and imprecise to serve as aesthetic descriptions. In fact, aesthetic description requires them. It does so because in just the way that aspects are essential to art, emergent meanings are essential to talk about art. The power of art to open up to us new ways of seeing goes hand-in-hand with the power of language to open up to us new ways of describing. It is always possible that a painting will change its meaning for us because we come to see some small part of it differently. This new seeing needn't require a description based on emergent meaning. A critic might point out some things we had not noticed, or he might get us to think about certain features of the painting together that we hadn't put together before. We still might not see what he sees or become able to discuss the painting with the insight such new seeing would give us. But his use of words with emergent meanings challenges us to go along with him and perhaps opens a way for us to see anew without being guided in a stepwise fashion. Emergent meanings, when grasped, allow us to leap to new understanding and new seeing, just the way that the sudden appearance of a new aspect propels us to a new place in our relationship to the work of art.

In music we see the use of emergent meanings in instructions on how to play a piece. Most instructions for playing will be of the sort of "allegro," or "andante," perhaps "allegro con brio" or "andante grazioso." The literal meaning of "allegro" is cheerful, but it has come to mean a certain quickness of pace, often also represented by a metronome value. "Andante" means something like "at a walking pace," though it, too, can be supplemented with a metronome value. "Allegro con brio" (used, for example, at the beginning of the first movement of Beethoven's fifth symphony) is a more suggestive instruction, meaning something like "quickly and with energy or spirit." "Andante grazioso" requires a slow tempo, played gracefully. While we might have some idea of what graceful walking is, it may take some considerable practice for us to translate this into the playing of an instrument or into an ability to recognize a performer's graceful playing. It might help to pay attention to examples of gracefulness from other areas of life in order to get the idea of how grace in a musical performance might manifest itself. Here I seem to be knocking on the door of emergent meaning, but there are far more compelling examples that one will simply get or not get, instructions and descriptions that will seem appropriate and make sense to some, but will be impossible for others. For example, in Edward MacDowell's "To a Wild Rose," the performer is told to play "*teneramente*" or "tenderly." I can search for an explanation, a paraphrase, of this instruction, but how far will I get before I realize that the attempt is misguided? How will I know that I have actually paraphrased or explained it anyway? I can, however, say that unless someone has experienced tenderness in life, or seen expressions of it, and therefore knows how the word is properly used in its ordinary senses, she will not be able to understand MacDowell's instruction. To get an emergent meaning requires that one already know from experience how the word is ordinarily used. In this sense, emergent meaning is indeed secondary or derivative, depending as it does on primary or ordinary meaning and emerging from it. The performer who can play MacDowell's piece as requested or the listener who can recognize a tender performance of "To a Wild Rose" will have had experience of tenderness in life. But emergent meanings needn't always show their connections to experience so directly. I recently read about a young and promising pianist, William Kapell, who was killed in a plane crash in 1953 at the age of thirty-one. Recently some homemade recordings of his performances were discovered, leading to an interview with the woman to whom he was married at the time of his death. She recalled something that the master pianist, Artur Schnabel, with whom Kapell studied briefly in his late twenties, had told him:

> She recalled in particular what Schnabel said about the soulful melody of the slow movement of Schubert's late Sonata in A.
> "He told Willy that this must sound like the first bird that sang in the world," she said. "Willy never forgot that." (Tommasini 2008a)[21]

Fanciful and imaginative, you say, but helpful and descriptive? Well, why not? You and I might have very little sense of what to do, given such instructions. And it is not likely we'd be able to hear when a performer got it right. This is a language-game we cannot play; we cannot obey this command, nor can we recognize when it is being obeyed. Might we be able to learn how to do so? Perhaps, with the right teacher giving us the right hints and examples. But this teacher would not pretend to teach us rules for performance or for listening. At best he could try to give us a feel for the thing, and this is the way it is in matters aesthetic. Our teacher can tell us to hold our fingers a certain way, to play faster or slower, to hesitate or accelerate at certain places. But how to play sweetly, or how to play a piece to sound like the dawn on the first day of creation cannot be transmitted except in those terms. Are you and I deaf to emergent meaning, the way we might be aspect-blind in some cases? I'm not sure I'm willing to describe our condition this way, because it is the condition of most of us. It will be a rare, well-trained, sensitive person who will grasp emergent meanings in art and music. It's as if they see and hear more intensely than we do, not that we are blind. But what they see and hear and feel is possible for a human being, and that is important.

The people I have been referring to as "critics" can be thought of simply as people more experienced or perceptive than most of us in thinking about art and looking at paintings. They might also be friends or colleagues with whom we share an interest, and with whom we spend time looking at art and talking about it. Some will doubtless be more helpful than others. Some have learned the language-games associated with art better than others, and some are simply more imaginative in their application of descriptions to what is right in front of us. What we don't need, I suppose, is a lot of historical and biographical information to clutter our eyes and keep us thinking rather than seeing. Such information may be both interesting and useful, but it often can obscure the most important features of a painting or piece of music: namely, how it looks and sounds. It generally doesn't help us to get a joke to learn something of its origin, though there surely are jokes we would not get without being aware of particular facts.[22]

If our friend, the critic, does not at first get us to see something in a painting or to hear something in a sonata, she can try various approaches. If we are told that Watteau's *L'embarquement pour Cythère* (*Embarkation for Cythera*) (fig. 47) expresses a feeling, we show our blindness to the painting when we ask, "What feeling?" The feeling's description is best given by the painting, not by a simple word such as "serenity" or "anticipation." If we can come to see this, then we come to have and to understand a new feeling, and our experience has grown accordingly. We show that we appreciate this feeling by how we go on to talk about the painting and by the sort of help we can offer others to see—not by attaching a name to the feeling.

Nevertheless, if someone tells us that to him the painting [Watteau's *L'embarquement pour Cythère*] or the piece of music [for example, *En Blanc et Noir* by Debussy] means nothing, there are many resources we have at our disposal for trying to get him to see what is expressed. In the case of the music, we could play it in a certain way, we could com-

Figure 47. *Embarkation for Cythera* by Antoine Watteau.

pare it with other music, we could appeal to the desolate circumstances of its composition, we could ask him why he should be blind to this specific piece: in the case of the painting, we could read to him *A Prince of Courtly Painters*, pausing, say, on the sentence "The evening will be a wet one," we could show him other paintings by Watteau, we could point to the fragility of the resolutions in the picture. It almost looks as though in such cases we can compensate for how little we are able to say by how much we are able to do. Art rests on the fact that deep feelings pattern themselves in a coherent way all over our life and behavior. (Wollheim 1980, 112)[23]

There's no guarantee that one who was blind or deaf to the Watteau or Debussy would now see or hear. He could remain blind and deaf to these aesthetic experiences just as someone might remain blind and deaf to aspects. He might be unable to go along with emergent meanings, stuck in a kind of literalness that, while admitting metaphor, rejects all uses of words that cannot be paraphrased. Such people will have a hard time not only with certain kinds of critical descriptions of art and music, but also with much poetry, where what a poem says cannot be said in any other way.[24] When viewing a painting, they might be able to figure out that the red over there is meant to be taken as a drop of blood, but they won't be able to *see* it as a drop of blood. Up to a point, they will be able to carry on a conversation about the painting, but they won't be able to see what others see. Their eyes will be literal eyes. They will be excluded from certain conversations because they won't be able to follow what is being said. It will be as if they just don't get the joke. When a joke is explained to someone who doesn't get it, the humor in it evaporates; so too when the details of a painting must be explained to someone, the pieces fit, but the heart is missing. Do these people lack aesthetic concepts or just the ability to apply the concepts? Well, we say of someone that he has the concept *tomorrow* when he uses words in certain ways: "The person who cannot play *this* game cannot have *this* concept" (*RC*, 115). The problem in getting the aesthetically blind and deaf to see and hear is really a problem of getting them to do certain things with words, which amounts to the problem of bringing them to have certain concepts or abilities. This may not always be possible.

A good art critic generally will not speak about how a piece makes him feel. A painting is not primarily the cause of feelings in the viewer, but rather an expression of feelings. A sad painting expresses sadness, but does not thereby necessarily cause sadness, just as someone else's sad face may not cause sadness in me. (I may even laugh at it if the context is right.) People who describe a painting or other art work by reference to how they feel fail to distinguish the cause of a feeling from the expression of a feeling. Aesthetic feelings are relatively weak, as I said earlier. This is because these feelings are essentially cognitive, not visceral. I notice, I recognize, I see things in a painting or hear them in a piece of music, and only incidentally feel them. If a piece of art were measured on the basis of how strong a feeling it aroused in its viewers, most great paintings would be judged inferior to violent and shocking ones. Pornography would be thought superior to Picasso, because after all its purpose is to arouse feelings.

The most important aesthetic aspects of a painting or a piece of music are those about which I cannot take another's word. On account of what someone says about a painting, I can believe what the subject is and what the dominant colors are. But that it is balanced or vibrant or expressive of something, I must see for myself. (It's not a coincidence, by the way, that I also cannot take the word of another that someone is morally good or that someone has heard the voice of God. More about this later.) We also don't hear good art critics use what are often thought of as especially aesthetic terms like "beautiful," "glorious," "lovely," "pretty." These words are not descriptive of the art work but rather of the viewer's feelings toward it. These terms are too vague to convey anything but a general positive or negative response from the viewer-critic.

When one has developed an eye or an ear for art, certain questions begin to sound appropriate; they are the right ones to ask. As one acquires such perceptual ability, his view of what is important changes. The progress one can make in understanding art—really, in coming to see and hear anew—parallels psychoanalytic therapy:

> The more one learns, so to speak, the hang of oneself, and mounts one's problems, the less one is able to *say* what he has learned. . . . There is no longer any question or problem which your words would match. You have reached conviction, but not about a proposition; and consistency, but not in a theory. . . . [Y]our world is different. . . . And this is the sense, the only sense, in which what a work of art means cannot be *said*. Believing it is seeing it. (Cavell 1965, 85)[25]

What then if anything does art change in the world? A work of art is not like a road or a factory or a building. Art does not make us go out of our way or help us get from one place to another. It can change the questions we think are important or suggest new questions we can address to our own experience and our own potentiality. Does it change ideas the way books might? Does it uncover new truths about the world or ourselves? Maybe, but this way of putting it seems to miss the central point I have been insisting on all along in this chapter. As we learn to appreciate art, we learn that there are other ways than our own of seeing the same things. "After we have responded to a work of art, we leave it, carrying away in our consciousness something which we didn't have before. . . . [T]he memory of the artist's way of looking at the world. The representation of a recognizable incident . . . offers us a chance of relating the artist's way of looking to our own" (Berger 2001, 8).[26] The good critic, the good writer, the good teacher, sees her job in large measure as trying to get us to experience these other ways of looking. That is, her job is to help us see, not help us understand or gain some knowledge about the painting or sonata or poem with which we are engaged. As we come to appreciate a painting, we simultaneously come to recognize how little we have come to know but how much we have come to see. What I come to see often cannot be taught to another, though I can give him hints. Perhaps with the help of these hints he will be able to have new experiences, which will show themselves in what he can then say about what he is seeing. "Well, what kind of experiences are these? Aren't you just saying that with some help I might be able to talk about a painting the way you do or the way a critic does? How is this a new experience?" But not even travel in strange places will necessarily result in new experiences for me unless someone helps me to see, points out things to me that I would not otherwise have noticed, and helps me compare my own way of seeing to a new one. We often depend on the guidance of others to see for ourselves what is right in front of us or to see it in a new way. We should not underestimate the difficulty of coming to see on our own. We often imagine that in order to break the mold in which our thoughts, beliefs, and experiences are formed, we need to think differently—that we need to go over in our mind different ways that the facts might be related, or need to solve some sort of puzzle. But I think this is not so. As long as we fail to change our eyes and ears, all we'll succeed in doing is to go around the same circle again and again. This is why coming to appreciate art has the air of successful psychotherapy and sometimes the feel of religious conversion. It is also a reason why totalitarian governments usually place a high priority on control of art.

When we look together with other people at a painting or three-dimensional display, it is crucial that we all agree on what we see. We can't begin a conversation if some of us are taken in by an illusion or by the angle from which we're viewing. It is also important that the possibility always be present that we disagree about what we see, in the sense that we see different aspects in the picture, or would describe what we see differently, or say that the picture's meaning is different. We agree and we disagree, and about our disagreement we can talk and perhaps come to some common ground, or perhaps not. At least discussion is possible. We can ask of each other that we try to see what the other is seeing, in the second sense of see, the "see the red as blood" sense. This possibility of talking about what we are seeing is what makes viewing art a social activity. It is not merely standing next to your friend in a museum or gallery or sitting next to her in a concert hall that makes experiencing art a way of sharing our humanity. It's talking about what we are seeing. The better we all become at that, the greater the likelihood that we will share unique experiences with others. We agree about the basic "perceivable stimuli" but then make various suggestions about how they fit in the painting as a whole. Some suggestions will go nowhere. They'll be fruitless or seem forced or unnatural. Others might open new doors. These suggestions could take the form of pointing out aspects of the picture that others haven't noticed, or using words with emergent meaning to describe what we all see. No one knows in advance what will come of this, but all are convinced that it is not knowledge of the philosophical, discursive kind that they are after. If they were, they could take a philosophy class. But art is difficult to teach and difficult to learn because it is essentially not based on a foundation of truth, but of vision. What is essential to getting it is not a rule or a bit of knowledge of history. Paintings cannot be paraphrased or reduced because they are, in a deep sense, individuals. We go up to paintings as we do to people. Adding or subtracting, noticing or failing to notice something very small can have tremendous impact on our aesthetic judgment and experience, as it can in our judgment and experience of people. Compare, for example, Edward Hopper paintings in which there are no living figures to those in which there are, even the smallest one. A bowl of water becomes a life-giving environment when a fish is added, even in a painting.[27]

Let's take another look at the words of critics. John Updike reviewed an exhibition at the Neue Galerie in New York of the paintings of Gustav Klimt (1862–1918), an Austrian who flourished early in the twentieth century. The occasion for the show was the recent purchase by the gallery of Klimt's 1907 portrait of society figure and art patron Adele Bloch-Bauer (see fig. 48 facing p. 211). Updike says that this painting was done in Klimt's Golden Style, which was influenced by a visit to Ravenna, Italy, well known for its startlingly luminescent mosaics. Updike seems disoriented by this painting. He offers two possible understandings of it and shows how an experienced critic sometimes does best when he illuminates for his reader multiple aspects of the same work and does not try to determine once and for all the place of the painting in the history of art. Here's what he says:

> *Adele Bloch-Bauer I* repels critical judgment. Does its subject's lush, heavy-lipped, dark-browed, green-eyed face beneath a black blob of hair and above a silver-encrusted collar, a pale stretch of upper chest, and a rather anxiously wrung pair of skinny pale hands, really mesh with the astonishing efflorescence of perspective-free patterns—eyes, spirals, squares, streaks, and splotches, ostensibly related to the wistful sitter's dress, robe, and armchair? Or does she look like a decal stuck onto a collage of tinselly wrapping paper? A witty and surprising patch of green in the lower left corner represents, it must be, a floor—otherwise the Vienna socialite . . . would seem to have been transported, bodiless, to a giddy Heaven of teeming ornament. Is such an abrupt juxtaposition of textures . . . a bold and necessary step in the direction of modernism, or an uneasy half-step, a cheaply bought glamour, a kind of higher kitsch? (Updike 2007)

Updike plays the role of a good critic, at least as I have been suggesting a good critic ought to behave. He makes no bones about his own ambivalent feelings toward the painting, reflected in his ambivalent description. He clearly sees the painting two ways, and while he seems to be merely reconciled to this ambiguity, not satisfied with it, he offers us no more. Perhaps the painting is both heavenly and earthly, Ravennesque mosaic and kitschy decal, seen one way now, another way a moment later. Can you manage to do that, too?

Perhaps our talk about seeing aspects and describing paintings using words with emergent meanings works well enough with representational art, picture-art, where mere paint takes on the look of objects. But so much art of recent decades has been so-called "abstract art." Now I know that such a categorization is superficial because the art of the twentieth and early twenty-first centuries has been divided into many groupings, such as cubism, abstract expressionism, fauvism, and futurism, while there are still many artists of note whose works are representational (for example, Edward Hopper, Andy Warhol, and Roy Lichtenstein). Still, what I mean by "abstract art" is art that does not aim to represent. I have wondered if aspect talk can help make sense of it. I haven't much to say about this question except to mention one clearly abstract painter and what has been said about his work. This may give us a sense of whether aspect criticism can make any sense with nonrepresentational art. I think it would be helpful to cast a glance at atonal music as well, because like abstract paintings, atonal works can be confusing or frustrating. Some of us may have the feeling that art and music took a wrong turn sometime around the early twentieth century, or that they have become so academic or esoteric or perverse or nonsensical that we'd rather spend our time looking at older paintings and listening to the great masters.

Brice Marden (b. 1938) is an American minimalist. In *Zen Study 6*, Cold Mountain Series (fig. 49), one of a series executed between 1989 and 1991, we see an example of one form his style can take. This is clearly a nonrepresentational painting, even though the title suggests that it is *of* something, or was executed under the influence of something, perhaps Cold Mountain near Asheville, North Carolina. We as viewers might search for the mountain in the paint-

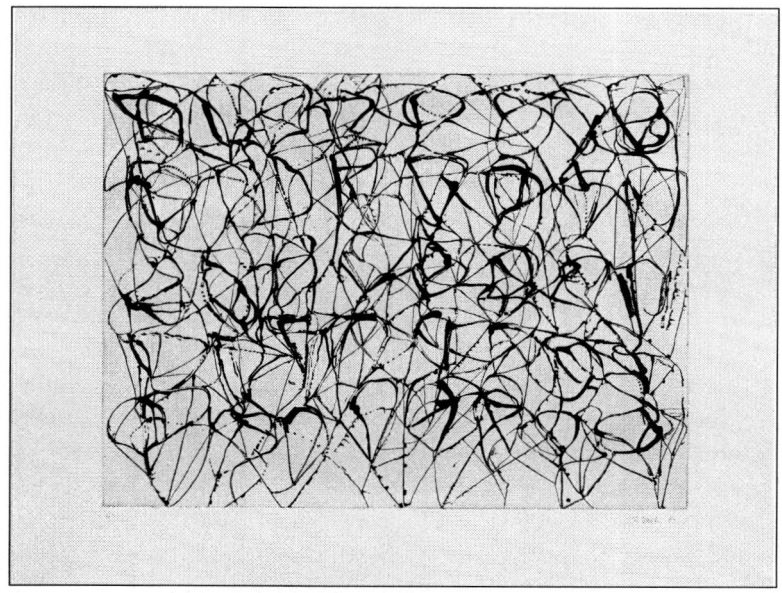

Figure 49. *Zen Study 6,* Cold Mountain Series by Brice Marden.

ing, much as contestants searched for the hairpin in the television game *Camouflage*, as we saw in chapter one. We might even find the mountain, but would we then understand the painting? I think not. In his review of the Brice Marden retrospective held at New York's Museum of Modern Art in 2006, Richard Dorment tries to get us to see Marden's work against the background of the depth perception and representation characteristic of older paintings. Marden's work makes sense only if we see it as a "struggle against pictorial illusion. The picture plane is an imaginary plane represented by the physical surface of the canvas or the paper. Behind it lies the picture space, the apparent space created by the use of perspective or other illusionist devices" (Dorment 2006). Marden tries to block the viewer's tendency to see into a painting, that is, to see the painting as a representation of something, even something as simple and spare as three-dimensional space. This is no mean feat. "For an artist who had always maintained the integrity of the picture plane, to introduce a linear element of any kind was to risk the possibility that spatial depth and illusionistic representation would enter his pictures" (Dorment 2006).[28] I would substitute "aspectual" for "illusionistic" in this description. Marden, then, tries to avoid aspects in his paintings. This is not to say that his paintings are to be seen unambiguously, but rather that "ambiguity" does not seem to have a place in their description. We do not see the painting first one way and then another as with the duck-rabbit, or suddenly see it changing orientation as with the Necker cube. When the artist is successful, such questions about multiple meaning and multiple seeing are no longer applicable. What makes his work noteworthy is that he can repel our very natural tendency to see paintings as something else. In some early paintings such as *Nebraska* (1966), Marden "undercuts any attempt to read the picture as a representation of anything in the natural world because when your eye comes to the bottom of the canvas, you see that it is, after all, a flat surface" (Dorment 2006). He has left an unpainted margin at the bottom wherein we can see for ourselves the drips left over from each layering of paint. Marden's paintings make sense because he deliberately makes them stand in opposition to representational paintings. In some ways, he wants to reveal to the eye that a painting is only paint on canvas and that paint on canvas can be devoid of aspect. In this sense, Marden's achievement is at the opposite end of the artistic spectrum from cubism, which attempts to represent all (or many) aspects of its subject simultaneously.[29]

Music has its counterpart to Marden. In music until the twentieth century, tonal dynamics were the norm:

> [M]usicians obeyed natural laws of physics. Pick up a rock, drop it, and it falls to the ground. Music was the same. Send a piece of music up in the air, doctor and twist it, make it major, minor or modal; in the end it wants to come down to where it started. You can call the process tonality or music's law of gravity. (Holland 2008)

Tonal center allows for variation from center and key, and thereby allows the composer to create dynamic pressure in melodies and harmonies. Classical music—most music—can be heard as an artfully constructed series of pulls and pushes with a final resting place back home, from where the music took off. Music of this form allows for aspects to be heard, as one and the same tone can take on different meanings. It can point in different dynamic directions, depending on what surrounds it musically, as we saw earlier. The absence of a tonal center would amount to an obliteration of aspects. There would be no way to hear a tone first in one key or mode, then in another, because there would be no keys or modes at all to provide the essential context for musical aspect. (Rhythm might still provide aspectual content to atonal music, but one could imagine even that being blurred beyond accessibility.) A master in this kind of music is Anton Webern (1883–1945). In his twelve-tone pieces, the primary rule to be followed is to avoid the slightest hint of a key or tonal center or dynamic tendency, which had defined Western music up to then. This is an accomplishment because just as the eye wants to see meaningful wholes in a painting, so too the ear wants to unify what it hears in a piece of music. The natural way to achieve this is through locating a tonal center almost instinctually and judging the place of all sounds by reference to it. Just as Marden tries to counter the eye's tendency to see things, Webern tries to thwart the ear's efforts to find a musical home base.

Figure 50 shows the opening measures of Webern's *Variations for Piano*, Opus 27.

Figure 50. *Variations for Piano*, Op. 27, by Anton Webern, opening measures.

How does he go about frustrating our efforts to hear a center while maintaining a sense of unity, which every work of art must possess? He begins with the twelve notes that make up the chromatic scale. On the piano, this would include all the white and black notes between C and B. This is his material, as it had been the material of his predecessors. Since the tonic note—the one that the others center around and towards which they tend or from which they strain away—is strongly emphasized in tonal music, Webern reasons that in atonal music every effort must be made to avoid dominance by any single tone. Here is what he says in his own words:

> [S]ince there was no tonic anymore . . . we felt the need to prevent one note being over-emphasized, to prevent any note's "taking advantage" of being repeated. . . . [T]he composition would have to be over when all twelve notes had been there. So no note must be repeated during a round of all twelve! But a hundred "rounds" could happen at once! That's all right, only when *one* has started, then the other notes of the row must follow it, without any of them being repeated. . . . There can even be a twelve-tone chord. (Webern 1963, 39 f)[30]

If you look carefully at the score of the opening of his Opus 27 Variations, you'll see that this is exactly what he does. Through measures 1–4, the tones follow a sequence of (F-E) B (F-sharp–G) C-sharp (A–B-flat) E-flat (C-D) G-sharp, where notes in parentheses are played together. The next four measures play the very same tone row backwards. I'll let you figure out what happens after that. You can be sure, however, that the sequence, no matter how it occurs, will be the same. "The round of twelve notes," as Webern calls it, gives the piece its unity. Perhaps we can say that the different permutations of this tone row are different aspects of the fundamental sequence with which we begin. That might be a way to rescue aspect-hearing in twelve-tone music. But it would not be like the hearing of aspects in tonal music, and in fact might be so different that we would be more comfortable saying that Webern successfully avoids aspects in his music, as Marden and Pollock avoid representation. Both art forms can be understood against the backdrop of aspects, as intentional and deliberate departures from aspect-seeing and aspect-hearing. It takes an understanding of the role of aspects in representational painting and in tonal music to begin to understand abstract painting and atonal music. Critical writers and teachers help us appreciate artists who work in these forms first by getting us to see and hear what they are not doing, and then bringing us to see what they are doing. We then might come to recognize that they are playing other games, related to those with which we are more comfortable and not entirely different from them. (Webern's Variations are *related* to Mozart's, though perhaps they are more difficult for our ears to hear.) As we become accustomed to the rules, we too can learn to talk about nonfigurative art with sensitivity and fluency. We can see that it, too, has a way of looking at the world that can help us attain new experiences.

A good critic of art helps our seeing along, provides us with new aesthetic experiences, and enlarges the scope of what is possible for us to see and imagine. David Hume (1711–1776), the Scottish philosopher and historian, provides a clear statement of the primary characteristics of a good critic: "strong sense, united to delicate sentiment, improved by practice, perfected by comparison, and cleared of all prejudice." He further describes the consequences when such qualities are lacking.

> When the critic has no delicacy, he judges without any distinction, and is only affected by the grosser and more palpable qualities of the object: The finer touches pass unnoticed and disregarded. Where he is not

aided by practice, his verdict is attended with confusion and hesitation. Where no comparison has been employed, the most frivolous beauties, such as rather merit the name of defects, are the objects of his admiration. Where he lies under the influence of prejudice, all his natural sentiments are perverted. Where good sense is wanting, he is not qualified to discern the beauties of design and reasoning, which are the highest and most excellent. (Hume 1993, 147)

Now, I don't know what part of Hume's description you believe. I'm not sure how many of us believe anyone at all can judge without prejudice. But I do know that most of us think it worth while, when evaluating a painting, a piece of music, a poem, or most anything else, to try our best to look with as unprejudiced an eye as we can. And what exactly Hume means by "delicacy" may not be immediately evident. Still, I think for the most part we appreciate that coming to see a work of art requires that we attend to *small* things that can have big implications. We do this every day when we immediately recognize a change in mood or opinion on the face of a friend.[31] The smallest differences, even ones we cannot point out, tell us something that can be very important. We do it with people, and we can do it with paintings, with music, with words.[32] If art is to mean to us more than simply "beauty," pleasant sounds, and "interesting" pictures, we must pay attention and learn to see and hear with more receptivity the aspects that works of art show us. In the end, however, when we try to bring another to see what we see in making an aesthetic judgment, "at some point we [must] be prepared to say in its support: don't you see, don't you hear, don't you dig? The best critic will know the best points" (Cavell 1965, 93).

CHAPTER FIVE

Ethics and Aesthetics
Are One

O UR ABILITY TO SEE aspects has its source not in our eyes
or brain, but in language, as we've seen. No amount of looking at retinas or brain scans will ever reveal to us the "what-it-is-to-
be" of aspects and aspect-seeing. This is so because of how we teach
language and learn it, how we use words in social settings, and how
we are justified in saying of others that they are now seeing. When
I say that I see the duck in the duck-rabbit, you know that I see it by
what I can go on to say and do. I can point to its eyes, draw the rest
of its body, maybe color it all in appropriately. But in a funny way I,
too, know that I see the duck because of what I can do. If I couldn't
go on to say or do appropriate things, then neither you nor I would
be justified in saying that I saw the duck.[1] This is how we teach children to use words. If a child claimed to see the rabbit in the duck-
rabbit but could do or say nothing else appropriate when asked, we
would be right to tell her that she wasn't seeing the rabbit at all. Even
if she insisted, we could not tell ourselves that maybe we're wrong,
maybe she actually is seeing the rabbit. No, if we are dealing with a
child who is still learning language, then we would not be *contradict-
ing* her by telling her she is not seeing the rabbit. Rather we would be
correcting her use of words in this context of describing ambiguous
pictures. No imaginable brain scan or other physiological information could stand as evidence that in fact the child was seeing the rabbit. Seeing aspects is a conceptual matter, but it is no less seeing than
seeing a chair. As Wittgenstein has said, it is an amalgam of seeing
and thinking—both at the same time and not separable from one

another. This seeing-thinking amalgam is also linguistic because for Wittgenstein thinking depends on language.

In cases where emergent word meanings play a prominent role, such as in talk about aesthetics, the meaning of a word may not be its use, but something more like a sack it carries from its usual language-games into new contexts. When this happens—when a word is used not metaphorically or figuratively, but not literally either—its emergent meaning cannot be explained. The word in its new context can, however, seem to be more or less appropriate for our goals, and if it is deemed appropriate—that is, if the hearer gets it—then a new use for it has entered the world. In a sense a new meaning and a new gesture, along with new possible experiences, enter the world, too. When we see a new aspect, a central part of our experience is that nothing has changed (the thing pictured or heard), while something has (the aspect). So, too, when we use a word with emergent meaning or hear it used that way, we recognize that the word now is doing different work while retaining the same meaning. The shift of a word's meaning from primary to emergent is akin to the seeing of a new aspect. Something happens to the world, or at least to a part of it, when this takes place.

In this final chapter, I want to expand the notions of aspect-seeing and emergent meaning to the areas of science, ethics, and religion. I think I am keeping true to Wittgenstein's notion of aspects when I broaden their application beyond the world of perception. Some of his remarks lead me to feel comfortable doing this.[2] But rather than simply state this, I'll take a look at how aspects and emergent meaning might help us get hold of what goes on in science, ethics, and religion, and how they can guide us to both a more generous and a more hopeful perception of all three. I won't give these topics the time that they deserve. Rather than giving arguments meant to persuade you, I will offer suggestions about directions that continuing investigation can take. I find the application of aspect-seeing and emergent meaning to these areas very exciting, but I also know that much more work needs to be done before the careful reader will be won over. I think such work can be done and that it will flower in a renewed appreciation for the place of *tolerance* throughout our work and our lives and in the world at large.

A. Science

> Getting hold of the difficulty *deep down* is what is hard. Because if it is grasped near the surface it simply remains the difficulty it was. It has to be pulled out by the roots; and that involves our beginning to think about these things in a new way. The change is as decisive as, for example, that from the alchemical to the chemical way of thinking. The new way of thinking is what is so hard to establish.
>
> Once the new way of thinking has been established, the old problems vanish; indeed they become hard to recapture. For they go with our way of expressing ourselves and, if we clothe ourselves in a new form of expression, the old problems are discarded along with the old garment. (*CV*, 48)

In June or July of 1609, word reached Galileo that someone in Holland, a lens grinder named Hans Lipperhey, had the previous year invented a device for magnifying objects that were far away, effectively bringing them closer. Ever his own craftsman, Galileo built one of these spyglasses (*perspicilla* in Latin) to his own exacting requirements. He then turned it toward the heavens, first to the moon. When Galileo and his contemporaries had looked at the moon before this, they had seen a round body, generally believed to be a sphere, the surface of which was covered with dark and light patches. The moon was not like the earth in that the moon's surface was thought to be smooth, though mottled. When he looked through the spyglass or telescope, Galileo saw that the markings on the moon were created by sunlight reflecting from the surface. He reported these findings (along with the discovery of the moons of Jupiter) in *The Starry Messenger* (*Sidereus Nuncius*).[3] He argues that the way the sun is reflected from certain lunar formations proves that the surface of the moon is not smooth at all, but is covered with "cavities and prominences" (Galileo 1957, 31). He describes how the changing distribution of light and darkness as the sun passes over the lunar surface can only (or best?) be explained by the presence of these depressions and heights.

Galileo is trying to allow others to *see* what he sees, when they look through a telescope. Without such a guide, I suspect that most people would not see these formations, though in some sense they would see just what Galileo saw. His words can bring them to see more than they could see left to their own. Galileo discovers something about the surface of the moon, something very important: it is rough, like the surface of the earth. But his discovery is also a new way of seeing the moon. Nowadays, when you and I look at the moon, we see craters and mountains. We have gone even beyond Galileo, for to call one of his cavities a crater is to say something about how it was created. Craters are formed by some kind of violent reaction, either an impact or a collapse from within, or some such thing. (A smoothed-out dry lake bed, for example, is not a crater, though it is a depression or cavity.) Through modern science education, we have come to see craters—and I do mean *see*—which means that we see something of the history of the moon. Galileo's account is essentially descriptive and ahistorical. I don't want to insist that we always see craters, but we know that what we see are craters because of things we've been told. But nowadays we would wonder why someone who said she saw "depressions or cavities" was speaking so strangely. Why doesn't she simply say that she sees "craters"? Today we would have to make an effort to see the moon's surface as smooth and covered with dark and light spots, or see simply cavities and prominences.[4] Before Galileo, no one saw anything like this, though people were looking at the same moon as we are. Perhaps the moon has changed, but if so it is in the way that the puzzle-picture of the man who looks something like Jesus changes when it suddenly becomes a portrait. Something changes, yet we know that nothing has changed.

A widespread belief holds that scientists follow, and for centuries have followed, the "scientific method," which runs something like: observation, hypothesis, experiment, analysis, accept or reject hypothesis, and so on. This is to some extent true, even since the advent of the highly theoretical physics of the twentieth century, which raises questions about what exactly is being observed in the first place. Bubble chamber observations of subatomic particles seem a far cry from Newton's experiments with pendulums and rotating pails of water. The tracks in the chamber are only made by subatomic particles if there exist subatomic particles that behave in just the ways that would produce those tracks. That is, the observation is itself dependent on a theory in order for it to be an observation of what it claims to be. For Newton, what you see is what you get: a bucket of water is a bucket of water.[5]

This is not the whole story, however. In *Patterns of Discovery*, the philosopher of science Norwood Russell Hanson (1924–1967) argues that throughout the history of science observation has involved something like aspect perception. For example, two microbiologists give different answers when asked what they see on a prepared slide. One sees "a cluster of foreign matter . . . an artifact," while the other sees a cell organ, a "Golgi body." Or perhaps these same researchers look at an amoeba. One sees a "one-celled organism," the other a "non-celled organism." Hanson is skeptical of the standard response to this, namely, that both observers see the same thing but interpret it differently. Their disagreement (if that's what it is) would then lie not in their eyes, but in their thinking. Do Galileo and his naïve contemporary see the same thing when they look at the moon? Do Ptolemy and Copernicus see the same thing when they view a sunset? We may be inclined to say "yes and no," and that tells us that once again we are talking about aspect perception. The way we describe what we see tells others *what we see*, and if your description differs from mine, then in an important way we see different things.

Hanson's arguments about the connection between scientific observations and their descriptions stem from Wittgenstein's insistence that seeing is often more complex than we take it to be. The complexity arises not from the smallness of things (like cells and atoms) nor from their great distance (like the moon). Rather, descriptions must be expressed in language, which is necessarily ambiguous. As a result, a request for "the facts, ma'am, just the facts," immediately lands us in trouble. For "the facts" can't be pried away from their descriptions in any obvious sense. In his first book, *Tractatus Logico-Philosophicus* (the only one published during his lifetime), Wittgenstein argues that "the world is the totality of facts, not of things" (*TLP*, 1.1). Sentences get their meaning by mirroring the form of these facts, so for the early Wittgenstein, facts and their descriptions can be kept separate. Scientists could find a way to agree on what they saw but disagree on what it meant for future research or for theory. Later, however, as he thought more about how language actually works, Wittgenstein moved away from this view. He no longer saw *facts* on the one hand and *descriptions* on the other. Words and sentences take their meanings from how they are used. Concepts such as force and energy are not simply present in the world to be observed and analyzed. Newton (1642–1727) argues that force is the central explanatory principle of moving things. In his *Principia Mathematica*, he introduces force in his opening definitions and laws, and from this unfolds a description of the workings of all moveable objects, from pendulums and colliding steel balls to the sun and the moon. When he looks at the universe (and when we do from a Newtonian point of view), he sees forces at work, pushing and pulling according to very simple, fixed laws. Leibniz (1646–1716), on the other hand, sees energy as the fundamental principle of motion. (He called it *vis viva*, "living force.") His laws are equally few, but different from Newton's. He emphasizes conservation principles, such as conservation of momentum and of *vis viva*. When he looks at the universe (and when we do from a Leibnizian point of view), he sees energy being transferred from place to place, all the while according to precise principles of conservation. It is perhaps amazing to note that problems in mechanics can be solved by either approach, and the answers will be exactly the same as far as their predictive power.[6] But the worlds inhabited by the two thinkers are remarkably different. Or are they? Is this the duck-rabbit once again?

When Newton and Leibniz see two steel balls collide, they both in a sense see the same thing. But if one sees force and the other energy, they see very different things. Jump off a short stool or ladder. Try to imagine yourself being pulled by the earth, rather than as falling. Can you do it? Falling is pulling, according to Newton's account. Neither Leibniz nor Newton interprets what he sees any more than we interpret the Necker cube when we see it one way or the other. Newton and Leibniz may have worked hard to get to the point where they could see the world of motion in the ways they did. But once they have done so, they see, just as once we have learned to read, we read—we don't interpret marks on a page.[7]

What we see is shown by how we respond and by what we can do: what we say, what we suggest for the next stage of research, what we reject as irrelevant and accept as relevant, and what connections we make between the thing in front of us and other things we know or other areas of research. These connections often cannot be said to be worked out by the scientist. Rather, they are seen in a way not unlike the way we see how parts of a painting illuminate one another. And because different descriptions of what we see may lead to different lines of research and different emphases within those lines, these descriptions are important. They are not simply another way of saying it.[8] Sometimes, seemingly innocent images and metaphors can have a big influence on the direction research takes, the sorts of things scientists will consider important, and the entire organization of a new theory. To ask, for example, where in the brain to locate consciousness or memory is already to have taken a stance on how to look at a problem—in this case problems about the relationship between mind and body.

Along with Wittgenstein and Hanson, I have been saying that prior knowledge shapes what we see. Wittgenstein is clear as to why this is so, and his reasons, as I have been repeating in various ways throughout this book, do not include neurological or physiological (or even mental) causes or accounts. Someone ignorant of mesons cannot see a meson shower because seeing is a kind of ability, not a passive receptivity. I am justified in saying of someone that he sees something—in this case, a meson shower—only if he can do something further. If I were to teach you what it means to see a meson shower, I would know that you had seen it only by what you say and do subsequently. This is the same sort of situation I am in when I try to teach a child how to use words as she is learning language. There is no inner picture of a meson shower that needs to be linked up with the words "meson shower" in order for me to be justified in saying that you have seen it. No, you have seen a meson shower if you can go on to ask questions, follow further discussion about meson showers, and help others see them, too. In a like way, someone ignorant of ducks cannot be said to see the duck-rabbit as a duck. No amount of poking around in his brain or retina will be able to leap over this conceptual wall, which is erected by the very ways we learn and use words, not by any limitations in our thinking or by transformations of neural connections that are too subtle for us to observe.

One more interesting example of how aspect-seeing plays a role in scientific investigation comes from Goethe's essay "On the Metamorphosis of Plants." Goethe (1745–1832) addresses the problem of how plants grow: where their parts come from, how the parts find their way to their proper stations on the plant, and in general how to make sense of the growth of plants from seeds. Preformationism was the dominant theory of the development of living things in the eighteenth century. In this view, all organisms were created at the same time. Succeeding generations grow from homunculi, animalcules, or other fully-formed but miniature versions of themselves that have existed since the beginning of creation. As strange a view as this seems to us today, it was adhered to by many respectable thinkers, such as van Leeuwenhoek (1632–1723) and Malebranche (1638–1715). It was a reasonable response to the discovery by microscope of spermatozoa, which could be considered fully developed organisms on a very small scale. (Plants were treated analogously to animals in this theory.) There was little available evidence for another view, epigenesis, which postulated that development took place from initial, undeveloped matter. Nevertheless, tension between the two views continued until cell theory replaced them in the late nineteenth century. Goethe offers yet a different approach to the development of plants, one that does not rely on discoveries by microscope. He tries to show that the growth of a plant can be seen as the alternating expansion and contraction of just one organ, the leaf. That is, "the same organ which expanded on the stem as a leaf and assumed a highly diverse form, will contract in the calyx, expand again in the petal, contract in the reproductive organs, and expand for the last time as fruit" (Goethe 1989, 77).[9]

Of course when we first look at a plant (any plant, according to Goethe), we don't think how alike all the parts appear, because they don't look alike. Goethe describes the growth of a plant in such a way that it begins to make sense that all the parts could arise from leaf if the process of development went along according to a certain sequence. This sequence is the sequence we actually see when plants grow. They do not emerge from the seed full of fruit and flowers, but the cotyledons do look like leaves. Goethe tries through description to change how we look at the plant and, in effect, to change what we see. He proposes a gradual expansion and contraction of each manifestation of leaf as the plant grows. The petal is a stamen in a state of expansion, while a stem leaf is a sepal "expanded by the influx of cruder saps" (Goethe 1989, 77). He places the parts of the plants in sequential juxtaposition, so that we can better see how one part literally can be the other. In a sense, he does what an artist might do by both placing together and talking about images we usually do not think to look at together, thereby helping us to see the similarities we might otherwise overlook. If we see what he sees, that is, if he succeeds in getting us to see the leaf in all the rest of the plant's parts, he will have brought us to see something new in something familiar. This is as much a discovery as Galileo's finding mountains and craters on the moon.

You may want to raise your hand at this point and ask how we can possibly understand modern physics—for example, quantum mechanics and the wave-particle descriptions of both light and matter—as involving a kind of aspect shift, when much of what has gone for theory in the last hundred years has been, quite literally, unimaginable. And this is true. But it is important to acknowledge that the radical *unpicturability* of these things is part of the theory. No picture can reflect the properties that quantum mechanics attributes to the constituents of the universe. In fact, any picture would immediately raise old questions that quantum mechanics has set aside, such as determining the precise location and momentum of particles. Heisenberg's indeterminacy principle tells us that the more we know about one of these properties, the less we can know about the other. This is not due to ignorance or to the inadequacy of our technology. Rather it is part and parcel of the theory of quantum mechanics.[10] We still can determine the position and momentum of, say, the moon, even though it consists of particles for no one of which we can determine both. This will seem paradoxical only to those who have not understood that it is possible to see and talk about the world in a number of ways without contradiction. You may say that this is nonsense, and that, too, may be true. We might say that quantum mechanics uses words with emergent meanings and, in so doing, speaks a kind of nonsense. To say that the experimental data suggest that light and subatomic particles behave sometimes like waves and other times like regular macroscopic physical objects—and sometimes like both simultaneously—sounds contradictory. It is certainly *unpicturable*, in the same way that the duck-rabbit cannot be seen both as a duck and as a rabbit at the same time. But perhaps the words "particle" and "wave," while retaining their ordinary meanings, take on new uses in this theory. This is not to say that physics is just like art or poetry—that you either get it or you don't (though there is that element in it, too). The concepts of physics, even when they are ordinary concepts put in new situations, must stand up to theory in a way that "fat" in "fat Wednesday" need not: "In a scientific perspective a new use is justified by a *theory*. And if this theory is false, the new extended use has to be given up" (*CV*, 44).

Galileo makes a discovery with the help of a new invention. His discovery signals an important moment in the transition from Aristotelean cosmology to what will become Newtonian cosmology. Rather than believing that the heavenly bodies are smooth spheres, radically different from the earth, Galileo and Newton point to the similarities between them and earth. The moon and earth have similar, irregular surfaces, and so the earth is no longer unique in the solar system in that regard. Jupiter is the center of the revolution of heavenly bodies (its moons), and so the earth is not unique as a center of a system of orbiting celestial bodies. And the forces that act on earth to cause objects to fall or move in just the ways they do are the very same forces acting to keep the earth and other planets in their orbits around the sun. Something is happening. Galileo's and Newton's observational aspect-changes lead to what Thomas Kuhn (1922–1996) calls a "paradigm shift" (Kuhn 1962). A whole new way of seeing and thinking about the physical world replaces a way that has run into difficulties. During times of relative stability in a theory, Kuhn argues, scientists pursue what he calls "normal science." Problems are framed in the context of an accepted theory, and answers are sought wholly within that context. In the Ptolemaic system of the universe, all heavenly bodies move in perfect circles around the earth as center. Sometimes, Ptolemy must hypothesize circles on circles (epicycles) in order to accommodate the data he has. Nevertheless, for centuries, the requirement that these bodies be described only by uniform circular motion (the most perfect according to Aristotle) precludes anyone from seriously asking, "What if the planets moved in elliptical orbits?" The stage is not set on which such questions could make sense.[11] When paradigms shift—when, for example, Newtonian mechanics gives way to Einsteinian relativity—new questions and problems, as well as new lines of research, come into existence.

A book, an article, a discovery, an invention—any one of these might draw people away from old ways of looking at phenomena and established modes of experimentation. When Lavoisier (1743–1794) in his chemical researches began to use the highly sensitive balances then being produced in France, he made weight a significant player in his arguments against phlogiston as an explanatory principle in oxidation. Phlogiston had been postulated to be what was released when substances burned or oxidized. Once careful measurements of weights before and after oxidation could be made (in particular the oxidation of mercury into mercuric oxide), it became clear that oxides actually weighed *more* than the substances from which they came. If the release of phlogiston were responsible for oxidation, then in order for the oxides to weigh more, phlogiston would have to have *negative weight*—so that when it left a substance, the substance's weight would increase. This is not entirely ridiculous: hydrogen and helium, for example, appear to have "negative weight," which is why balloons filled with them float. At least this is the way an argument to save phlogiston could go. But Lavoisier's emphasis on weight as it is determined on a balance simply overwhelmed the phlogiston theory and allowed a new, simpler, and more inclusive way of organizing the data to emerge. Still, in one sense, it was not discovered that phlogiston does not exist. Instead a new paradigm replaced the old, and phlogiston was swept under the conceptual rug.[12]

Paradigm shifts are much like aspect changes. What did or did not make sense when looked at one way makes sense when seen a different way. This may be accompanied by a shift in the hierarchy of what sorts of data are important. Science tends not to waffle back and forth between paradigms—as we do when we view the Necker cube, for example—except at times of transition when no paradigm dominates. Paradigm shifts in Kuhn's sense are more like recognizing what one did not recognize before, such as the portrait in the puzzle-picture. Paradigm shifts are not discoveries. A discovery is more like: "Falling bodies increase in speed in proportion to the time they are falling," or "The speed of light is finite." Copernicus did not discover that the earth moved around the sun. Nor did Einstein discover that nothing can travel faster than the speed of light in a vacuum. Such changes in how we view the physical world can be catalyzed by a discovery, but they are not themselves discoveries any more than my seeing the rabbit in the duck-rabbit for the first time is a discovery. If anything, it is the realization that, yes, it could be this way, too. This could be the picture of a rabbit, this cube could be pointing down, those fingers could be pressing on the table, the earth could be moving around the sun.

Kuhn's book had a profound impact on the way philosophers and historians of science viewed the development of scientific theories and the everyday work of scientists in the laboratory and the armchair. He presents interesting details from many fields and makes what I take to be a persuasive argument.[13] (Hanson does something similar.) I have tried merely to suggest (very briefly!) that what Wittgenstein says about aspects—and how I have developed his remarks in this book—opens a door for us to see some connections between science and aesthetics. This is not to say that science develops and evolves the way art does. The influences on them may be very different. But the similarities are hard to avoid.[14]

B. From a Religious Point of View

> I am not a religious man, but I cannot help seeing every problem from a religious point of view. —Wittgenstein (mentioned in Rhees [1984], 94)

Can sensitivity to aspects help us when we talk about ethical and religious matters? Can we find ways to talk productively even with those with whom we disagree strongly on ethical and religious beliefs? Is there a truth about the ethical, or are claims about what is good and right entirely relative to our time and our culture? Are claims about the existence of God, an afterlife, and miracles sensible, or are they mere nonsense that science has shown to be without foundation and that enlightened people ought to reject? Can we find ways to keep the conversation alive between believers and atheists, the religious and the scientific, absolutists and relativists?

It seems to me that we must always look for ways to keep talking together, because when conversation ends, misunderstanding and conflict ensue. My intention is to suggest that what we've learned about aspect-seeing and the emergent meaning of words can provide a foundation for finding common ground and keeping talk alive. Once again, I can give only the barest outline of how we might take steps toward understanding the very people and beliefs we now find most difficult to fathom. We can do so without simultaneously abandoning our own convictions. Wittgenstein tended to view ethical and religious questions and problems together, without clearly demarcating the purview of each. I shall do the same, though I am fully aware that nonreligious people can take their ethical beliefs very seriously and that one needn't believe in any sort of God or supernatural aspect of life in order to try to be good and to do the right sorts of things. I am one of those people. If I had to say where on the spectrum of religious belief I fall, I would say "atheist," though not born an atheist. I'm not comfortable with such labels, however, because there is usually a much longer story to be told about someone's relation to these ideas than is suggested by a mere word.

In 1929 Wittgenstein delivered a "Lecture on Ethics" to the Heretics Society at Cambridge University.[15] In the lecture, he adopts a working definition of ethics that is based on something G. E. Moore (1873–1958) writes in his book, *Principia Ethica*: "Ethics is the general inquiry into what is good" (Moore 1959, 2). Wittgenstein broadens the topic to include what he says is generally called "aesthetics." He eventually takes into account some ideas we usually think of as falling under the umbrella of the religious or supernatural—for example, miracles. As you might guess, he is primarily interested in how we *talk* about the good and the right and the beautiful. But as I have mentioned before, this in no way implies that he is not interested in the good, the right, and the beautiful themselves, because *how* we talk about something tells us what it *is* if we pay attention to what we say. Thinking about how we talk about the good and miracles is very close to thinking about the good and miracles.[16]

Wittgenstein goes on to distinguish between relative value and absolute value. "Every judgment of relative value is a mere statement of facts and can therefore be put in such a form that it loses all the appearance of a judgment of value" (*PO*, 38). For example, to say that a man is a good runner simply means that he satisfies certain criteria, such as being able to complete a marathon or to run a certain number of miles in a certain time. A good car is one that does what a car is meant to do and doesn't do what can make a car a headache to own. According to Wittgenstein, descriptions of objects or people or actions in terms of relative value can never imply any sort of ethical judgment. One might know all the facts about an event yet not have come one bit closer to knowing if the event was good or bad. In other words, according to this extreme view, no proposition of science (fact) can in any sense be sublime, important, or trivial, terms that express absolute value.

At this point in his life, Wittgenstein believes that language can only express relative value, not absolute value—though it is full of sentences that seem to be about absolute value. These are the propositions of ethics, aesthetics, and religion. They are not facts in the sense of what can be properly expressed by language. Yet such propositions (if they can be called such) have a place in life and in our conversations and thoughts. We use them seriously, and they often are the way we determine other people's characters. What is their status? "Then what have all of us who, like myself, are still tempted to use such expressions as 'absolute good,' 'absolute value,' etc., what have we in mind and what do we try to express?" (*PO*, 39). Wittgenstein gives a personal example of a feeling that for him expresses something absolute. Perhaps you have had such a feeling or one like it. He describes it as a sense of wonder at the existence of the world as a whole, not of any single thing in it. That there is anything at all rather than nothing seems to be another way to express this feeling of absolute value. Another example that is meaningful to him is the feeling of being *absolutely safe*, such that nothing can harm him.

Wittgenstein has a surprising answer to the question of what absolute value statements are about. They are *nonsense*. The verbal expressions that we give to these experiences about wonder at the existence of the world or feeling absolutely safe are nonsense because they use words that have meaning in ordinary contexts but extend their use far beyond the ordinary. Someone can wonder about the existence of a fossil or even about the existence of, say, trees—which I sometimes do. Sometimes I'm struck by the fact that there are trees at all. I don't know why I am. This sense of wonder contrasts with the absence of such a feeling about most everything else. I wonder at the existence of trees, but not of rocks, dirt, air, or even animals. My wonder has a place amid my taking so much else for granted. But when I extend this sense to *everything*, and wonder about the existence of it all, what am I doing? I am taking a perfectly good word ("wonder") which expresses a perfectly good experience (wonder), and removing it from the very context that gives it the power to express such an experience. I cannot, according to Wittgenstein, imagine the whole world not existing, so how can I wonder at its existence? I can imagine a world without trees or fossils, but can I imagine no world at all? Wittgenstein thinks not, and I agree with him. Similarly I can feel safe or protected to an extent, safe *from*, say, falling bricks or lightning: "To be safe essentially means that it is physically impossible that certain things should happen to me" (*PO*, 42). It is nonsense, though, to say that I am absolutely safe—that is, safe no matter what happens to me. To be absolutely safe is to be safe from everything, and this makes no sense.

When we speak about absolute experiences or when we give words absolute meanings—meanings that refer to feelings of absolute value in ethics, aesthetics, or religion—we are literally speaking nonsense or speaking literal nonsense. Someone might say that when we talk this way, when we say for example that Jack is a good man, we are speaking in similes or analogies or in some other figurative or metaphorical way. The words we are using are not being used with their normal meanings (their "relative" meanings), but are connected in some way to their normal meanings. When we say that a man's life is valuable, we don't mean it in exactly the same way as when we say some jewelry is valuable. Perhaps we mean it in an analogous way. It is often the case that when we speak of God we speak analogically.[17] When we say, for example, that God is wise, we might mean something like "As human beings are to human wisdom, so is God to divine wisdom." Wittgenstein says that the experience of feeling absolutely safe is sometimes thought of as arising because we believe we are in the hands of God. Also, we sometimes feel guilty about our actions and this is sometimes expressed by saying that God disapproves.[18] And so perhaps the feeling of absolute safety or guilt can also be understood by analogy, because these feelings sometimes involve a conception of God. As the feeling of human safety (from specific dangers) is to relative experience (of facts), so is the feeling of absolute safety (from all dangers) to our experience of God. Maybe something like that makes sense.

Wittgenstein, however, does not think the problem of the non-sensicality of ethical and religious expressions can be solved in this way. If I can describe a fact figuratively, I must also be able to drop the figure and describe it literally. This is in line with what he says later in his life about metaphor. Metaphors give words new meanings by placing them in new contexts, and these meanings can be explained. If all we're interested in is meaning, we can do without the metaphor. "Thou foster-child of silence and slow time" is a metaphor that takes a poem to explain.[19] But it can be explained. The problem with feelings of absolute value and their expression, however, is that once we remove the simile or analogy or metaphor, there are no facts left to serve as explanation. "And so, what at first appeared to be simile now seems to be mere nonsense" (*PO*, 43). The paradox in this case is that a fact—my experience of safety or wonder or guilt—should take on what seems to be supernatural value. The expression of the experience in terms of feeling absolutely safe or wondering at the existence of things cannot be reduced to an expression of facts. Once I try to do so—once I try to explain the feeling in relative (factual) terms—I can no longer capture what is essential about the feeling, and so the best I can do is to speak nonsense. But we might not call it plain nonsense. This nonsense has a point.

This is beginning to sound an awful lot like what Wittgenstein later calls the secondary meaning of a word. We've called it emergent meaning, and here he calls it the expression of absolute value. We might call it "absolute meaning" in the context of this book. Absolute meaning is sheer nonsense in the same way that "fat Wednesday" is nonsense if one insists that it is not a metaphor and that "fat" is being used with its usual meaning. We have seen how such emergent meanings of words have an important place in aesthetics. In fact, they seem to be indispensable in describing aesthetic qualities that cannot be expressed in any other way. Might it be the case that in ethical and religious expression, the emergent meanings of words play a similar role? We must not be afraid of talking nonsense, because not all meaning resides in the sensible. This at least seems to be Wittgenstein's belief.

Wittgenstein gives one last example of how ethical and religious talk, while nonsensical, still has a place in human life and understanding. In fact, it has a place precisely *because* it is nonsense. He says that a miracle is "simply an event the like of which we have never yet seen" (*PO*, 43). I am tempted to think of a miracle as something that happens contrary to the laws of nature, like walking on water or rising from the dead. I think Wittgenstein's formulation, however, is more general and captures the sense of the miraculous that we feel regardless of whether a natural explanation is available for it.[20] Now perhaps most of us would respond to some extraordinary event—Wittgenstein suggests someone's growing a lion's head and beginning to roar—by calling a doctor or other expert to try to figure out what was going on. Let's say the doctor succeeds in locating the man's problem (and a serious problem it would be!). Where then has the miracle gone? Wittgenstein says that looking at matters this way does indeed destroy the miracle, because "the scientific way of looking at a fact is not the way to look at it as a miracle" (PO, 43). According to Wittgenstein, it is absurd to say that science has proved there are no miracles. The scientific way of looking is the relative way, the way of facts, while the miraculous way is the absolute way, the way of nonsense: "And I will now describe the experience of wondering at the existence of the world by saying: it is the experience of seeing the world as a miracle" (PO, 43). Seeing the world as full of facts and seeing it as a miracle are two ways of seeing, or the seeing of two aspects of the world. The one is expressed through propositions with ordinary or relative meaning (including figurative meaning), the latter through nonsensical propositions that nevertheless strike us (some of us, some of the time) as appropriate, fitting, and the right way to put it, despite our inability to explain their appropriateness. You get it or you don't. Aspect-seeing seems to tie in most closely here with emergent (or absolute) meaning. We experience things in certain ways and express these experiences. Some of our deepest experiences seem to *require* nonsense in order to be expressed. What could that mean? Wittgenstein takes these experiences seriously. These expressions have nonsense as their very essence, and Wittgenstein thinks that maybe they have the power to carry us beyond the significations of ordinary language. He doesn't pretend to offer an explanation of the effect of emergent meanings, but he does think that if we pay attention to them, we might be better able to appreciate people whose ideas and beliefs differ substantially from ours. How might this work out?

Most religious and ethical words, like those used in the best descriptions of works of art, are ordinary words first and foremost. They do not belong to any special groups, and they have not acquired their meanings because of theories or experiments, as many scientific words have. (They will not go out of use if it's shown, for example, that God does not exist, the way "phlogiston" has.)[21] This means that believers and nonbelievers can find some sort of common ground without necessarily having an initial introduction to dogma or theory. I ought to be able to ask an atheist to *try* to see the hand of God at work in the world or to *try* to imagine life after death. When looking at a painting, I can ask someone to see the hand of Matthew as pressing against the table, and I can ask that he hear some measures in a piece of music as an introduction or a variation. There are, however, two considerations that can make such dialogue difficult to initiate and sustain when it comes to ethical and religious experiences. To see the world as the work of God is not entirely like seeing Matthew's hand pressing against a table. Except for the fact that I am looking at paint on canvas, I know exactly what hands are and what "press" means, even in the context of a painting. And even though there are literally no hands and no pressing in the painting, these words are not being used with emergent meanings. I talk easily about facial expressions, arm movements, and so forth, in paintings, and so I am also at ease asking another to see some of these features differently. But when I talk about the work of God, I may be using "work" with emergent meaning. It is not a metaphor, because I really do mean work. Yet I don't imagine God with tools or sitting at a computer or in fact doing anything I would ordinarily call work, not even *thinking*. Still it seems appropriate (at least in a religious context) to call the world the work of God, just as it might be to call this man "good" in an ethical sense. In religious talk, as in aesthetic and ethical talk, we are sometimes forced to take words out of their normal contexts and use them where they are not at home. "The world is the work of God" is one of those uses. We then ask another to *see* the world this way, *as* the work of God. This might be doubly hard to do, and there needn't be any method for getting someone to do it, just as there is no method for getting him to see the figure of a man in the chaos picture or to find "velvety" an appropriate description of a wine. Custom, upbringing, common language and experience can all play roles in whether or not another person gets it. This means that some kind of community of discourse is presupposed in the very effort to get someone to understand the meaning of "the world is the work of God," and to *see* the world that way (Verbin 2000, 17).

A second problem concerns seeing for oneself. I can believe a lot of what another person tells me. I can believe that the weather in Brazil is tropical, that cyanide can make me very sick, and that atoms exist. It is hard to imagine living any kind of ordinary, normal life without taking the words of others as conclusive reason for holding certain beliefs. But the beautiful, the good, and the religious have in common that about them we *cannot* take the word of another. We cannot take another's word for it that a painting that we are both looking at is beautiful. If I don't see its beauty, his telling me that it is beautiful means very little. It may make me want to work harder at educating myself about how to see the painting, but his word does not allow me, too, to say that the painting is beautiful.[22] Unless I see the beauty of the painting or hear the delicacy of the sonata or experience the coherence of image in the poem, I will not act in other ways as if I believed these qualities inhered in these works of art. I may feel stupid or blind that I don't see what my friend sees or what the well-known critic sees, and I may take steps to become less stupid. But if I don't see, then I cannot take his word for it. I cannot *believe* that a joke is funny simply because another tells me it is. If I don't think it's funny, I can't even see what might be funny about it. If others seem to get it, I will feel left out. And of course explaining the joke to me usually won't help much, because the humor comes from getting it all at once, not from understanding it when it's explained.[23] While I can believe another that a certain make of car is good, that is, does the sorts of things a car should do, I cannot likewise believe that a person is good, in the absolute sense of good that transcends any and every particular sense. This I must see with my own eyes, just as I must see the duck in the duck-rabbit, or else I won't even know what I'm being asked to believe on the word of the other. Some things demand that I see for myself in order for me even to understand what the experience of seeing is like. So, too, with religious experiences in the broad sense. I cannot take another's word for it that I am forgiven or that I am hearing the voice of God telling me what to do. The very nature of aesthetic, ethical, and religious experiences and problems involves how they are seen, not the beliefs one holds. No one can do my seeing for me, and so no one can frame my ethical and religious experiences for me. In art, in ethics, and in religion, what you see is what you get, and what you get must be what *you* see.

Two powerful stories come to my mind about hearing God's voice: those of Abraham and of Augustine. The story of Abraham and Isaac in Genesis is brief and simple, completely told in the opening verses of chapter 22. Abraham hears God's voice ordering him to sacrifice his only son, the very son God had promised him and Sara, his wife, in their old age, and who was to be the sign of the covenant or agreement between God and Abraham. Abraham begins to do what God has commanded, without questioning and without telling anyone what he is up to. Then, at the moment Abraham is about to plunge the knife into Isaac's breast, God sends an angel telling him to stop and to sacrifice a nearby ram instead. Abraham does this and returns home with Isaac.[24] In *Fear and Trembling*, Kierkegaard (1813–1855) looks at this story from different perspectives and wonders if faith can be understood. He concludes that it cannot be: Abraham, while the "father of faith," cannot be a lesson to any of us from which we can learn either what faith is or how to achieve it. We cannot even really understand what it means for Abraham to have heard the voice of God. From one point of view, Abraham is crazy and needs to be restrained from carrying out an obviously heinous and absurd murder. And we would be right to think of him that way, because we do not see what he sees and we haven't heard what he has. Even if we had heard God's voice, it would have been meant only for us anyway. We cannot share in this kind of experience.[25] Abraham's behavior has all the appearances of insanity or wickedness. Abraham could not explain his actions because any explanation based on what God has told him could also be understood as the ravings of a madman. And it would be right to understand it in this way. Had he tried to explain, his explanation would have made no sense, and so Abraham tells no one why he is taking Isaac to Mount Moriah.[26]

To hear God's voice or the voice of an angel is not to hear a voice in any ordinary way, nor to hear any ordinary voice. We might say that "hear" and "voice" in this context have emergent meanings. We don't know *how* Abraham heard these voices. We've no reason to think he hallucinated them or dreamt them or heard them in his head. If hearing in this context carries emergent (or absolute) sense, then it can take any form at all, even Abraham's simply conceiving a notion first to kill Isaac, then not to. From the relative or primary point of view, Abraham *hears* nothing. From the absolute or secondary or emergent point of view, Abraham's hearing is nonsense. But whatever moves Abraham throughout this story, the writer thinks it is appropriate to express Abraham's experience in terms of God's speaking to him.

The story of Augustine's (354–430) conversion as he describes it in his *Confessions* recounts a coming to see, a true aspect change. Augustine had been well educated in the Roman style, and he was very intelligent and a successful teacher of rhetoric. His mother, Monica, was a Christian, but he was not. I won't tell his whole story here; for that, you must read the book. But eventually in his search for answers to rather deep questions about the meaning of life, he is led almost to a state of hopelessness and despair. He cannot make the turn to Christian belief, towards which he is pulled by some part of himself. One day, at his lowest emotional point, he finds himself in a garden. His own words describe what next happens:

I went on talking like this and weeping in the intense bitterness of my broken heart. Suddenly I heard a voice from a house nearby—perhaps a voice of some boy or girl, I do not know—singing over and over again, "Pick it up and read, pick it up and read." My expression immediately altered and I began to think hard whether children ordinarily repeated a ditty like this in any sort of game, but I could not recall ever having heard it anywhere else. I stemmed the flood of tears and rose to my feet, believing that this could be nothing other than a divine command to open the Bible and read the first passage I chanced upon; for I had heard the story of how Antony had been instructed by a gospel text. He happened to arrive while the gospel was being read, and took the words to be addressed to himself when he heard, *Go and sell all you possess and give the money to the poor: you will have treasure in heaven. Then come, follow me.* So he was promptly converted to you by this plainly divine message. Stung into action, I returned to the place where Alypius was sitting, for on leaving it I had put down there the book of the apostle's letters. I snatched it up, opened it and read in silence the passage on which my eyes first lighted: *Not in dissipation and drunkenness, nor in debauchery and lewdness, nor in arguing and jealousy; but put on*

the Lord Jesus Christ, and make no provision for the flesh or the gratifi-
cation of your desires. I had no wish to read further, nor was there need.
No sooner had I reached the end of the verse than the light of certainty
flooded my heart and all dark shades of doubt fled away. (1997, 168)

When Augustine leaves the garden, the world will in some sense
be entirely different, but it will in another sense be exactly the same.
This is a sign that he has experienced a change in aspect, one unusu-
ally deep and penetrating. Augustine's hearing is ordinary, at least
to the degree that he hears a child's voice. We're not sure what the
child was saying. Augustine may have *heard* whatever the child was
saying *as* "take and read." (He seems to think that children don't
have an obvious reason to say this. It's not, say, part of a game or
song.) The entire situation is full of possibilities for aspect-hearing.
The telling moment, however, comes when he takes what he hears as
a divine command. I don't doubt that if you and I were there with
him, we might have heard a child say something, maybe even just
what Augustine said he heard the child say (in Latin, "tolle, lege,"
"take and read"). But I don't think that I would have heard the child's
words as a command from God. Augustine's hearing a command
is not something he could share with others, or that others around
him would necessarily experience, just as I might see the Necker
cube as pointing up while you saw it pointing down or as flat. Someone might give another person instruction on how to see the cube
one way then another, or how to see a Cubist painting as a woman.
Whether the other will see as I see is not entirely in my control. That
is, no set of instructions can guarantee that she will see what I see,
the way she would see the moon if I directed her attention to it. If we
were with Augustine and heard the child's voice, I think there would
be nothing he could say to us that would lead us to hear the voice as a
command, though we might hear the voice and might even hear the
same words. Hearing a command from God is more like seeing the
man in the moon than it is like seeing the moon, so while you and I
can hear what Augustine hears, we might not be able to hear what he
hears. And this can make all the difference in a life.

To Augustine, the voice as a command fits into the weave of his
life. He has reached a low point after trying to find a way to "put
an end to [his] depravity" (Augustine 1997, 167). The fittingness or

appropriateness of the child's voice as a vehicle to convey God's will is confirmed for Augustine by the thought he has of how Anthony had a similar experience. We still might wonder why that specific thought came to him at this critical moment. Still, if God is talking to Augustine, then everything in his life finally fits, which is to say that it has meaning with respect to the work of God's will in his life. What was perhaps a jumble of experiences, emotions, misdirections, and frustrations now becomes a coherent whole, much like the chaotic puzzle-picture of chapter one, or the confusion in electrodynamics before special relativity. The child's voice might not have that effect on you or me, perhaps because our lives are different from Augustine's or because we see our lives differently from the way he saw his. If Augustine's moment of conversion is a kind of miracle, it is not a miracle of fact but of vision. It is not an event contrary to nature, but a natural event seen in a new way. Augustine's entire book can be seen as an expression of the reordering of the events of his life in such a new way as to provide for them the coherence that sheer intellectual pursuit could not.

Wittgenstein says that Freud (1856–1939), too, believed that mental illness could be cured by bringing about a rearrangement of things in a person's waking and dream life:

> When a dream is interpreted we might say that it is fitted into a context in which it ceases to be puzzling. In a sense the dreamer re-dreams his dream in surroundings such that its aspect changes. It is as though we were presented with a bit of canvas on which were painted a hand and part of a face and certain other shapes, arranged in a puzzling and incongruous manner. Suppose this bit is surrounded by considerable stretches of blank canvas, and that we now paint in forms—say an arm, a trunk, etc.—leading up to and fitting on to the shapes on the original bit; and that the result is that we say: "Ah, now I see why it is like that, how it all comes to be arranged in that way, and what these various bits are . . ." and so on. (*LA*, 45–46)

Freud knew from experience that his patients had to come to see for themselves the meaning of their dreams. The therapist may have a good understanding of what the sources of a patient's problems are from very early in therapy, but he cannot divulge this to the patient.[27] In this way the work of the therapist is like that of an art teacher or preacher, whose goal is to get others to see differently, rather than like the work of a physician, who deals with bodily ailments. I generally believe what my doctor tells me after my yearly physical. If he says my cholesterol is elevated and I should eat less cheese and ice cream, I believe he is probably right (even if I can't abide by his suggestions for more than a couple of weeks). I wasn't feeling bad when I went for my physical and don't feel particularly better when I abstain from the foods that might be causing me trouble. I simply believe what he says. A psychoanalyst does not have this luxury. If he simply announced his analysis to the patient, the patient would not be helped by knowing, even if she believed what she was told. Belief does not have the efficacy that seeing has; in fact, seeing for myself is the crux for regaining health through psychoanalysis. What the patient sees comes about through a rearrangement of things.[28] Therapy can be filled with "aha!" moments, in which something that was right in front of us all along is suddenly recognized or takes on new meaning. This can be something like Kuhn's paradigm shifts in science, where elements that were not meshing before come together in a brand new way, leaving old questions and problems behind and generating new ones. What troubled us before no longer does, not because some reasoning process has enabled us to see a truth we did not see before, but because we see differently—taking together what we did not take together before, comparing what we had not been accustomed to compare. And the questions that bothered us, while not being answered, no longer nag: "How words are understood is not given by words alone" (Z, 144).

The most interesting disagreements we can have in ethics and religion are not about facts. They are not even about the validity of arguments. Both sides in an ethical or religious dispute can agree to the facts and agree about how an argument on one side or the other goes. No, the most interesting and important disagreements are about what we see, because these are disagreements about what things mean. Vision determines what we consider important in the first place and what we will consider as evidence for or against a belief. Evidence is not independent of our valuing it. In order to have an effect in a discussion, something must be seen as relevant. A fact needs to be taken for evidence, and new evidence is only evidence if it is first considered relevant.

Several scientists and philosophers have recently published popular books arguing that belief in God is not supported by the scientific findings of the past several centuries—Darwin's theory of evolution, in particular.[29] The tone of their remarks ranges from shrill to sanguine. I'll leave it to you to explore them and draw your own conclusions. While reading these books, I'm tempted to say on the one hand, "Of course, those of us who adopt Enlightenment values and who revere reason as the final arbiter of conviction find what you say to be right on target, if not always generously expressed." On the other hand, however, I find myself thinking that these writers have missed the point about religious faith and, in fact, about our convictions of what is right, what is beautiful, and maybe even what is funny. The existence or nonexistence of miracles is not a fact to be decided on the basis of evidence, on whether or not a purported miracle can be otherwise explained scientifically. We might be willing to say that all events necessarily have a scientific explanation, even if it is not now known to us. One who says this says no more—and no less—than that the scientific point of view has merit and that from this point of view nothing happens contrary to nature. Adopting this point of view—that is, seeing this aspect of the world—eliminates miracles. One does not see the world or any event in the world as miraculous. And this is all well and good. Trouble begins with the claim that the scientific point of view is the only rational point of view or the true point of view or the privileged point of view. This would be like taking a drawing of the duck-rabbit, placing it on a Cartesian coordinate grid, and deriving an (admittedly complicated) algebraic expression for it, all the while claiming that this expression is what the picture of the duck-rabbit really is. The equation has gotten to the heart of the matter of the duck-rabbit.[30] But just as the equation can be a description of the drawing, so too, calling it a duck or a rabbit can be a description. Seeing miracles is also an aspect experience. It makes sense to ask of someone that she try to see "the heavens as declaring the glory of God," just as it makes sense to ask that she try to see "his laughter as courageous rather than cowardly," or "her wrinkles as beautiful rather than ugly," or this drawing as a duck rather than as a rabbit (Verbin 2001, 505). To see courage, beauty, and miracles already requires that one be able to entertain the possibility of their existing in the world. That is, to see in these ways requires not that one believe in their existence, but that one can *imagine* what seeing courage, beauty, and miracles would be like. That is why an atheist such as myself can still try to make sense of the religious experiences of others, even if I do not share their experiences. If I cannot put myself in their place and at least try to see as they do, perhaps I am at fault. If we let what we think we know do our seeing for us, we stand in our own way (Baz 2000, 121).

The atheist writers who are most adamant about the sheer wrongness of religious belief focus their attention on a similar but contrary stubbornness that afflicts some (perhaps many) believers. This is the conviction that science cannot be the whole answer and that there must be questions forever beyond the reach of science to answer or even grasp—not because of their difficulty, but because of their supernatural nature. The existence of the soul or of our own persistence after bodily death comes to mind here, both as a religious and an ethical concern. These are questions that have puzzled and even troubled me. The confirmed atheist who sees the world only from a scientific point of view might dismiss them as not being real questions. To explain why people continue to ask them and find them troubling, he might offer an account based on upbringing, psychology, and tradition. But if we take to heart what Kuhn says about paradigms in science, perhaps we would do well to counsel our atheist friend to consider not normal science as his model when trying to understand religious belief, but paradigm shift science. That is, just as during a paradigm shift in the history of science old questions die and new ones take their place, so too perhaps we can *imagine* the religious point of view as being a place from which certain kinds of questions make sense that do not make sense from another point of view. I want to say that this is at least imaginable regardless of where you find yourself in your own life. It is the power of the imagination that comes to our rescue when we are trying to see as others see without necessarily abandoning our own convictions.[31]

Wittgenstein addresses the question of how to take the nonfactual expressions of others with which we do not agree so that we can at least keep discussion between us alive:

> Suppose someone is ill and he says: "This is punishment," and I say: "If I'm ill, I don't think of punishment at all." If you say: "Do you believe

the opposite?"—you can call it believing the opposite, but it is entirely different from what we would normally call believing the opposite. I think differently, in a different way. I say different things to myself. I have different pictures. (*LA*, 35)

Wittgenstein suggests that what can appear to be disagreement between people regarding religious and ethical beliefs may be more like differences in judgment concerning the aesthetic value of a painting or the humor of a joke. It is one thing to claim the opposite to someone else in the sense of opposite that precludes both positions' making sense and co-existing. It's another to disagree in a way that allows both views (and perhaps additional ones) to live in the same moral space. Wittgenstein seems to be suggesting that each expression makes sense as part of a whole, not as an isolated fact whose truth or falsity we are called on to judge. To understand my believer friend, I need to place his remarks in the context in which he is making them, to step into his shoes fully, which means to try to understand his life: "When we first begin to *believe* anything, what we believe is not a single proposition, it is a whole system of propositions. Light dawns gradually over the whole" (*RC*, 141). So, too, in our efforts to understand those who disagree with us not about the facts but about their meaning, we need to become aware that to disagree is not always to be at opposite ends of a spectrum. Rather, we may be looking at the same things from different points of view. At times, this seems so obvious to me as to appear trite and not helpful to emphasize right now. But I find myself frequently engaged in discussions in which the notion of a transcendent truth exerts a guiding but unacknowledged pressure, even in these days of cultural relativism and political correctness. Perhaps it is time once and for all to replace truth, even relative truth, with something else:

> If someone who believes in God looks round and asks "Where does everything I see come from?," "Where does all this come from?," he is *not* craving a (causal) explanation; and his question gets its point from being the expression of a certain craving. He is, namely, expressing an attitude to all explanations.—But how is this manifested in his life?
>
> The attitude that's in question is that of taking a certain matter seriously and then, beyond a certain point, no longer regarding it as serious, but maintaining that something else is even more important. (*CV*, 85)

This is not to say that those who do not see God in the world suffer from a kind of aspect blindness of the sort we discussed at length in chapter three. You might ask, "Isn't it a consequence of what you've been saying all along that those who don't see the hand of God in their lives are missing something? After all, people who can't see both the duck and the rabbit or who can't experience the Necker cube shifting from one orientation to another are missing something that most others can experience. More to the point, isn't someone who cannot see in a painting or hear in a symphony what a good critic can simply not getting it? Isn't a consequence of what you've said simply that atheists don't get the joke?" Perhaps an even thornier question concerns someone like me, who early in life did recognize and accept the religious nature of the world but who has lost such vision. Well-meaning believers cannot ask the atheist to mistrust his own perception of the world and to trust their own. Belief of this sort can be acquired and maintained only if one sees for oneself: "Calling [the atheist] deprived, condemning her way of seeing the world as sinful or ungrateful, comparing her inability to see God to color blindness or lack of a musical ear does not amount to a reason" for her to begin believing (Verbin 2001, 510–511). On the flip side, can't the atheist urge the believer to open himself up to the power of scientific explanation and not spend his energy believing in what can't be seen or proved? Can't the atheist say that the believer is hallucinating, just as the believer might be tempted to call the atheist blind? This head-butting doesn't seem to get us very far, does it?

While I'm not sure that Wittgenstein proposes a solution to seemingly intractable disagreements about fundamental values and convictions such as these, he does think that we can make sense of all sorts of things we might not be inclined to believe. We need to remember that for the most part, the way a word is used tells us what it means, and we need to let our imaginations guide us when reason gives out: "How about religion's teaching that the soul can exist when the body has disintegrated? Do I understand what it teaches? Of course I understand it—I can imagine a lot here. (Pictures of these things have been painted too. And why should such a picture be only the incomplete reproduction of the spoken thought? Why should it not perform the *same* service as what we say? And this service is the point.)" (*RPP I*, 265). Wittgenstein seems to be suggesting that as long as someone who professes belief in God can give voice to this belief and say something that serves a purpose in his speech and life, then even confirmed atheists can find a way to understand what he is saying. That my friend believes in God and I do not needn't prevent us from finding in one another sources of comfort and enjoyment. Must we avoid discussing religion in order to remain friends? Not necessarily. Such a discussion need not separate us any more than our disagreeing about what we see in a painting. It depends on so much, but most of all on how our beliefs work themselves out in our lives. Just as the use of our words gives them meaning, so too the actions we perform ground our beliefs. We ought to be able to "try on" the beliefs of others by reflecting about how those beliefs manifest themselves in life. If we don't try, we shall stand accused of laziness of the imagination. If we do try but can't succeed, perhaps we are blind: "What must the man be called, who cannot understand the concept 'God,' cannot see how a reasonable man may use this word seriously? Are we to say he suffers from some *blindness*?" (*RPP I*, 213). That Wittgenstein considers this failure of the imagination to be a form of blindness indicates that he thinks most of us ought to be able to understand a serious person's beliefs and the concepts that shape them, even if we cannot hold them ourselves.

Not all disagreements in religious and ethical matters can be smoothed over by considering them as expressions of aspect-seeing and by asking each person to try to see in a different way. I might not always be in a position to do that. At some points or about some beliefs, I might just not get it. Or if I do get it, there's no guarantee that I could get someone else to see what I've come to see. It might be more like what we said about emergent meanings, such as "fat Wednesday." Something sounds right about an expression, even if in another sense I think the expression is nonsense: Wittgenstein says, "Suppose someone, before going to China, when he might never see me again, said to me: 'We might see one another after death'—would I necessarily say that I don't understand him? I might say simply, 'Yes. I *understand* him entirely.'" A student of Wittgenstein's, Casmir Lewy, then says, "'In this case, you might only mean that he expressed a certain attitude.'" But Wittgenstein objects, "I would say 'No, it isn't the same as saying "I'm very fond of you"'—and it may not be the same as saying anything else. It says what it says.

Why should you be able to substitute anything else?" (*LA*, 71). Just as some descriptions of wines, paintings, and pieces of music "say what they say" and can be understood only through hints and experience, not explanations, so too, with certain expressions of religious and ethical belief. Wittgenstein rejects Lewy's translation of "meeting after death" because any reformulation of it would be an attempt to explain it away. The effect of such an explanation would be something like saying that atheists can come to understand the words of believers by saying what believers must really mean. This reductionism is exactly what Wittgenstein tries to avoid. Language-games can't be pressured into appearing more like one another than they are. Wittgenstein seems to think that there needn't be any privileged position from which to view the world, whether it be the viewpoint of physics, of psychology, of physiology, or of religion. Sometimes we can see as others see, entertaining their perspectives without adopting them. Other times we simply have to get what they're saying, and if we don't, conversation along those lines might need to come to a pause while we search out common ground. There may, of course, come a time when we give up the search. But because *seeing* is at stake, not *knowing*, the possibility always remains that something can be said or done that will bring us to see similarly, or get something to click for us. In the *Phaedo*, Plato's dialogue on the death of Socrates, Socrates and his friends engage in a discussion about the immortality of the soul, an especially poignant topic for their final conversation together. Somewhere near the middle of the dialogue, after what had seemed a powerful argument for the soul's immortality is shown to be undependable, Socrates' friends begin to despair of ever being able to rely on dialogue to help them address their worries. Socrates responds in effect by saying that misology—hatred of reason, or *logos*, or genuine conversation—is a monster that must be slain. While reason might not deliver the truth to us today, we cannot on that account give up the pursuit, that is, give up talking together.[32] We might add something further, in the light of what we have been saying about disagreements in art, in ethics, and in religion: To believe we *have* found the truth is at least as powerful an enemy to carrying on conversations and common projects as is the belief that the truth is unattainable. Dogmatism and misology are opposite sides of the same coin, whose only value is to keep us divided.

When I started thinking about aspects and about what role they play in our lives, I thought that I'd end up touting the merits of tolerance. Tolerance seemed to be the attitude towards which my thinking about Wittgenstein's ideas of aspects and emergent meanings was taking me. But I've come to see things differently in the course of writing this book. I've no complaints about tolerance in a democratic society. It seems, in fact, to be our premier political virtue. If, however, tolerance only means letting others do and believe what they wish, so long as they allow me the same freedom, then it seems to fall short of the kind of understanding that I think Wittgenstein is proposing. I can let another believe what he wants about God, about art, even about right and wrong, up to a point. But I can be tolerant without ever really trying to see things the way he does. While tolerance requires that I not impose my beliefs and values on others, it does not insist I make an effort to try on a different way of seeing. "You see a duck, I see a rabbit; I'm okay, you're okay." If this is tolerance then it is not okay because it is not enough. It is not enough to enable us to "achieve agreement among human beings about what to do, to bring about consensus on the ends to be achieved and the means to be used to achieve those ends" (Rorty 1999, xxv). Neither does the pursuit of truth for its own sake help us achieve goals together. Rather, in the spirit of American pragmatism as championed by Peirce, James, Dewey, Putnam, and Rorty, our first goal is to keep the conversation going.[33] This means not merely to tolerate the opinions of others (though this would be better than vilifying them). The kind of conversation Rorty (and Wittgenstein) have in mind demands what I call "active tolerance." When we are being actively tolerant, we not only allow others to hold their own opinions and values—to paint their own pictures of the world—but we try to see the world through their eyes. This is hard, I know. It may require new forms of education to bring about a generation of adults capable of switching between the duck and the rabbit while not succumbing to a vacuous relativism. We require, or perhaps demand, a new kind of freedom, one which allows us to go beyond our original situation, while still remaining the same (Merleau-Ponty 2004, 285). For it is not that we want to change ourselves but rather to move ourselves forward, up, beyond, towards a life in which we are not held captive by a picture (*PI*, sec. 115). Rorty suggests that the picture that has held us is that of "a mind seeking to get in touch with a reality outside itself" (Rorty 1999, xxii). There is no doubt that people change, but frankly they do so rarely on account of an argument. Rather, they change when they begin to realize that "it can be that way, too." This is the lure of aspect-seeing: "Imagination is the source both of new scientific pictures of the physical universe and of new conceptions of possible communities. It is what Newton and Christ, Freud and Marx, had in common: the ability to redescribe the familiar in unfamiliar terms" (Rorty 1999, 87).

I began with a duck, a rabbit, and a problem whose form morphed like Proteus himself as I made my way. How can what we see change when nothing changes? How can we see and yet be blind? How can nonsense open us to new experiences? How can we go beyond tolerance while maintaining our own intellectual and moral integrity? I'm sure you have your own questions that have arisen from what you've just read, and I hope you will continue to have questions and the passion to think and talk about them. You never know when— click!—something will happen and you, too, will enter a new world. Or at least your old one will perk up a bit.

BIBLIOGRAPHY

Works by Wittgenstein

Works by Ludwig Wittgenstein are identified by the following abbreviations:

(BB)   *The Blue and Brown Books.* New York: Harper and Row, 1958.

(CV)   *Culture and Value.* Ed. G. H. von Wright. Trans. Peter Winch. Chicago: Univ. of Chicago Press, 1984.

(LA)   *Lectures and Conversations on Aesthetics, Psychology, and Religious Belief.* Ed. Cyril Barrett. Los Angeles: Univ. of California Press, 1967.

(LWPP I) *Last Writings on the Philosophy of Psychology, Volume I.* Ed. G. H. von Wright and Heikki Nyman. Trans. C. G. Luckhardt and M. A. E. Aue. Chicago: Univ. of Chicago Press, 1990.

(LWPP II) *Last Writings on the Philosophy of Psychology, Volume II.* Ed. G. H. von Wright and Heikki Nyman. Trans. C. G. Luckhardt and M. A. E. Aue. Oxford: Blackwell, 1992.

(PE)   *Lectures on Personal Experience.* From the Michelmas Term of 1935–36. Ed. Cora Diamond from notes by Margaret Macdonald, unpublished.

(PI)   *Philosophical Investigations.* Trans. G. E. M. Anscombe. New York: Macmillan, 1953.

(PO)   *Philosophical Occasions 1912–1951.* Ed. James Klagge and Alfred Nordmann. Indianapolis: Hackett, 1993.

(PR)   *Philosophical Remarks.* Ed. Rush Rhees. Trans. Raymond Hargreaves and Roger White. Chicago: Univ. of Chicago Press, 1975.

(RC)   *Remarks on Colour.* Ed. G. E. M. Anscombe. Trans. Linda McAlister and Margarete Schaettle. Los Angeles: Univ. of California Press, 1977.

(RPP I)   *Remarks on the Philosophy of Psychology, Volume I.* Ed. G. E. M. Anscombe and G. H. von Wright. Trans. G. E. M. Anscombe. Chicago: Univ. of Chicago Press, 1980.

(RPP II) *Remarks on the Philosophy of Psychology, Volume II.* Ed. G. H. von Wright and Heikki Nyman. Trans. C. G. Luckhardt and M. A. E. Aue. Chicago: Univ. of Chicago Press, 1988.

(TLP)   *Tractatus Logico-Philosophicus.* Trans. D. F. Pears and B. F. McGuiness. London: Routledge and Kegan Paul, 1969.

(Z)   *Zettel.* Ed. G. E. M. Anscombe and G. H. von Wright. Trans. G. E. M. Anscombe. Los Angeles: Univ. of California Press, 1975.

Works by Other Authors

Amerine, Maynard, and Edward Roessler. 1976. *Wines: Their Sensory Evaluation.* New York: W. H. Freeman and Co.

Anscombe, G. E. M. 1969. *Intention.* Ithaca: Cornell Univ. Press.

261

Aquinas, Thomas. 1981. *Summa Theologica*. Trans. Fathers of the English Dominican Province. Notre Dame, Ind.: Christian Classics.

Aristotle. 1984. *On Dreams*. Vol. One, in *The Complete Works of Aristotle*. Ed. Jonathan Barnes. Trans. J. I. Beare. 729–35. Princeton: Princeton Univ. Press.

———. 1995. *Physics*. Trans. Francis M. Wicksteed and Philip H. Cornford. Vol. 2. 2 vols. Cambridge: Harvard Univ. Press.

Augustine of Hippo. 1998. *The Confessions*. Trans. Maria Boulding. New York: Vintage.

Austin, J. L. 1961, 1979. *Philosophical Papers*. Ed. J. O. Urmson and G. J. Warnock. Oxford: Oxford Univ. Press.

———. 1962. *How To Do Things with Words: The William James Lectures Delivered at Harvard University in 1955*. Ed. J. O. Urmson. Oxford: Clarendon.

———. 1964. *Sense and Sensibilia*. Oxford: Oxford Univ. Press.

Ayer, A. J. 1952. *Language, Truth and Logic*. New York: Dover.

———. 1963. *The Foundations of Empirical Knowledge*. London: Macmillan.

Baker, G. P., and P. M. S. Hacker. 1983. *An Analytical Commentary on Wittgenstein's Philosophical Investigations*. Chicago: Univ. of Chicago Press.

Barrett, H. C., and R. Kurzban. 2006. "Modularity in Cognition: Framing the Debate." *Psychological Review* 113, no. 3: 628–47.

Baz, Avner. 2000. "What's the Point of Seeing Aspects?" *Philosophical Investigations* 23, no. 2: 97–121.

Berger, John. 2001. *Selected Essays*. Ed. Geoff Dyer. New York: Vintage International.

Bickard, Mark H. 2003. "Some Notes on Internal and External Relations and Representations." *Consciousness and Emotion* 4, no. 1: 101–10.

Bloom, P. 1997. "Intentionality and Word Learning." *Trends in Cognitive Sciences* 1: 9–12.

Brain, Russell. 1941. "Visual Object Agnosia with Special Reference to Gestalt Theory." *Brain* 64: 43–62.

Butterfield, Andrew. 2002. "Leo's Last Supper." *New York Review of Books*, July 18: 14–17.

———. 2007. "Brush with Genius." *New York Review of Books*, April 26: 10–14.

Carroll, Lewis. 1946. *Through the Looking Glass*. New York: Random House.

Carruthers, P., and P. K. Smith, eds. 1996. *Theories of Theories of Mind*. Cambridge: Cambridge Univ. Press.

Carse, James P. 2008. *The Religious Case Against Belief*. New York: Penguin.

Cavell, Stanley. 1976. "Aesthetic Problems in Modern Philosophy." In *Must We Mean What We Say?*, by Stanley Cavell, 73–96. New York: Cambridge Univ. Press.

Cervantes, Miguel de. 2003. *Don Quixote*. Trans. Edith Grossman. New York: Ecco.

Chalmers, David. 1996. *The Conscious Mind*. Oxford: Oxford Univ. Press.

Churchland, P., V. Ramachandra, and T. Sejnowski. 1994. "A Critique of Pure Vision." In *Large-Scale Neuronal Theories of the Brain*, by C. Koch and J. Davis, 23–60. Cambridge: MIT Press.

Churchland, P. 1985. "Reduction, Qualia, and Direct Introspection of Brain States." *Journal of Philosophy* 82, no. 1: 8–28.

Conant, James B. 1957. *The Overthrow of the Phlogiston Theory: The Chemical Revolution*. Vol. 1, in *Harvard Case Studies in Experimental Science*, ed. James B. Conant, 65–115. Cambridge: Harvard Univ. Press.

Damasio, Antonio. 1994. *Descartes' Error*. New York: Penguin.

Dante. 2002. *Inferno*. Trans. Robert and Jean Hollander. New York: Anchor.

Dawkins, Richard. 2006. *The God Delusion*. New York: Houghton Mifflin.

Dennett, Daniel. 1991. *Consciousness Explained*. Boston: Little, Brown.

———. 2006. *Breaking the Spell: Religion as a Natural Phenomenon*. New York: Viking.

Descartes, Rene. 1993. *Meditations on First Philosophy*. Trans. Donald Cress. Indianapolis: Hackett.

Deutsch, Diana. 2004. "The Octave Illusion Revisited Again." *Journal of Experimental Psychology: Human Perception and Performance* 30: 355–64.

Diamond, Cora. 1995. "Secondary Sense." In *The Realistic Spirit*, by Cora Diamond, 225–41. Cambridge, Mass.: MIT Press.

Doherty, M. J., and M. Wimmer. 2005. "Children's Understanding of Ambiguous Figures: Which Cognitive Developments Are Necessary to Experience Reversal?" *Cognitive Development* 20, no. 3: 407–21.

Dorment, Richard. 2006. "Journey from 'Nebraska.'" *New York Review of Books*, December 21: 8–14.

Eckman, Paul. 2007. *Emotions Revealed, Second Edition: Recognizing Faces and Feelings to Improve Communication and Emotional Life*. New York: Henry Holt.

Edelman, G. 1989. *The Remembered Present*. New York: Basic Books.

Einhauser, W., J. Stout, C. Koch, and O. Carter. 2008. "Pupil Dilation Reflects Perceptual Selection and Predicts Subsequent Stability in Perceptual Rivalry." *Proceedings of the National Academy of Sciences* 105, no. 5: 1704–9.

Einstein, Albert. 1998. "On the Electrodynamics of Moving Bodies." In *Albert Einstein's Special Theory of Relativity*, by Arthur I. Miller, 370–93. New York: Springer.

Ellis, S., and L. Stark. 1978. "Eye Movements During the Viewing of a Necker Cube." *Perception* 7: 575–81.

Emerson, Ralph Waldo. 1903. *The Complete Works of Ralph Waldo Emerson*. New York: Houghton Mifflin.

Engelmann, Paul. 1967. *Letters from Ludwig Wittgenstein, with a Memoir*. Ed. B. McGuinness. Trans. L. Furtmuller. New York: Horizon Press.

Euclid. 2008. *Elements*. Ed. and trans. Richard Fitzpatrick. Richard Fitzpatrick.

Fann, K. T. 1967. *Ludwig Wittgenstein: The Man and His Philosophy*. Atlantic Highlands, N. J.: Humanities Press.

———. 1971. *Wittgenstein's Conception of Philosophy*. Los Angeles: Univ. of California Press.

Fleck, Ludwig. 1979. *Genesis and Development of a Scientific Fact*. Chicago: Univ. of Chicago Press.

Freud, Sigmund. 1965. *The Interpretation of Dreams*. Trans. James Strachey. New York: Avon Books.

———. 1977. *Introductory Lectures on Psychoanalysis*. Ed. and trans. James Strachey. New York: W. W. Norton.

Freyd, J. J. 1987. "Dynamic Mental Representations." *Psychological Review* 94: 427–38.

Freyd, J. J., and R. A. Finke. 1985. "A Velocity Effect for Representational Momentum." *Bulletin of the Psychonomic Society* 23, no. 6: 443–46.

Frith, U., and F. Happé. 1999. "Theory of Mind and Self-consciousness: What Is It Like To Be Autistic?" *Mind and Language* 14, no. 1: 1–22.

Gadamer, Hans-Georg. 1999. *Truth and Method*. New York: Continuum.

Galileo. 1957. "The Starry Messenger." In *Discoveries and Opinions of Galileo*, trans. Stillman Drake, 27–58. New York: Anchor.

———. 1974. *Two New Sciences*. Trans. Stillman Drake. Madison: Univ. of Wisconsin Press.

Gallistel, C. R. 2001. "Psychology of Mental Representations." In *International Encyclopedia of the Social and Behavioral Sciences*. Elsevier Science, Ltd.

Gardner, Howard. 1976. *The Shattered Mind*. New York: Vintage.

Gladwell, Malcolm. 2005. *Blink: The Power of Thinking Without Thinking.* New York: Little, Brown.

Glock, H.-J. 1996. *A Wittgenstein Dictionary.* Oxford: Blackwell.

Goethe, Johann Wolfgang von. 1970. *Italian Journey.* Trans. W. H. Auden and Elizabeth Mayer. New York: Penguin.

———. 1986. "Giuseppe Bossi: On Leonardo da Vinci's Last Supper at Milan." In *Essays on Art and Literature,* ed. J. Gearey, trans. E. von Nardoff and E. H. von Nardoff, 37–59. New York: Suhrkamp.

———. 1989. "On the Metamorphosis of Plants." In *Goethe's Botanical Writings,* trans. Bertha Mueller. Woodbridge, Conn.: Ox Bow Press.

———. 2008. *Faust: Part One.* Trans. David Luke. New York: Oxford Univ. Press.

Goodwin, Charles. 2003. "Conversational Frameworks for the Accomplishment of Meaning in Aphasia." In *Conversation and Brain Damage,* ed. Charles Goodwin, 90–116. Oxford: Oxford Univ. Press.

Gopnik, A., and A. Rosati. 2001. "Duck or Rabbit? Reversing Ambiguous Figures and Understanding." *Developmental Science* 4, no. 2: 175–83.

Gregory, Richard L. 1968. "Perceptual Illusions and Brain Models." *Proc. R. Soc. Lond. B,* 171: 279–96.

———. 1970. *The Intelligent Eye.* London: Weidenfeld and Nicolson.

———. 1997. "Knowledge in Perception and Illusion." *Phil. Trans. R. Soc. Lond. B,* 352: 1121–27.

Hacker, P. M. S. 1986. *Insight and Illusion.* Oxford: Oxford Univ. Press.

Haggard, Patrick, and Benjamin Libet. 2001. "Conscious Intention and Brain Activity." *Journal of Consciousness Studies* 8, no. 11: 47–63.

Hallett, Garth. 1977. *A Companion to Wittgenstein's Philosophical Investigations.* Ithaca: Cornell Univ. Press.

Hanson, Norwood Russell. 1958. *Patterns of Discovery.* Cambridge: Cambridge Univ. Press.

Hardy, G. H. 1999. *Ramanujan: Twelve Lectures on Subjects Suggested by His Life and Work.* Providence, R. I.: American Mathematical Society.

Harvey, William. 1993. *On the Motion of the Heart and Blood in Animals.* Trans. Robert Willis. Buffalo, N.Y: Prometheus Books.

Hegel, G. W. F. 1977. *The Phenomenology of Spirit.* Trans. A. V. Miller. Oxford: Clarendon Press.

Holland, Bernard. 2008. "Rocketing to Inner Space, Defying Tonality." *New York Times,* April 20: 22.

Holt, Jim. 2008. "Stop Me If You've Heard This: A History and Philosophy of Jokes." *New York Review of Books,* July 17.

Homer. 1999. *The Odyssey.* Trans. Robert Fagles. New York: Penguin.

Hubbard, T. L. 1995. "Environmental Invariants in the Representation of Motion: Implied Dynamics and Representational Momentum, Gravity, Friction, and Centripetal Force." *Psychonomic Bulletin and Review* 2: 322–38.

Hubel, D., and T. N. Weisel. 1965. "Receptive Fields and Functional Architecture in Two Nonstriate Visual Areas (18 and 19) of the Cat." *Journal of Neurophysiology* 28: 229–89.

Hume, David. 1978. *A Treatise of Human Nature.* Oxford: Clarendon Press.

———. 1992. "Of the Standard of Taste." In *Four Dissertations and Essays on Suicide and the Immortality of the Soul,* 203–40. South Bend, Ind.: St. Augustine's Press.

Humphrey, Nicholas. 2006. "Consciousness: the Achilles Heel of Darwinism? Thank God, Not Quite." In *Intelligent Thought: Science versus the Intelligent Design Movement*, by John Brockman, 50–64. New York: Vintage.

Intraub, H. 2002. "Anticipatory Spatial Representation of Natural Scenes: Momentum without Movement?" *Visual Cognition* 9, no. 1/2: 93–119.

Jackson, Frank. 1982. "Epiphenomenal Qualia." *Philosophical Quarterly* 32: 127–36.

———. 1986. "What Mary Didn't Know." *The Journal of Philosophy* LXXXIII, no. 5 (May): 291–95.

James, William. 1950. *The Principles of Psychology*. Vol. 1. 2 vols. New York: Dover.

Janik, A., and S. Toulmin. 1973. *Wittgenstein's Vienna*. New York: Simon and Schuster.

Jastrow, Joseph. 1900. *Fact and Fable in Psychology*. Boston: Houghton Mifflin.

Kant, Immanuel. 1964. *Groundwork of the Metaphysic of Morals*. Trans. H. J. Paton. New York: Harper and Row.

———. 1996. *Critique of Pure Reason*. Trans. Werner S. Pluhar. Indianapolis: Hackett.

Kay, J., R. Lesser, and M. Coltheart. 1992. *Psycholinguistic Assessments of Language Processing in Aphasia (PALPA)*. East Sussex: Lawrence Erlbaum.

Kennerknecht, I., et al. 2006. "First Report of Prevalence of Non-syndromic Hereditary Prosopagnosia (HPA)." *American Journal of Medical Genetics. Part A* 140, no. 15: 1617–22.

Kierkegaard, Søren. 1983. *Fear and Trembling*. Ed. and trans. Howard and Edna Hong. Princeton: Princeton Univ. Press.

Kleist, Heinrich von. 1982. *An Abyss Deep Enough: Letters of Heinrich von Kleist, with a Selection of Essays and Anecdotes*. Ed. and trans. Philip B. Miller. New York: Dutton.

Köhler, W. 1947. *Gestalt Psychology*. New York: Signet.

Kuhn, Thomas. 1962. *The Structure of Scientific Revolutions*. Chicago: Univ. of Chicago Press.

Kurtz, Richard M. 1969. "A Conceptual Investigation of Witkin's Notion of Perceptual Style." *Mind* 78, no. 312 (October): 522–33.

Lanchester, John. 2008. "Scents and Sensibility." *New Yorker*, March 10.

Lavoisier, Antoine. 1965. *Elements of Chemistry*. New York: Dover.

Leibniz, Gottfried Wilhelm von. 1989. *Philosophical Essays*. Ed. and trans. Roger Ariew and Daniel Garber. Indianapolis: Hackett.

Leopold, D. A., et al. 2002. "Stable Perception of Visually Ambiguous Patterns." *Nature Neuroscience* 5: 605–9.

Lewis, Clarence I. 1929. *Mind and the World-Order*. New York: Charles Scribner's Sons.

Locke, John. 1987. *An Essay Concerning Human Understanding*. Oxford: Clarendon Press.

Long, G. M., T. C. Toppino, and J. F. Kostenbauder. 1983. "As the Cube Turns: Evidence for Two Processes in the Perception of a Dynamic Reversible Figure." *Perception and Psychophysics* 34: 29–38.

Long, G. M., and T. C. Toppino. 2004. "Enduring Interest in Perceptual Ambiguity: Alternating Views of Reversible Figures." *Psychological Bulletin* 130: 748–68.

Long, G. M., J. A. Stewart, and D. E. Glancy. 2002. "Configural Biases and Reversible Figures: Evidence of Multilevel Grouping Effects." *American Journal of Psychology* 115: 581–607.

Longfellow, Henry Wadsworth. 1975. *The Poetical Works of Longfellow*. New York: Houghton Mifflin.

Lundquist, D., and A. Öhman. 2005. "Caught by the Evil Eye: Nonconscious Information Processing, Emotion, and Attention to Facial Stimuli." In *Emotion and Con-*

sciousness, ed. L. Barrett, P. Niedenthal, and P. Winkielman, 97–122. New York: The Guilford Press.

Malcolm, Norman. 1994. *Wittgenstein: A Religious Point of View?* Ithaca: Cornell Univ. Press.

———. 2001. *Ludwig Wittgenstein: A Memoir.* New York: Oxford Univ. Press.

Marr, D. 1982. *Vision.* San Francisco: Freeman.

Marx, Karl. 1967. *Capital: A Critical Analysis of Capitalist Production.* Ed. F. Engels. New York: International Publishers.

McGinn, Colin. 1991. *The Problem of Consciousness.* Oxford: Blackwell.

Merleau-Ponty, Maurice. 2004. *Maurice Merleau-Ponty: Basic Writings.* Ed. Thomas Baldwin. London: Routledge.

Michelangelo. 1998. *The Complete Poems of Michelangelo.* Trans. John Frederick Nims. Chicago: Univ. of Chicago Press.

Mitchell, P., and D. Ropar. 2004. "Visuo-spatial Abilities in Autism: A Review." *Infant and Child Development* 13, no. 3: 185–98.

Mitroff, S., D. Sobel, and A. Gopnik. 2006. "Reversing How to Think about Ambiguous Figure Reversals: Spontaneous Alternating by Uninformed Observers." *Perception* 35: 709–15.

Moir, Alfred. 1989. *Caravaggio.* New York: Harry N. Abrams.

Moore, G. E. 1953. *Some Main Problems of Philosophy.* London: Allen and Unwin.

———. 1959. *Principia Ethica.* Cambridge: Cambridge Univ. Press.

Mulhall, Stephen. 1990. *On Being in the World: Wittgenstein and Heidegger on Seeing Aspects.* London: Routledge.

Necker, L. A. 1832. "Observations on Some Remarkable Phenomena Seen in Switzerland: And an Optical Phenomenon Which Occurs on Viewing a Figure of a Crystal or Geometrical Solid." *The London and Edinburgh Philosophical Magazine and Journal of Science* 3: 329–37.

Nelson, C. 2001. "The Development and Neural Bases of Face Recognition." *Infant and Child Development* 10: 3–18.

Newton, Isaac. 1934. *Principia Mathematica.* Ed. Florian Cajori. Trans. Andrew Motte. Los Angeles: Univ. of California Press.

Ovid. 1999. *Metamorphoses*, Books I–VIII. Trans. Frank Miller. Cambridge: Harvard Univ. Press.

Peterson, M. A., J. F. Kihlstrom, P. M. Rose, and M. L. Glisky. 1992. "Mental Images Can Be Ambiguous: Reconstruals and Reference-frame Reversals." *Memory and Cognition* 20, no. 2: 107–23.

Petry, G. E., and S. Meyer, eds. 1987. *The Perception of Illusory Contours.* Heidelberg: Springer.

Plato. 1991. *The Republic.* Trans. Allan Bloom. New York: Basic Books.

———. 1998. *Phaedo.* Trans. Eva Brann, Peter Kalkavage, and Eric Salem. Newburyport, Mass.: Focus Publishing.

Porter, Paul B. 1954. "Another Puzzle-Picture." *American Journal of Psychology* 67: 550–51.

Ptolemy. 1952. *Almagest.* Ed. Mortimer Adler. Trans. R. Catesby Taliaferro. Chicago: Encyclopedia Britannica.

———. 1984. *Almagest.* Trans. G. J. Toomer. London: Duckworth.

Rhees, R., ed. 1984. *Ludwig Wittgenstein, Personal Recollections.* Oxford: Oxford Univ. Press.

Rock, I., A. Gopnik, and S. Hall. 1994. "Do Young Children Reverse Ambiguous Figures?" *Perception* 23: 635–44.

Rock, I., S. Hall, and J. Davis. 1994. "Why Do Ambiguous Figures Reverse?" *Acta Psychologica* 87: 33–59.

Rorty, Richard. 1981. *Philosophy and the Mirror of Nature.* Princeton: Princeton Univ. Press.

———. 1999. *Philosophy and Social Hope.* New York: Penguin.

Ruggieri, V., and M. Fernandez. 1994. "Gaze Orientation in Perception of Reversible Figures." *Perceptual and Motor Skills* 78: 299–303.

Sacks, Oliver. 1987. *The Man Who Mistook His Wife for a Hat.* New York: Simon and Schuster.

Schwartz, S. 2007. "The Hogarth Show." *New York Review of Books*, June 28: 16–19.

Scruton, Roger. 1997. *Art and the Imagination: A Study in the Philosophy of Mind.* South Bend, Ind.: St. Augustine's Press.

Searle, John. 1992. *The Rediscovery of Mind.* Cambridge: MIT Press.

Shepard, R. N., and J. Metzler. 1971. "Mental Rotation of Three-dimensional Objects." *Science* 171: 701–3.

Sobel, D., L. Capps, and A. Gopnik. 2005. "Ambiguous Figure Perception and Theory of Mind Understanding in Children with Autistic Spectrum Disorders." *British Journal of Developmental Psychology* 23: 159–74.

Steinberg, L. 1973. "Leonardo's Last Supper." *The Art Quarterly* 36, no. 4: 297–410.

Strawson, Galen. 1994. *Mental Reality.* Cambridge: MIT Press.

Struber, D., and M. Stadler. 1999. "Differences in Top-down Influences on the Reversal Rate of Different Categories of Reversible Figures." *Perception* 28: 1185–96.

Swift, Jonathan. 2003. *Gulliver's Travels.* New York: Penguin.

Tanakh: The Holy Scriptures. 1985. Philadelphia: Jewish Publication Society.

Taylor, Charles. 1975. *Hegel.* New York: Cambridge Univ. Press.

Thompson, P. 1980. "Margaret Thatcher: a New Illusion." *Perception*, 9(4): 483–84.

Tommasini, Anthony. 2008a. "Found Gems from a Pianist Gone Too Soon." *New York Times*, June 6: AR 25–26.

———. 2008b. "From a Veteran at the Keyboard." *New York Times*, July 25: B4.

Updike, John. 2007. "Gold & Geld." *New York Review of Books*, December 20: 26–28.

———. 2008. "Splendid Lies." *New York Review of Books*, August 14: 14–16.

Verbin, N. K. 2000. "Religious Beliefs and Aspect Seeing." *Religious Studies* 36: 1–23.

———. 2001. "Seeing-As and the Justification of Religious Belief." *Faith and Philosophy* 18, no. 4: 501–22.

Vetter, G., J. D. Haynes, and S. Pfaff. 2000. "Evidence for Multistability in the Visual Perception of Pigeons." *Vision Research* 40, no. 16 (July): 2177–86.

Virsu, V. 1975. "Determination of Perspective Reversals." *Nature*, October: 786–87.

Webern, Anton. 1963. *The Path to the New Music.* Bryn Mawr, Penna.: Theodore Presser.

Weinberg, Steven. 2008. "Without God." *New York Review of Books*, September 25: 73–76.

Wheelock, A. K. 1981. *Jan Vermeer.* New York: Harry N. Abrams.

Wollheim, Richard. 1980. *Art and Its Objects.* New York: Cambridge Univ. Press.

Woolf, Virginia. 1984. "On Not Knowing Greek." In *The Common Reader, First Series*, 23–38. San Diego: Harcourt Brace Jovanovich.

NOTES

Chapter One: The Aspects Family

1. "Wittgenstein once said that a serious and philosophical work could be written that would consist entirely of jokes (without being facetious)" (Malcolm 2001, 27 f.). If there is a joke here, it lies in the fact we often refer to pictures like those in Figs. 1 and 2 by the names of the animals they depict. We can leave out "picture of" and be perfectly comfortable. How many of you balked at the opening sentences of this chapter, in which I called the pictures "a duck" and "a rabbit"? Figure 3 likely fooled no one; you knew it was the *picture* duck-rabbit to which I referred, because you knew that there are no duck-rabbits. (There are turduckens in some parts of the United States around Thanksgiving.) Perhaps we should say that *because* the duck-rabbit is a joke (albeit a low-grade one) we ought to take it seriously.
2. Kant, in the *Critique of Pure Reason*, said something similar: "Concepts without percepts are empty, percepts without concepts are blind" (B75).
3. "'Where do you feel grief?'—In my mind.—And if I had to give a place here, I should point in the region of the stomach. For love to the breast and for a flash of thought, to the head" (*RPP I*, 438).
4. Hamlet: My father,—methinks I see my father.
   Horatio: O, where, my lord?
   Hamlet: In my mind's eye, Horatio. (*Hamlet*, I. iii, 184–85)
5. Further examples:

Figure A. More Duck-Rabbits.

6. Ovid, *Metamorphoses*, 2, 351 (*Proteaque ambiguum*).
7. For example, see M. A. Peterson, J. F. Kihlstrom, P. M. Rose, and M. L. Glisky (1992). For examples of tristable and polystable figures, take a look at http://mto.societymusictheory.org/issues/mto.02.8.1/ex01.html.
8. If the cube could easily be seen also as flat, that is, with both dots at the same distance from the viewer, then it would be *tri*stable.
9. L. A. Necker (1832).
10. "*Optische oder geistliche.*" This corresponds roughly to what modern psychologists call "bottom up" or "top down" processing. That the question is still a very live one

can be seen by a glance at some of the psychological experiments done in the past thirty years on ambiguous figures and how we "disambiguate" them. An excellent summary can be found in G. M. Long and T. C. Toppino (2004). I shall have more to say about these experiments in chapter two.

11. In Plato's dialogue *Meno*, Socrates poses the following question to Meno: What is it that all virtues have in common by which we call them virtue? Meno is confused by the question and answers only with a list of different virtues for different kinds of people, without ever being able to answer Socrates' initial question. Meno comes across as stubborn and perhaps dull-witted. But if "virtue" is a "family resemblance" concept, then we would not expect to find any one thing common to all virtues. Had Socrates been willing to entertain the possibility that the same word could be used to refer to things that may share no common trait, Meno's answer might have been the beginning of a new kind of dialogue.

12. Diana Deutsch has done a lot of research on pitch reversals and other auditory illusions. For example, see Deutsch (2004).

13. For example, R. L. Gregory (1968) calls ambiguous figures "*perceptual* illusions. They arise from misinterpretations by the brain of sensory information."

14. Invented by the Italian psychologist Gaetano Kanizsa in 1955 while he was studying "quasi-perceptual margins."

15. Henry Wadsworth Longfellow (1807–1882), *Michel Angelo: A Fragment*, Part III, sec. 6 (Longfellow 1975). See also poem 151 in Michelangelo (1998): "Nothing the best artists can conceive/but lies, potential in a block of stone,/superfluous matter round it. The hand alone/secures it that has intelligence for guide." And in the most universal terms, Michelangelo wrote: "Beauty is the purgation of superfluities" (Emerson 1903, VI, 8, 294).

16. This figure first appeared in the *American Journal of Psychology*, 67, 1954, pp. 50–51. The short article accompanying it was written by Paul B. Porter. See also N. R. Hanson's use of it in *Patterns of Discovery* (1958), where his interest in it focuses on the concept of observation in the sciences.

Chapter Two: Aspects and Words

1. Algebraic "Camouflage": find the circle in $x^2 + y^2 - 4x - 2y = -1$. It's there, right before your eyes. Rearrange the equation a bit and it takes on the textbook form of the equation for a circle with radius = 2 and center = (2, 1): $(x - 2)^2 + (y - 1)^2 = 4$. (You didn't think you would have to do algebra to read this book, did you?)

2. I have modified Jackson's story by introducing a wavelength detection device, changing his tomato to a rose, and introducing Mary's twin sister, who remains behind.

3. For several years, this was the slogan for the home delivery service of the *Washington Post*.

4. For the reader who would like to pursue the current debate on qualia more, here are some good resources: D. Chalmers, *The Conscious Mind* (1996); P. Churchland, "Reduction, Qualia, and Direct Introspection of Brain States" (1985); D. Dennett, *Consciousness Explained* (1991); C. McGinn, *The Problem of Consciousness* (1991); J. Searle, *The Rediscovery of Mind* (1992).

5. The opening to this report reads: "Every view of our visual world gives rise to an infinite number of interpretations. Only through a series of inferential processes do we perceive a consistent and stable environment. These inferences occur so

smoothly that they are rarely noticed. However, certain stimuli can create problems for the visual system and in so doing allow for a glimpse into the inferential processes." Other researchers say similar things. For example, Gregory (1997): "visual perceptions [are] unconscious inferences from sensory data and knowledge derived from the past . . . similar to predictive hypotheses of science."

6. See, for example, D. Hubel and T. N. Weisel (1965). Also D. Marr (1982).
7. P. Churchland, P. Ramachandra, and T. Sejnowski (1994). Also G. Edelman (1989).
8. While it makes sense to say that it would be useful to an animal's survival to see things in similar situations similarly, there remains the question of how the animal (or person) determines in the first place that *this* situation is sufficiently similar to a previous one, so that what I learned *then* ought to inform what I see *now*. The problem of recognizing similarity is already an "aspect question." As an example of errors that can attend selection of the wrong model, Malcolm Gladwell, in *Blink: The Power of Thinking Without Thinking* (2005), recounts the story of two policemen in New York City who, in a split-second reaction, were sure that a cornered suspect had a gun in his hand. They *saw* the gun and reacted accordingly. After many shots were fired, they discovered that there was no gun, that there never had been a gun.
9. For example, S. Ellis and L. Stark (1978); V. Ruggieri and M. Fernandez (1994).
10. For example, D. A. Leopold et al. (2002); G. M. Long et al. (2002); V. Virsu (1975).
11. For example, D. Struber and M. Stadler (1999).
12. Here's a version of the ice-cream story in detail:

> A toy town is laid out on a table in front of the child so that the child can see the whole town. The experimenter then tells the following story, moving dolls and an ice-cream truck accordingly.
> This is Pete and Nancy. They live in this town. Here they are in the park. Along comes the ice-cream man. Pete would like to buy an ice-cream but has left his money at home. He is very sad. "Don't worry" says the ice-cream man, "you can go home and get your money and buy some ice-cream later." "Oh, good," says Pete. "I'll be back here later to buy an ice-cream." So Pete goes home. He lives in this house. Now, the ice-cream man says: "I am going to drive my truck to the school to see if I can sell my ice-cream outside there instead." The ice-cream man drives over to the school. On his way, he passes Pete's house. Pete sees him and says, "Where are you going?"
> The ice-cream man says, "I'm going to sell my ice-cream outside the school," and off he drives to the school. Now Nancy goes home. She lives in this house. Then she goes over to Pete's house. She knocks on the door and asks, "Is Pete in?" "No," says his father, "he's gone out to buy an ice-cream."
> Question: Where does Nancy think that Pete has gone to buy an ice-cream? (Correct answer: the park)

13. For example, G. Long et al. (1983).
14. For example, I. Rock, S. Hall, and J. Davis (1994).
15. Some people can't do it. About 2.5 percent of the population suffers from prosopagnosia, the inability to recognize faces. Often their disability goes undetected for some time, because these people learn to rely on cues of which they are conscious, such as distinctive facial features, gait, and voice, to recognize others.
16. See, for example, D. Lundquist and A. Öhman (2005).

17. And others like it. For example, *RPP I*, 292, 1039, 1093.
18. On other "long ways," see Plato *Republic*, Book II, and Dante, *Inferno*, cantos 1 and 2.
19. Cf. Jastrow (1900, 285): ". . . the thing or idea is more important than the sign."
20. Children's television shows are full of such games. Tom Lehrer wrote a song titled "Silent E" for an episode of the television series *The Electric Company* in 1971. "Who can turn a can into a cane? / Who can turn a pan into a pane? / It's not too hard to see, / It's Silent E." There's more, but you probably get the idea.
21. In chapter four, we'll return to music from the point of view of seeing aspects and experiencing changes in aspect.
22. Though were I to say, "I sincerely promise," I may not have promised sincerely. My sincerity might very well depend on my state of mind.
23. I am reminded of the line from Goethe's *Faust*: "In the beginning was the deed" (*"Im Anfang war die Tat"*), Part One, line 1235.
24. One contrary case comes to mind. We may sometimes not be sure if violent tickling is painful or not. This seems to be more an uncertainty about what word best to use in such a situation, and indicates that even the use of a word like "pain" can have an uncertain application in some cases. This is the nature of language in practice.
25. "Why doesn't one teach a child the language-game 'It looks red to me' from the first? Because it is not yet able to understand the rather fine distinction between seeing and being?" (*RPP II*, 315).
26. See, for example, Descartes, *Meditations*, especially Meditation VI.
27. The "inverted spectrum" has had a venerable history at least since John Locke (1632–1704) suggested the possibility in his *Treatise on Human Understanding*. Locke writes:

> Though one man's idea of blue should be different from another's, neither would it carry any imputation of falsehood to our simple ideas, if by the different structure of our organs it were so ordered, that the same object should produce in several men's minds different ideas at the same time; e. g. if the idea that a violet produced in one man's mind by his eyes were the same that a marigold produced in another man's, and vice versa. For, since this could never be known, because one man's mind could not pass into another man's body, to perceive what appearances were produced by those organs; neither the ideas hereby, nor the names, would be at all confounded, or any falsehood be in either. For all things that had the texture of a violet, producing constantly the idea that he called blue, and those which had the texture of a marigold, producing constantly the idea which he as constantly called yellow, whatever those appearances were in his mind; he would be able as regularly to distinguish things for his use by those appearances, and understand and signify those distinctions marked by the name blue and yellow, as if the appearances or ideas in his mind received from those two flowers were exactly the same with the ideas in other men's minds. I am nevertheless very apt to think that the sensible ideas produced by any object in different men's minds, are most commonly very near and undiscernibly alike. For which opinion, I think, there might be many reasons offered: but that being besides my present business, I shall not trouble my reader with them; but only mind him, that the contrary supposition, if it could be proved, is of little use, either for the improvement of our knowledge, or conveniency of life, and so we need not trouble ourselves to examine it" (Book II, chap. 32, sec. 15).

Recent authors relate the possibility of an inverted spectrum (also inverted musical scale and other sensory inversions) to "qualia," which we met earlier in this book. Those who are interested can follow up by reading the entry in the Stanford Dictionary of Philosophy (online) and look at the extensive bibliography that follows. The site is http://plato.stanford.edu/entries/qualia-inverted/.

28. "For philosophical problems arise when language *goes on holiday*" (*PI*, sec. 38).
29. Or the duck-rabbit picture you see as a duck I see as a rabbit? Are the cases similar?
30. "*I would say that he knows no more whether he has this experience than we do.* If you say 'Of course he knows that *this* is red,' I would say 'How does he know that it is *red?*' Can't he be wrong about this? *He has learned the word 'red' from us and uses it together with us.* He cannot know better than we whether he is blind because he has learned from us the language which includes the word 'blind.' Similarly with the word 'red.' For in the first stage of learning we *correct* him, we do not *contradict* him, or think he contradicts us" (*PE*, 14).
31. G. W. F. Hegel (1770–1831) expresses a similar insight in the opening section of his influential work, *The Phenomenology of Spirit*. "Sense-Certainty is a view of our awareness of the world according to which it is at its fullest and richest when we simply open our sense to the world and receive whatever impressions come our way, prior to any . . . conceptual activity" (Taylor 1975, 140–41). When the subject of sense-certainty is asked to *say* what he experiences, however, he finds that his attempts are empty. If he tries to speak of the "here" and "now" that he is experiencing, not even he himself can know what he means by "here," "now," and "I," unless he means something universal, beyond the immediate place, moment, and person. The pure particular is inexpressible and therefore untrue and irrational, according to Hegel.
32. In *Gulliver's Travels* by Jonathan Swift (1667–1745), Gulliver visits the "grand academy of Lagado," a proto-think tank. Here he meets people working on various absurd projects. One of these is "a scheme for entirely abolishing all words whatsoever; and this was urged as a great advantage in point of health, as well as brevity. . . . An expedient was therefore offered, that since words are only names for things, it would be more convenient for all men to carry about them such things as were necessary to express a particular business they are to discourse on . . . [M]any of the most learned and wise adhere to the new scheme of expressing themselves by things; which has only this inconvenience attending it, that if a man's business be very great, and of various kinds, he must be obliged, in proportion, to carry a greater bundle of things upon his back, unless he can afford one or two strong servants to attend him. I have often beheld two of those sages almost sinking under the weight of their packs, like pedlars among us, who, when they met in the street, would lay down their loads, open their sacks, and hold conversation for an hour together; then put up their implements, help each other to resume their burdens, and take their leave" (part III, chap. V). One reason we find this passage funny suggests that we already know that words do not "stand for" objects, but instead perform a variety of functions.
33. "You must bear in mind that [a] language-game is so to say something unpredictable. I mean: it is not based on grounds. It is not reasonable (or unreasonable). It is there—like our life" (*RC*, 559).
34. "One thing we always do when discussing a word is to ask how we were taught it. Doing this on the one hand destroys a variety of misconceptions, on the other hand gives you a primitive language in which the word is used. Although this language is

not what you talk when you are twenty, you get a rough approximation to what kind of language game is going to be played. Cf. How did we learn 'I dreamt so and so'? The interesting point is that we didn't learn it by being shown a dream" (*LA*, 1–2).

35. David Hume, *A Treatise on Human Nature* (1978); G. E. Moore (1953); A. J. Ayer (1963).

36. Karl Marx, *Capital*, book one, section three, part two (and elsewhere).

37. "The description of the subjectively seen is closely or distantly related to the description of an object, but does not function like the description of an object. How does one compare visual sensations? How do I compare my visual experiences with someone else's?" (*RPP I*, 1099).

38. Also *LWPP I*, 565: "*Astonishment* is essential to a change of aspect. And astonishment is thinking."

39. "I meet someone whom I have not seen for years; I see him clearly, but fail to know him. Suddenly I know him, I see the old face in the altered one. I believe that I should do a different portrait of him now if I could paint" (*PI*, sec. 169). Might this new portrait be part of a description of what I now see?

40. I'm not hallucinating because I'm really looking at something and seeing it. No one questions this. If you can't see it too, then it makes more sense to say that you are blind to the aspect I am seeing than to say that I'm seeing something that isn't. Perhaps the line between these is not always clear. It is especially unclear, and important, in aesthetics, ethics, and theology.

41. "When I compare wild flowers and garden flowers, this may make me conscious of the difference of character; but that is not to say that I already earlier on perceived their characters as well as the flowers themselves, or that I must after all have perceived them as having some character or other" (*RPP I*, 419). Similarly, until we hear another language than our own, we can hardly be aware of the characteristic features of our mother tongue. We might not even be aware that we are speaking a *language*.

42. "Someone has always seen the duck-rabbit as a rabbit and now he sees it as a duck for the first time. From this he might learn that a rabbit's head and a duck's head can have the same contours. . . . But the dawning of the rabbit aspect is not the perception of that relation. Couldn't someone perceive the relation and still not be able to experience the change or the dawning of an aspect?" (*LWPP I*, 492).

43. Among experiences, Wittgenstein does *not* include intending, thinking, believing, hoping, remembering, and others. "There is no cry of intention, anymore than there is one of knowledge or belief" (*RPP II*, 179). It would take us too far from our main topic to explore in detail what he says about all these psychological concepts. His remarks are scattered throughout a number of his books, especially *PI*, *RPP I*, *RPP II*, *LWPP I*, *LWPP II*, and *RC*. Also you might find Elizabeth Anscombe's book *Intention* useful.

44. Let us also assume his eyes are open. (The old children's joke: "I can't see! I can't see!" "What's the matter?" "I've got my eyes closed!" This underscores the assumption.)

45. Also: "How does seeing an aspect hang together with the ability to perform certain operations (for example, in mathematics)? Think of seeing three-dimensionally in descriptive geometry and operating within the drawing. He moves his pencil on the surface of the drawing as if he were moving with the real object. But how can this be proof of *seeing*?

"Well, don't we accept it as proof of seeing if somebody moves about a room with confidence? There are simply different criteria for seeing" (*RPP II*, 506).

46. You can find a fuller discussion of external and internal relations in Bickard (2003). Also at www.lehigh.edu/~mhb0/Int.ExtRelations.pdf.

47. "One may note an alteration in a face and describe it by saying that the face assumed a harder expression—and yet not be able to describe the alteration in spatial terms. This is enormously important" (*RPP I*, 919). "Anyone with an eye for family resemblance can recognize that two people are related to each other, even without being able to say wherein the relation lies" (*RPP II*, 551). Malcolm Gladwell's *Blink* is full of examples of such "implicit seeing."

48. I don't want to be held to this bit of child psychology. It is enough that comparisons between physical objects seem to be the most straightforward to make.

49. "We could easily imagine people who . . . would be repelled by our photographs because a face without color is sinister and ugly" (*LWPP I*, 679).

50. For example, C. R. Gallistel (2001).

51. "When the light dove parts the air in free flight and feels the air's resistance, it might come to think that it would do much better still in space devoid of air" (Kant, *Critique of Pure Reason*, Introduction, Part III, A5/B8). "We want to walk: so we need *friction*. Back to the rough ground!" (*PI*, sec. 107)

52. R. N. Shepard and J. Metzler (1971).

53. J. J. Freyd and R. A. Finke (1985). Helene Intraub (2002) says this: "Freyd and Finke's (1985) choice of the term 'representational momentum' reflected the idea that the mental extrapolation was analogous to physical momentum. In terms of Shepard's theory, the characteristics of physical momentum in the physical world were internalized during evolution. Thus, when the inducing stimulus disappears, without this external stimulation (just as in the case of circadian rhythms), the mental representation nevertheless continues (perhaps with some 'drift' across individuals)."

54. For example, T. L. Hubbard (1995).

55. Mixing language-games, like those of "picture" and "mental image," can lead to trouble. Which brings to mind the story of the day that Socrates ran into his old, but less "grammatically" astute, friend, Crito, who was coming out of one of the baths in Athens. Socrates: Hello, Crito! Have you taken a bath? Crito: Why, Socrates? Is one missing?

56. For similar reasons, thinking cannot be a form of "inner dialogue" or "private conversation." There are questions that can be asked in an ordinary conversation between people that cannot be asked in a "private conversation," such as, "When you said to meet you at the bank, did you mean the riverbank or the savings bank?"

57. For example, a recent study by Christof Koch of Cal Tech shows that while viewing the Necker cube, subjects' pupils dilate slightly just before they report that the cube "jumps." This study establishes a correlation between a physiological response and a conscious reaction on the part of the subject, namely pressing a key on a keyboard to signal that the cube had changed for her. "The scientists found a significant increase in the diameter of the pupil at the instant preceding the perceptual switch. The pupil, which is about 2 mm wide in bright light, dilated by as much as 1 mm at that moment—a change that, in theory, could be noticeable to a casual observer. Koch and his colleagues also found that the more the pupil dilated, the longer the period of time before the switch from one interpretation to the other" (http://mr.caltech.edu/media/Press_Releases/PR13103.html; also in *Proceedings*

of the National Academy of Sciences, February 8, 2008). Note, however, that the description of the experiment does not distinguish between the subjects' keyboard pressing and their seeing the cube jump. What the psychologists are really interested in is the experience of a change of aspect. What they measure is pressing a key.

58. "[Among psychologists] the reassuring atmosphere created by complex and expensive laboratory apparatus . . . and the formidable magic of statistics often act as an insurance policy in our mind against the fear of being taken in; all this tends to keep many psychologists from a serious examination of the grammar of basic concepts. But there is more to it than this. There is, I believe, a deeply ingrained resistance to the examination of the workings of language, especially among psychologists. Part of this resistance is linked with their intense distrust of what psychologists contemptuously consider 'just semantics' or 'doing philosophy.' This distrust is understandable. The history of psychology is steeped in the struggle of psychology to free itself from the metaphysical sterilities of philosophy and of faculty-psychology . . . But over and beyond these forces is the implicit belief of many psychologists that language is a *given*, once and for all, and that it does not need any examination" (Kurtz 1969, 532).

59. R. L. Gregory (1968); D. Sobel, L. Capps, and A. Gopnick (2005); G. M. Long and T. C. Toppino (2004); and many others.

60. William Harvey (1578–1657), *On the Motion of the Heart and Blood in Animals*. Galileo Galilei, *Two New Sciences*.

61. Greek, *phaimomenon*: "that which appears or is seen," from the verb *phainesthai*, to appear.

62. Seeing: *RPP II*, 77; remembering: *RPP I*, 905; *LWPP I*, 504, 837–39; intending: *PI*, p. 205, secs. 588, 653; more: *PI*, sec. 148, pp.185–86.

63. I include the neuter pronoun "it" because Wittgenstein's challenge is directed also to how we talk about animals and machines.

64. I like to ask my friends who have newborns to let me know when their children have their "first thought." The same question could be asked about speaking their first word. The questions point out that both concepts, thinking and speaking, are not *single-event* concepts, but require a whole field of activities to make sense, like checkmate in a chess game.

65. Heinrich von Kleist (1777–1811) wrote a short piece in 1805 titled "On the Gradual Fabrication of Thoughts While Speaking," in which he argues that "speak before you think" may often be the way to get our thought going when we are stuck: "Whenever you seek to know something and cannot find it out by meditation, I would advise you . . . to talk it over with the first person you meet. He need not be especially brilliant, and I do not suggest that you *question* him; no, *tell* him about it. . . . As they say in France, *l'appétit vient en mangeant* ["the appetite comes as we are eating"] and from our own experience we might in parody assert, *l'idée vient en parlant* ["ideas come as we are speaking"] (Kleist 1982, 218).

66. Other concepts too apply only to beings with language: "Can only those hope who can talk? Only those who have mastered the application of a language. The phenomena of hope are modes of this very complicated pattern" (*LWPP I*, 365). "Why can a dog feel fear but not remorse? Would it be right to say 'Because he can't talk'?" (*Z*, 518).

67. This talk about how the philosopher's role is to remind us of things reminds me of a comic strip I once read about: Two adolescents are talking and the first says, "Every-

day I ask myself those age-old philosophical questions—Who am I? Where am I? Why am I here? That, my friend, is philosophy." Whereupon his friend responds, "Sounds more like amnesia" (Fann 1971, 108).
68. See Rorty (1981).

Chapter Three: Aspect Blindness

1. Children younger than about four generally never experience a spontaneous change of aspect. See, for example, A. Gopnick and A. Rosati (2001), 175–83. Also I. Rock, A. Gopnik, and S. Hall (1994), 635–44.
2. This is the one that he uses: ⌐⊢ (*PI*, sec. 210).
3. "A poet's words can pierce us. And that is of course *causally* connected with the use that they have in our life. And it is also connected with the way in which, conformably to this use, we let our thoughts roam up and down in the familiar surroundings of the words" (*Z*, 155).
4. *PI*, pp. 200, 209; *LWPP I*, 549; *RPP I*, 71, 362.
5. "Can we describe to a blind person what it is like for someone to *see*?—Certainly, the blind learn a great deal about the difference between the blind and the sighted. But the question was badly put; as though seeing were an activity and there were a description of it" (*RC*, 81).
6. "[It is] impossible to attribute visual imagery to a blind man or auditory images to one who is deaf. This is a logical truth, not a contingent fact" (Scruton 1997, 104).
7. From the Greek, πρόσωπον (prosopon), meaning "face," and ἀγνωσίας (agnosia), meaning "ignorance" or "lack of knowledge." I mentioned earlier that while prosopagnosia can be the result of a stroke or other brain trauma, recent studies suggest that about 2.5 percent of the population are prosopagnosic from birth. See I. Kennerknecht et al. (2006), 1617–22.
8. Sacks (1987), 13.
9. "I say: 'I can think of this face (which gives an impression of timidity) as courageous too.' We do not mean by this that I can imagine someone with this face perhaps saving someone's life (that, of course, is imaginable in connection with any face). I am speaking rather of an aspect of the face itself. Nor do I mean that I can imagine that this man's face might change so that, in the ordinary sense, it looked courageous; though I may very well mean that there is a quite definite way in which it can change into a courageous face. The reinterpretation of a facial expression can be compared to the reinterpretation of a chord in music, when we hear it as a modulation first into this, then into that key" (*PI*, sec. 536).
10. P. Thompson (1980), 483–84. Thompson used pictures of Margaret Thatcher, while I have substituted pictures of George Bush. (These pictures were designed by Dr. Tania Lombrozo, who graciously gave me permission to print them here.)
11. Some psychologists suggest that in viewing inverted faces, we focus on the individual features of the face in isolation. Eyes, nose, lips all look normal in both pictures when they are looked at individually. When the face is turned upright, the position in which we normally see faces, we recognize the relationships among the parts. We see these relationships, which determine facial expression. ("A smiling mouth *smiles* only in a human face" [*PI*, sec. 583]. We might add: only in an *upright* human face.)
12. "Thus we could imagine someone who would see only a painted face as a face, but not one that consists of a circle and four dots" (*RPP II*, 482).

13. In a slightly more technical sense, we can say that aspect blindness is not like color blindness because color is an *external* relation of an object, not an *internal* relation. That is, the color of an object in general does not essentially relate it to something else, as the arc of a circle is related to the center of that circle. In those cases where color can be considered an internal relation (as, for example, in paintings, where color and meaning might be related in a nonconventional way), the color-blind will be at a considerable disadvantage compared to the normally sighted.

14. Sacks (1987), p. 15. Sacks's Dr. P. has a more far-reaching agnosia, which extends beyond representations to objects and people.

15. With respect to the regular solids, it would have been interesting to know if Dr. P. could have recognized them from drawings.

16. Sacks suggests (p. 16) that Dr. P. can still visualize schemata, although his visualization of faces, scenes, narrative, and drama is profoundly impaired. His support for this is that Dr. P. can still play a good game of "mental chess" and therefore must be imagining a chessboard, chessmen, and the moves. But is that necessarily so? "Mental chess" may no more require a "mental chessboard" than "calculating in the head" requires "mental paper and pencil."

17. In 1918, Kurt Goldstein and Adhemar Gelb reported a case of a soldier injured in the back of the head by shrapnel. They referred to him as *Schn.* (later revealed to be *Schneider*), and the lengthy case study they wrote was widely read and achieved a kind of notoriety. Schneider seemed normal except that on close examination he could not identify words and objects when shown to him briefly on a tachistoscope (a machine for very briefly displaying words and pictures on a screen, from the Greek, *tachus*, swift). In *The Shattered Mind* (1976), Howard Gardner, following Goldstein and Gelb, describes Schneider in the following terms:

    > Schn. found it easiest to identify objects and pictures that contained some clear defining feature. . . . He had special difficulty in apprehending groups of objects, or making sense of configurations in which the relationship between objects was critical. . . . He claimed not to understand what was meant by perception of motion. (144–45)

    Schneider could recognize the parts of what he viewed but seemed unable to synthesize them into "forms suffused with meaning" (146–47). He exhibits many of the characteristic deficits of someone who has become *aspect-blind*. In 1941, Russell Brain, a neurologist, published "Visual Object Agnosia with Special Reference to Gestalt Theory," about a fifteen-year-old boy who could not see a rectangular shape as a book, a box, or a tray. He could not see it as something other than a rectangle. Brain suggests that his visual memory was grossly deficient, and so he could not "match up" what he saw with "schemes" of forms he had previously seen. But in our account, memory may have little to do with his problem. He is aspect-blind.

18. Named for Paul Broca and Carl Wernicke, who first localized the brain lesions responsible for the kinds of aphasia associated respectively with their names. It's not important for our discussion of aspect blindness to know exactly where in the brain these areas lie, but if you are interested, take a look at any neuroanatomy book. A web search will also turn up many useful pictures and diagrams.

19. For example, a patient interviewed by Howard Gardner (*The Shattered Mind*, 1976) spoke on and on in the following vein: "Boy, I'm sweating, I'm awful nervous, you know, once in a while I get caught up, I can't mention the tarripoi, a month ago, quite a little, I've done a lot well. I impose a lot, while, on the other hand, you

know what I mean, I have to run around, look it over, trebbin and all that sort of stuff" (68).

20. I have not been able to discover if work has been done on the ability of any aphasic to experience changes in aspect. As far as I know, showing a stroke victim an ambiguous figure like the duck-rabbit or Necker cube is not part of the standardized battery of tests currently administered to determine the kind and severity of their injury.

21. I have added the italics.

22. Proponents of mind modularity disagree on whether it includes brain modularity. For a nice overview of the wider discussion about modularity, see H. C. Barrett and R. Kurzban (2006).

23. J. Kay, R. Lesser, and M. Coltheart (1992).

24. Normal speakers can also play language games with themselves, such as thinking and talking to oneself, because they are able to bring context to bear on words *through* words. Their imaginations are intact. This is why they are able to see aspects and experience aspect changes.

25. See, for example, P. Carruthers and P. K. Smith (1996); P. Bloom (1997).

26. Those with Asperger's syndrome tend to develop better and better social skills as they get older, and "pass" theory of mind tests. But when young, they, too, perform significantly worse than normal children of the same age and intelligence.

27. And to *ourselves*, some believe. The argument of Frith and Happé (1999) is that autistics fail even to attribute correct mental states to themselves and so may lack "self-consciousness" and an ability to "introspect."

28.

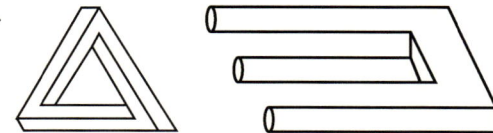

Figure B. Penrose Triangle and Devil's Fork.

29. "Do not try to analyze your own inner experience" (*PI*, sec. 174). ". . . if the possible uses of a word do float before us in half-shades as we say or hear it—this simply goes for *us*. But we communicate with other people without knowing if they have this experience too" (*PI*, sec. 155). "For one needs only to ask, 'What do I care about inner events, whatever they are?!,' to see that a different attitude is conceivable. . . . Would I know that pain, etc., etc., is something inner if I weren't told so?" (*RPP II*, 643).

30. Augustine's account of how words work, that they are connected somehow to the objects or ideas they stand for, would tell us that because words carry their meanings along with them we shouldn't be surprised that an isolated word would still *have* a meaning. As we've seen, however, Wittgenstein has given us ample reason to doubt any Augustinian-type account in which meanings are other than uses.

31. ". . . if the inflection of voice, for example, seems to me to determine whether I mean one thing or the other—then I would be experiencing meaning" (*LWPP I*, 60).

32. Wittgenstein alludes to the hairdresser-sculptor pun at *LWPP I*, 711.

33. Comedy routine. Pick your favorite pair of comedians. Mine are Abbott and Costello. Abbott on stage, Costello enters stage right, both dressed in togas. Abbott raises his right arm with the fingers of his hand held together pointing upward, and

says "Hail!" Costello immediately ducks down, covers his head with his toga, and looks up fearfully. We laugh. Did Abbott do something wrong?

34. Repetition is one way to bring about this loss of meaning, but there are others. Might not the usual experience of some stroke victims be similar to our own experience when we repeat a word over and over? Perhaps the aphasic condition is one of "emptied words," with which nothing can be done. Several subtests on PALPA (Psycholinguistic Assessment of Language Processing in Aphasia) ask patients to identify isolated words, to read them, to associate them with pictures, and so forth. People with most forms of aphasia perform poorly on many of these subtests. When we consider how to assess the results of such isolated word tests, we should bear in mind what Goodman's Chil achieved by communicating with other people in a real context.

35. *PI*, p. 210. See also note 2 to chapter three, above.

36. We are not interested in *how* people can do this. (Not everyone can.) Psychologists might be able to tell us. But we are concerned with the relationship between the concepts of "chess" and "mental chess," no matter what the explanations are of how people can play the two games.

37. "The mental picture is the picture which is described when someone describes what he imagines" (*PI*, sec. 367).

38. Picture-image: *PI*, sec. 367; talking-thinking: *PI*, sec. 185; waking-dreaming: *PI*, sec. 157; *LWPP I*, 898.

39. Even *Mardi Gras*, Fat Tuesday, can be explained without recourse to secondary or emergent meaning. The "fat" in "Fat Tuesday" and the "fat" in "fat Wednesday" are not the same.

40. They may not "sound right" to you. Can you think of other similar nonmetaphorical examples that do?

41. Srinivasa Ramanujan (1887–1920) was one of those people. The British mathematician G. H. Hardy told an anecdote about a time he visited Ramanujan. "I remember once going to see him when he was ill at Putney. I had ridden in taxi cab number 1729 and remarked that the number seemed to me rather a dull one, and that I hoped it was not an unfavorable omen. 'No,' he replied, 'it is a very interesting number; it is the smallest number expressible as the sum of two cubes in two different ways.'" (The pairs of cubes are $10^3 + 9^3$ and $12^3 + 1^3$.)

42. In Book Four of Swift's *Gulliver's Travels*, Gulliver describes the years he spent among the Houyhnhnms, perfectly rational and enlightened horses. He thought he was in paradise, so perfect their lives seemed to him. Before Gulliver's arrival, they detect no ambiguities in life and have no understanding of what an "opinion" could be. A case might be made, I think, that they are aspect-blind, meaning-blind—and happy.

Chapter Four: Aspects and Art

1. I have seen some extraordinary painted fluting on columns in churches that demanded I go right up and touch it to be convinced that it was flat.

2. The Italian titles of these three paintings are, respectively, *La Vocazione di San Mateo*, *Il Martirio di San Mateo*, and *L'Ispirazione di San Mateo*.

3. Part of the preceding description is adapted from Alfred Moir's *Caravaggio* (1989) and also from his article on Caravaggio at http://artchives.com/critics.

4. I have used the Revised Standard Version of the Bible for these and subsequent passages unless I indicate otherwise.
5. See, for example, *Allegory on the Blessings of Peace* by Rubens (1577–1640), among many other allegorical paintings that this Flemish Baroque artist produced.
6. "While they were eating he said, 'I tell you solemnly, one of you is about to betray me.' They were greatly distressed and started asking him in turn, 'Not I, Lord, surely?' He answered, 'Someone, who has dipped his hand into the dish with me, will betray me . . .' Judas, who was to betray him, asked in his turn, 'Not I, Rabbi, surely?' 'They are your own words,' answered Jesus" (Matt. 26:21–25). See also Mark 14: 17–21, Luke 22: 21–23, John 13:21–30.
7. The institution of the Eucharist appears in the three synoptic gospels, so-called because they share a common view of the life of Jesus and tell similar stories (Matt. 26:26–29, Mark 14:22–25, Luke 22:19–20). John's gospel differs in that, while he recounts the Last Supper, he makes no mention of a Eucharist. In John's gospel, Judas leaves the dinner immediately after Jesus reveals that he is the traitor, while the synoptic accounts do not mention Judas's leaving.
8. In some of their poems, Wallace Stevens (1879–1955) and e. e. cummings (1894–1962) emphasize looking at different aspects at once (for example, Stevens's "Thirteen Ways of Looking at a Blackbird") or the taking apart of ordinary language and putting it back together in different ways (cummings's "nonsun blob a"). They might be said to have written "Cubist poems."
9. His brother Paul was a concert pianist who had lost his right arm in World War I. Ravel wrote his well-known "Concerto for Left Hand" for him (Janik and Toulmin 1973, 171). Brahms was a close friend of the family (Malcolm 1958, 2).
10. This comes from Engelmann (1967).
11. *RPP II*, 494: "Does it take imagination to hear something as a variation? Yet I am also perceiving."
12. Mozart also wrote variations for piano on "Ah vous dirai-je, Maman," the melody of which is the same as "Twinkle, twinkle." You might find these easier to hear as variations than those in the A-major sonata. Considerably more challenging than either of these are the "Variations on a Theme of Hayden" by Brahms, written for full orchestra.
13. See *LA*, 33.
14. "Soulful expression cannot be recognized by rules" (*RPP II*, 695).
15. "Understanding a Gregorian mode doesn't mean getting used to the sequence of notes in the sense in which I can get used to a smell and after a while cease to find it unpleasant. No, it means hearing something new, which I haven't heard before, much in the same way—in fact it's a complete analogy—as it would be if I were suddenly able to see 10 strokes //////////, which I had hitherto only been able to see as twice five strokes, as a characteristic whole. Or suddenly seeing the picture of a cube as 3-dimensional when I had previously only been able to see it as a flat pattern" (*PR*, 281).
16. The first wine is Argentinean and was given a point score of 97 out of 100, which is very high. (So is the price.) The second is a French Rhône wine, rated 95, while the third is a California Cabernet Sauvignon, rated 85 (*Wine Spectator*, November 15, 2008).
17. One more might need to be added. "The tongue can detect only five tastes, salty, sweet, bitter, sour, and a taste whose receptors have only begun to be identified: umami—the savory, brothy sensation that is amply present in Parmesan, seaweed,

and ripe tomatoes. All other taste sensations are really smells, as a very simple experiment will confirm: all you have to do to prove it is hold your nose while you taste something" (Lanchester 2008). In fact, can you distinguish a raw apple from a raw potato with your mouth alone? Not easy.

18. Lanchester cites a seminal study, *Wines: Their Sensory Evaluation* (1976) by Maynard Amerine and Edward Roessler, who were both against the "Romantic" tradition in writing about wines. He also quotes an outrageous description from Evelyn Waugh's *Brideshead Revisited* of some tasting notes: "It is a little, shy wine like a gazelle." "Like a leprechaun." "Dappled, in a tapestry meadow." "Like the last unicorn." It goes on. The tasters are growing progressively more intoxicated as their notes grow more imaginative.

19. "We learn certain things only through long experience and not from a course in school. How, for instance, does one develop the eye of a connoisseur? Someone says, for example: 'This picture was not painted by such-and-such a master'—the statement he makes is thus not an aesthetic judgment, but one that can be proved by documentation. He may not be able to give good reasons for his verdict.—How did he learn it? Could someone have taught him? Quite.—Not in the *same* way as one learns to calculate. A great deal of *experience* was necessary. That is, the learner probably had to look at and compare a large number of pictures by various masters again and again. In doing this he could have been given *hints*. Well, that was the process of *learning*. But then he looked at a picture and made a judgment about it. In most cases he was able to list reasons for his judgment, but generally it wasn't *they* that were convincing [to him]" (*LWPP I*, 925). In the opening chapter of *Blink*, Gladwell describes such a case.

20. On Tintoretto, see Butterfield (2008); for Turner, see Updike (2008).

21. And here is a description full of emergent meanings of a recent performance by Philippe Entremont: "For an encore, Mr. Entremont played Chopin's *Polonaise* in C sharp minor, conveying both the burly vigor and the ruminative tenderness of this mercurial work" (Tommasini 2008b).

22. This seems too obvious to belabor, but sometimes the best jokes are the ones that depend least on particular facts and most on general "grammatical" features of our language. I think Abbott and Costello's "Who's on First?" routine would be funny even if you knew nothing about baseball, as long as you knew English. To the extent that "getting" a painting is something like "getting" a joke, then perhaps we can say something similar about the sort of knowledge that is required to appreciate the best paintings: It is often very general knowledge about culture, and a "cultured" person possesses this.

23. *A Prince of Courtly* (or *Court*) *Painters* is an imaginary word-portrait of Watteau by Walter Pater, published in *Macmillan's Magazine* in October, 1885.

24. For a discussion of the debate about the paraphrasability of poetry, see Cavell (1965).

25. See also T. S. Eliot as cited in Wollheim (1980), p. 187 to the effect that "the critic imposes a new meaning on a work of art, making old meanings irrelevant or uninteresting." Also *LA*, 46: "In considering what a dream is, it is important to consider what happens to it, the way its aspect changes when it is brought into relation with other things remembered." Also *PI*, sec. 133: "For the clarity that we are aiming at is indeed *complete* clarity. But this simply means that the philosophical problems should *completely* disappear." And *TLP*, 6.521: "The solution of the problem of life is seen in the vanishing of the problem. (Is not this the reason why those who have

found after a long period of doubt that the sense of life became clear to them have then been unable to say what constituted that sense?)"

26. See also Wollheim (1980), 102: ". . . what is peculiar to art . . . [is] a new conjunction of elements already in existence."

27. Two Hopper paintings that illustrate this are the watercolor *House with a Big Pine* (1935) and the oil *High Noon* (1949).

28. Dorment suggests that Marden's *Grove Group IV* is an example of a painting where he fails. Two canvases, one blue-grey, the other green-gray, join in a horizontal line, which the eye sees as a horizon. "And the moment the eye sees the picture as a seascape, it also sees the green [upper] panel as receding into endless space, even though it knows it is actually looking at a flat plane." This is aspect-talk, simply.

29. Another painter who consciously attempts to avoid references to the outside world—to all representation—is Jackson Pollock (1912–1956). His paintings "have no focal center for the eye to travel towards or away from. They are designed as continuous surface patterns which are perfectly unified without the use of any obvious repeating motif" (Berger 2001, 16). Not all abstract art avoids aspects so assiduously; Marden and Pollock clearly make an effort to do so.

30. In the last movement of his Symphony Number 40 in G minor, Mozart uses a chromatic sequence that touches eleven of the twelve tones, leaving out only G, the tonic. (Follow only the notes that sound out most when you hear the piece, that is, D-flat, C, E, A-flat, B-natural, E, F-sharp, B-flat, C-sharp, F, and G-sharp.) But this "tone row" does not sound at all like a Webern row, in part because the context isn't right. Just as the duck-rabbit will not be seen as a duck when viewed against a background of rabbits, so too this chromatic section in Mozart does not sound like a foreshadowing of atonal music.

Figure C. A few measures from the last movement of Mozart's Symphony No. 40, K. 550.

31. "I may recognize a genuine loving look, distinguish it from a pretended one. . . . But I may be quite incapable of describing the difference" (*PI*, p. 228).

32. "It is possible—and this is important—to say a *great deal* about a fine aesthetic difference.—The first thing you say may, of course, be just: 'This word fits, *that* doesn't'—or something of the kind. But then you can discuss all the extensive ramifications of the tie-up effected by each of the words. That first judgment is *not* the end of the matter, for it is the field of force of a word that is decisive" (*PI*, p. 219).

Chapter Five: Ethics and Aesthetics Are One

1. Normally, however, I do not need justification for my own seeing of the duck if I am an experienced speaker of the language I am using. It is enough that I know what the word "duck" means and what it means "to see the duck-rabbit as a duck." So my being unable to go on in other ways might indicate to you that something is wrong with me. If this condition persisted, then even I would no longer be in a position to claim that I was seeing the duck.

2. "What a Copernicus or a Darwin really achieved was not the discovery of a true theory but of a fertile new point of view" (*CV*, 18). "The miracles of nature. One might say: art *shows* us the miracles of nature. It is based on the *concept* of the miracles of nature. (The blossom, just opening out. What is *marvelous* about it?) We say: "Just look at it opening out!" (*CV*, 56). "Ethics and aesthetics are one and the same" (*TLP*, 6.421).

3. Drake (1957). *The Starry Messenger* is a very accessible, short work full of the best of scientific thinking at the cusp of a new way of looking at the heavens. I recommend it highly.

4. "What I saw when I looked at the famous duck-rabbit was either the duck or the rabbit, but not the lines on the page—at least not until after much conscious effort. The lines were not the facts of which the duck and rabbit were alternative interpretations" (Kuhn in Fleck 1979, ix).

5. Along a similar line, the pictures of atoms taken by electron microscopes, as thrilling as they may be, cannot constitute evidence that "atoms exist," in the way that discovering fossils can be taken as evidence for the prior existence of species of animals no longer extant. The description of how an electron microscope works tells us that it depends on the existence of electrons, which are constituent parts of atoms with certain important wave-length properties. Therefore the electron microscope allows us to "see" atoms only if we have already accepted that atoms exist.

6. For example, the question of how long the period of a pendulum will be, given a certain string length and a certain mass, can be answered either in terms of the gravitational force on the pendulum bob or in terms of the transformation of potential energy to kinetic energy. I will not present those solutions here, since they are secondary to our main interest. I'll ask you to take my word for it—or try to work out the solutions yourself.

7. You and I may be blind to what the physicist sees. Sometimes with help we can be brought to see what is right in front of us. Hanson cites a passage from Babbage's *The Decline of Science in England* (1830), which refers to the discovery by Fraunhofer of dark lines in the spectrum of sunlight:

> An object is frequently not seen *from not knowing how to see it*, rather than from any defect in the organ of vision . . . [Herschel said] "I will prepare the apparatus, and put you in such a position that [Fraunhofer's dark lines] shall be visible, and yet you shall look for them and not find them: after which, while you remain in the same position, I will instruct you *how to see them*, and you shall see them, and not merely wonder you did not see them before, but you shall find it impossible to look at the spectrum without seeing them." (Hanson 1958, 184)

You may have come to see the portrait of the man in figure 23 from the first chapter in a similar way.

8. "The dawning of an aspect and the dawning of an explanation both suggest what to look for next. In both, the elements of inquiry coagulate into an intelligible pattern. The affinities between seeing the hidden man in a cluster of dots and seeing the Martian ellipse in a cluster of data are profound" (Hanson, 1958, 86).

9. He also says of his realization: "While walking in the Public Gardens of Palermo, it came to me in a flash that in the organ of the plant which we are accustomed to call the leaf lies the true Proteus who can hide or reveal himself in all vegetal forms. From first to last, the plant is nothing but leaf, which is so inseparable from the future germ that one cannot think of one without the other" (Goethe 1970, 366).

10. This is not the place to explain why this is so. Hanson's book makes a good case for it in Chapter Six. In fact, I heartily recommend this book to anyone interested in pursuing further the relationship between physics and aspects.

11. You can find Ptolemy's account by Ptolemy himself in a number of editions, two of which are listed in the bibliography. Aristotle's remark about the perfection of circular motion can be found in his *Physics*, Book VIII, and elsewhere.

12. An excellent source for the paradigm shift away from phlogiston and toward the theory of combustion as we now accept it can be found in Conant (1957).

13. In other words, read this book, if you haven't already. It is very accessible to the educated and interested reader.

14. If I were to pursue the relation of aspects to science in greater depth, I would talk more about the place of language in science, and especially how Wittgenstein's claim that "meaning is use" helps illuminate the actual work of scientists, both practical and theoretical. Hanson puts it this way: "Can one understand the logic of statements without understanding how people use the sentences which express them? How? Can we say 'It is irrelevant how anyone or everyone uses dynamical law formulae or what anyone or everyone thinks about mechanical laws. The question is whether or not the laws *themselves* are necessary or contingent'? What are the laws of dynamics *themselves*? What are they other than what dynamicists express by the use of law formulae? . . . Can the logic of a proposition be grasped in any way other than by learning how the sentence expressing it is used on particular occasions by particular people?" (Hanson 1958, 114). I don't know where such a line of thought would eventually take me, but I suspect it would serve to narrow the gap between science and art even further.

15. *PO*, 36–44. See also "Secondary Sense," in Diamond (1995), 225–41. The Heretics Society consisted of a general audience of interested people who had no particular training in philosophy.

16. "Now instead of saying 'Ethics is the enquiry into what is good' I could have said Ethics is the enquiry into what is valuable, or, into what is really important, or I could have said Ethics is the enquiry into the meaning of life, or into what makes life worth living, or into the right way of living" (*PO*, 38). You can see that Wittgenstein construes ethics broadly.

17. In fact Thomas Aquinas (1225–1274) argues in Question 13 of the first part of *Summa Theologica* that all of our talk about God is analogical.

18. Wittgenstein runs together different kinds of figurative language that perhaps ought to be kept separate, such as analogy, simile, and allegory. I think we need not worry about that here, because his general point is clear enough.

19. John Keats (1795–1821), "Ode on a Grecian Urn."

20. In *Two New Sciences*, section 60, Galileo has Sagredo say: "Nothing is contrary to nature save the impossible, and that never happens" (Drake 1974, 21).

21. There are of course exceptions, what we might call "technical religious words," which in a way depend on a whole theology. "Transubstantiation" and "Holy Eucharist" might fall into this category. "Grace," "word," and "forgiveness" are ordinary words. Some technical words fall out of use when beliefs change, much as did "phlogiston" and "caloric."

22. A friend or critic may tell me that a new movie release is very good, but this can serve only to encourage me to see the movie myself, not to convince me that it is very good. Further, "Do we know of anyone who was converted to faith by means of her hearing of another's person's religious experience?" (Verbin 2001, 503). No.

23. This reminds me of something Niels Bohr, the physicist, once said. He was seen by a colleague to be hanging a "lucky" horseshoe over the door to his office. The colleague said, "You don't believe that stuff, do you?" Bohr replied, "Of course not. But I heard that it works even for those who don't believe" (Holt 2008). Why did you find this funny, if you did?

24. The entire story is worth repeating as it is written. This is the Tanakh (1985) version.

> 1 Sometime afterward, God put Abraham to the test. He said to him, "Abraham," and he answered, "Here I am." 2 And He said, "Take your son, your favored one, Isaac, whom you love, and go to the land of Moriah, and offer him there as a burnt offering on one of the heights that I will point out to you." 3 So early next morning, Abraham saddled his ass and took with him two of his servants and his son Isaac. He split the wood for the burnt offering, and he set out for the place of which God had told him. 4 On the third day Abraham looked up and saw the place from afar. 5 Then Abraham said to his servants, "You stay here with the ass. The boy and I will go up there; we will worship and we will return to you." 6 Abraham took the wood for the burnt offering and put it on his son Isaac. He himself took the firestone and the knife; and the two walked off together. 7 Then Isaac said to his father Abraham, "Father!" And he answered, "Yes, my son." And he said, "Here are the firestone and the wood; but where is the sheep for the burnt offering?" 8 And Abraham said, "God will see to the sheep for His burnt offering, my son." And the two of them walked on together. 9 They arrived at the place of which God had told him. Abraham built an altar there; he laid out the wood; he bound his son Isaac; he laid him on the altar, on top of the wood. 10 And Abraham picked up the knife to slay his son. 11 Then an angel of the Lord called to him from heaven: "Abraham! Abraham!" And he answered, "Here I am." 12 And he said, "Do not raise your hand against the boy, or do anything to him. For now I know that you fear God, since you have not withheld your son, your favored one, from Me." 13 When Abraham looked up, his eye fell upon a ram, caught in the thicket by its horns. So Abraham went and took the ram and offered it up as a burnt offering in place of his son.

25. "'You can't hear God speak to someone else, you can hear him only if you are being addressed.'—That is a grammatical remark" (*Z*, 717).

26. Kierkegaard also tells about a preacher who one Sunday gave a glorious sermon about Abraham and Isaac, a sermon that led a parishioner to determine to kill his own son, so as to be like Abraham. When he told the preacher of his intent, the preacher was horrified and tried to explain to the man that one does not become like Abraham by imitating him. Nor does one understand Abraham by hearing the words of another. Faith is radically particular, not universal. One must see it for oneself because it is something akin to a way of looking at the world, not a belief or a fact. Kierkegaard calls it a "passion" (1983), 28–29.

27. "Knowledge is not always the same as knowledge: There are different sorts of knowledge, which are far from equivalent psychologically. . . . If a doctor transfers his knowledge to a patient as a piece of information, it has no result. . . . The patient knows after this what he did not know before—the sense of his symptom; yet he knows it just as little as he did. Thus we learn that there is more than one kind of ignorance" (Freud 1977, 281).

28. You can find many examples of this in Freud's *The Interpretation of Dreams.*

29. For example, Richard Dawkins, *The God Delusion* (2006); Steven Weinberg, "Without God" (2008); Daniel Dennett, *Breaking the Spell: Religion as a Natural Phenomenon* (2006).

30. We can also imagine a neuropsychological account of the change in aspect of the duck-rabbit being considered the "true explanation" of the visual phenomenon of aspect change.

31. "A proof of God's existence ought really to be something by means of which one could convince oneself that God exists. But I think that what *believers* who have furnished such proofs have wanted to do is give their 'belief' an intellectual analysis and foundation, although they themselves would never have come to believe as a result of such proofs. Perhaps one could 'convince someone that God exists' by means of a certain kind of upbringing, by shaping his life in such and such a way" (*CV*, 85). James Carse, in *The Religious Case Against Belief*, argues that an enlightened skepticism is truer to the believer's experience than are the over-the-top positions criticized by Dawkins and others. Perhaps Wittgenstein's "religious point of view" allows him to find "questions at the heart of the most certain of answers" (Carse 2008, 20).

32. A good translation of the *Phaedo* is that by Brann, Kalkavage, and Salem (1998).

33. Charles Sanders Peirce (1839–1914), William James (1842–1910), John Dewey (1859–1952), Hilary Putnam (b. 1926), and Richard Rorty (1931–2007).

ACKNOWLEDGMENTS

I OWE DEBTS TO MANY people who helped me, directly and indirectly, in thinking these thoughts and writing this book. After I gave an hour-long lecture on seeing aspects at St. John's College, where I have taught since 1975, Eva Brann suggested that I write a book about Wittgenstein. Before I had time to consider what I might be undertaking, Paul Dry asked me for a copy of the lecture, at Eva's suggestion, and before long asked me to write a book based on it. A sabbatical leave from St. John's allowed me to begin work on the book. The college then offered me the Schmidt tutorship, which gave me the time both to finish the book and to participate in a very lively and helpful faculty study group on *Philosophical Investigations*. I want to thank the members of that group, Eva Brann, Tom Crouse, George Doskow, Marilyn Higuera, Alan Pichanick, Debbie Renaut, and Jon Tuck, for forcing me to make as clear as I could some of Wittgenstein's central ideas.

I also want to thank four friends who are connected with the college in different ways for reading all or substantial parts of drafts of this book and returning extremely useful and at times very challenging comments: alumnae Jennifer Donnelly and Blakely Phillips, and tutors Robert Druecker and Steve Houser. I appreciate their time, patience and insight more than I can express. John Corenswet, John Goldman, Ann Martin, and Will Schofield all raked over various versions of the manuscript, at the behest of Paul Dry. They made many very helpful comments, especially stylistic ones.

Reaching further back in my intellectual development, I would like to remember the late Martin Lean, then chair of the philosophy department at the University of Southern California, who introduced me to Wittgenstein in graduate school, and whose persistent, calm questioning of my rather conventional philosophical objections to Wittgenstein eventually resulted in an "aha!" moment for me. Two other faculty members at USC, John Dreher and Dallas Willard, were also significant influences on whatever skills I developed in reading difficult books. While I was a graduate student in cognitive psychology at the University of California at San Diego, I learned much from Norman Anderson about how to think critically about the design and results of experiments in psychology. This helped broaden my perspective on the difficulties of achieving reliable knowledge in the sciences in general. The late Robert Bart, who took me under his wing (even though I never fit there very comfortably) when I joined the St. John's faculty, also offered me intellectual gifts of which I was able to appreciate only a few. I hope that I have come to appreciate more. I also want to thank St. John's College—the institution at which I have taught, talked, and prospered for thirty-five years—simply for being what it is: a place where Platonists and pragmatists can rub shoulders collegially, and in the process lose their labels, which is the beginning of real learning.

My wife, Eleanor, showed tact, patience, and encouragement through all stages of the long writing of this book. She always had an ear for a thought I needed to express, develop, or criticize. My children, Antonia and Luca, have shown appropriate enthusiasm for the project, and are awaiting the actual physical book, which might make more of an impression on them than a few fleeting ideas.

A substantial part of Section B of Chapter Two originally appeared in *The St. John's Review* (44.3, 1998). It is reprinted here with permission.

Figures 6, 7, and 8
From Hanson, N. R., *Patterns of Discovery*
Cambridge University Press, 1958

Figures 24 and 25(b)
Reprinted by permission of Dr. Gerald Long and Dr. Thomas Toppino
From Long and Toppino (2004)

Figure 25(a)
Reprinted by permission of Elsevier Limited
From Long and Toppino (2004)

Figure 29
Reproduced with the permission of Dr. Tania Lombrozo
Department of Psychology, University of California, Berkeley

Figure 30
Hals, Frans (1580–1666)
Portrait of Rene Descartes.

Location: Louvre, Paris, France
Photo Credit: Erich Lessing/Art Resource, NY

Figure 31
Caravaggio (Michelangelo Merisi da) (1573–1610)
Calling of Saint Matthew. Contarini Chapel.
Location: S. Luigi dei Francesi, Rome, Italy
Photo Credit: Scala/Art Resource, NY

Figure 35
Vermeer, Johannes
Woman Holding a Balance
Widener Collection
Image courtesy of the Board of Trustees, National Gallery of Art,
    Washington, DC

Figure 36
Leonardo da Vinci (1452–1519)
The Last Supper. 1498. Post-restoration.
Location: S. Maria delle Grazie, Milan, Italy
Photo Credit: Scala/Ministero per i Beni e le Attività culturali/
    Art Resource, NY

Figure 37
Ghirlandaio, Domenico (1448–1494)
Last Supper. Fresco.
Location: Museo di S. Marco, Florence, Italy
Photo Credit: Nicolo Orsi Battaglini/Art Resource, NY

Figure 38
Rembrandt Harmensz van Rijn (1606–1669)
The Last Supper, after Leonardo da Vinci. 1634–1635.
Robert Lehman Collection, 1975 (1975.1.794).
Location: The Metropolitan Museum of Art, New York, NY, U.S.A.
Photo Credit: Image copyright © The Metropolitan Museum of Art/Art
    Resource, NY

Figure 39
Claesz, Pieter (c. 1590–1661)
The Last Supper, ca. Peter Paul Rubens copy, after a drawing by Leonardo
    da Vinci. Etching, 29.8 × 50.3 cm.
Location: Herzog Anton Ulrich-Museum, Braunschweig, Germany
Photo Credit: Foto Marburg/Art Resource, NY

Figure 40
Picasso, Pablo (1881–1973)
Women of Algiers (after Delacroix), 1955. Oil on canvas, 114 × 146 cm.
Location: Coll. Victor M. Ganz, New York, NY, U.S.A.

Figure 46
Hogarth, William (1697–1764)
Mrs. Salter, 1741. Oil on canvas
Location: Tate Gallery, London, Great Britain
Photo Credit: Tate, London/Art Resource, NY

Figure 47
Watteau, Jean Antoine (1684–1721)
Departure for Cythera. Ca. 1717. Oil on canvas
Location: Charlottenburg Castle, Stiftung Preussische Schlösser & Gärten
    Berlin-Brandenburg, Berlin, Germany
Photo Credit: Bildarchiv Preussischer Kulturbesitz/Art Resource, NY

Figure 48
Klimt, Gustav (1862–1918) *Adele Bloch-Bauer I*. 1907. Oil, silver, and gold
    on canvas. This acquisition made available in part through the gener-
    osity of the heirs of the Estates of Ferdinand and Adele Bloch-Bauer.
Location: Neue Galerie New York, New York, NY, U.S.A.
Photo Credit: Neue Galerie NewYork/Art Resource, NY. Reprinted by per-
    mission of the Neue Galerie.

Figure 49
Marden, Brice (1938–)
Zen Study 6 (Early State) from Cold Mountain Series. 1990.
Location: The Museum of Modern Art, New York, NY, U.S.A.
Photo Credit: Digital Image © The Museum of Modern Art/Licensed by
    SCALA/Art Resource, NY. Reprinted with permission

Figure 50
Webern, Anton, *Op. 27*
© 1936 by Universal Edition
All Rights Reserved
Used by permission of European American Music Distributors LLC, U.S
    and Canadian agent for Universal Edition

INDEX

A

ability, concept of, 112–14
Abraham, 248–49
amalgams, 27
ambiguous figures: bird-antelope, 5; duck-rabbit, 1–6, 23, 25, 27–28; Necker cube, 7–10, 26, 27–28
ambiguous words, 137–40
Anderson, Leroy, 188
aphasia, 128–33; modular explanations of, 130–31
Aristotle, 162
art: abstract vs. representational, 221–24, 226; conversations about, 219–20, 227
art criticism, 206–27. *See also* emergent meaning, and art criticism
artworks: as physical objects vs. representations, 163–68
aspect blindness, 116, 118–55; facial expressions and, 120; language and, 119, 122–23, 125
aspect-hearing, 250
aspect-seeing: as an ability, 111–14; as an amalgam of thought and vision, 159; as discovery, 28; vs. illusions, 17–18, 24, 27, 69; vs. imagination, 70; insufficiency of descriptions for, 27; vs. interpretive seeing, 171–73; not contained in the drawing, 24; as *quale*, 31–33; vs. seeing, 24, 70–89, 173; volitional studies of, 36–38; voluntary nature of, 25–6, 28
aspect shifts: in animals, 103–4; vs. continuous seeing of an aspect, 71–72; criteria for, 77–89; duration of, 72; experience of, 73–75; mental images and (*see* mental images); role of imagination in, 114–16, 124–25
aspects of a triangle, 172–73
Asperger's syndrome, 133. *See also* Autistic Spectrum Disorder

B

Augustine, 42–43, 249–51
Augustinian account of language-learning, 42–43, 58, 102, 132–33; and our understanding of psychological terms, 102–3; vs. Wittgenstein's, 43–44
Autistic Spectrum Disorder (ASD), 133–35, 155, 176
Ayer, A. J., 67

Beethoven, Ludwig van, 18, 165, 188, 194
"beetle in the box" thought experiment, 63, 74
blindness, 116–17; aspect blindness (*see* aspect blindness); change blindness, 117–19; color blindness, 117; face blindness (*see* prosopagnosia); inattentional blindness, 117–18; meaning blindness, 137, 151–56
blueprints, 158
Bourdon, Sebastien, 162
Brahms, Johannes, 188
Butterfield, Andrew, 164

C

The Calling of St. Matthew, 165–70, 174, 203; composition of, 166–67; religious conversion in, 167
Camouflage, 18, 84
Caravaggio, 165, 167–70, 174
Carroll, Lewis, ix, 42
Cavell, Stanley, 218
Il Cenacolo. See The Last Supper (Leonardo)
Cervantes, Miguel de, 71
change of aspect. *See* aspect shifts
Church of San Luigi dei Francesi, 165–66
Confessions, 249–51
conversation: about art, 219–20, 227; about religious experience, 254–58
conversion, religious, 219, 249–51

Copernicus, Nicolaus, 239
cubism, 186–87

D

Descartes, René, 29–30
Don Quixote, 71
double-cross figure, 23, 26

E

1812 Overture, 188
Einstein, Albert, 28, 238–39
L'embarquement pour Cythera, 215–16
emergent meaning, 145–56, 162, 195–98,
    200–227; and art criticism, 206–8,
    211–27; and music, 213–15; and wine,
    200–203
Euclid, 78
experience: role of brain processes in,
    103; visual, 74–84, 158–61. *See also*
    perception
experiencing the meaning of a word,
    136–56, 196
experimental psychology: ordinary lan-
    guage and, 92–105; vs. physics, 96–98

F

face-recognition, 85–86; experimental
    studies of, 39
family resemblance: aspect-seeing and,
    12–13; among concepts, 65–66
"fat Wednesday," 150–51, 153, 197–98,
    202–3, 205
Fear and Trembling, 248
feelings, aesthetic vs. visceral, 217
Fifth Symphony (Beethoven), 213
figure reversals: effect of learning and
    expectation on, 38; spontaneous,
    37–38
finding the right word, 143–44, 151
Freud, Sigmund, 251

G

Galileo Galilei, 97–98, 112, 231–33, 238
Gardner, Howard, 129–31
gestalt, 127
Ghirlandaio, Domenico, 177–78
Goethe, Johann Wolfgang von, 179,
    182–83; on plants, 235–37
Goodwin, Charles, 131–33

Grammatical or conceptual error, 59
Gregory, Richard, 34

H

Hals, Franz, 162–63
Hanson, Norwood Russell, 233, 235, 240
Harvey, William, 98
Heisenberg's indeterminacy principle, 237
Hogarth, William, 177, 206–12
Hume, David, 29–30, 66–67, 123; on criti-
    cism, 226–27
humor, philosophy and, 58, 60–62, 106,
    139, 149, 152–54

I

illusions, 13–18; vs. aspect-seeing, 17–18,
    24, 69; boundary or contour, 15–16;
    brightness, 16–28; devil's fork, 135;
    Hermann's grid, 16–17; Kanizsa's Tri-
    angle, 15, 17; Müller-Lyer illusion, 14,
    17; Penrose triangle, 135; as explained
    through physiology, 17–18; Ponzo illu-
    sion, 14
imagining: vs. aspect-seeing, 70; vs. see-
    ing, 26, 92–95
introspection: as a way of understand-
    ing aspect-seeing, 28–33, 40; William
    James on, 40
inverted spectrum, 61

J

Jackson, Frank, 30
James, William, 40–41
Jastrow, Joseph, 3–5

K

Kant, Immanuel, 50
Kapell, William, 214
Kierkegaard, Søren, 248
Klimt, Gustav, 220–21
knowledge, in question only in the con-
    text of doubt, 59–60, 95
knowledge argument, the. *See* Mary the
    color scientist
Kuhn, Thomas, 238–40, 252, 254

L

language: comparison with chess, 45–46;
    comparison with ancient city, 94; role

of convention in, 46; "grammar" in,
45–46, 49–50, 60; ordinary, 59–60;
private (*see* private language); rule-
following in, 49–58
language comprehension, 131
language-games, 44–49, 59, 65, 132–33,
145–50
The Last Supper (Ghirlandaio), 177–78
The Last Supper (Leonardo), 177–87;
Eucharist vs. betrayal in, 181–83; as
visual paradox, 184–85
The Last Supper (Rembrandt), 179–80
The Last Supper (Rubens), 181
Lavoisier, Antoine, 239
Leeuwenhoek, Antonie van, 236
Leibniz, Gottfried, 234; vs. Newton on
motion, 234
Leonardo da Vinci, 177–87
Lewis, C. I., 30
light, wave-particle duality of, 237

M

MacDowell, Edward, 213–14
Malebranche, Nicolas, 236
man in the moon, 73
Marden, Brice, 222–24, 226
Mary the color scientist, 30–33
meaning: absolute vs. relative, 244–45
(*see also* value); emergent (*see* emergent meaning); figurative, 196, 242–43
(*see also* emergent meaning); primary
(or non-metaphorical), 150; secondary (*see* emergent meaning); as use,
43–44, 64
melodies, hearing variations on, 190–95;
first vs. third-person questions about,
192–93; in Mozart's *Piano Sonata* in
A-Major, 190–95
mental chess, 146–47, 148–49
mental images, 89–98, 147–48; example of
the Statue of Liberty, 91
mental state attributions, 133–35
method of projection, 55
Michelangelo, 18–19
miracles, 245, 253
misology, 258
modularity. *See* aphasia, modular explanations of
Moore, G. E., 67, 241

Mozart, Wolfgang Amadeus, 190–95
Mrs. Salter, 206–12
music (*see* melodies; tonal theory): atonal,
224–26

N

Nebraska: as aspectless, 223
Necker cube (*see also* ambiguous figures,
Necker cube): after-image experiment,
34; Necker's explanation of the reversal of, 34
Newton, Isaac, 232–34, 238
nonsense, 242–45
noticing an aspect. *See* aspect-seeing

O

Odysseus, 157

P

pain, 74, 157
paintings: allegorical, 176–77; role of artist's intent in understanding, 184–85
paradigm shift, 238–40, 252, 254
perception, 158–61; bottom-up theories
of, 33–35, 89; as requiring language,
160–61; satiation in, 33–34; top-down
theories of, 34, 35–38, 89; "thoughtless," 158–61
Phaedo, 258
phlogiston, 239
physicalism, 31
Piano Sonata in A-Major (K. 331), 190–95
Picasso, Pablo, 186–87
plant development, preformationism
about, 236
Plato, 258
Portrait of Adele Bloch-Bauer, 220–21
Portrait of Descartes, 162–64
pragmatism, 259
private language argument. *See* private
language, impossibility of
private language, 49, 57–64, 66, 74,
193–94; impossibility of, 193–94
prosopagnosia, 119–20, 126–28
Proteus, 6, 18, 25
psychotherapy, 251–52
Ptolemy, 238
puzzle-pictures, 18–21, 84

Q

qualia, 30–33
quantum mechanics, 237–38
questions, conceptual vs. causal, 5

R

reading: as a rule-guided activity, 51–54
religious experience, conversations about,
254–58
religious experience, expressions of,
242–58; emergent meaning in,
244–46
religious point of view vs. scientific,
252–54
Rembrandt van Rijn, 179–80
representationalism, 162
resemblance, of faces, 11–12, 23, 25,
27–28; vs. ambiguous figures, 11–12;
experience of, 87–89
Rorty, Richard, 259–60
Rubens, Peter Paul, 181
rule-following. *See* language, rule-
following in

S

Sacks, Oliver, 120, 126–28, 176
Schubert, Franz, 143
Schwartz, Sanford, 206–8, 211–12
science: aspect-seeing in, 231–40; role of
theory in, 232, 238
scientific method, 232–40
seeing for oneself, 217–20, 247–52
sensations, private, 61–64, 107
sense-data, 67
sense that something has changed though
nothing has changed, 23, 25, 27–28,
124, 160, 192, 230, 232
similarity, concept of, 88–89
Sixth Symphony (Pastoral) (Beethoven),
188
Starry Messenger, The, 231–32
Steinberg, Leo, 179–87

Strawson, Galen, 31
symptoms, vs. expressions, 98–100

T

Tchaikovsky, Pyotr Ilyich, 188
theory of mind, 133–35
thinking: concept of, 99–102; speech and,
100–102
Tintoretto, 164
To a Wild Rose, 213–14
tolerance, active, 259–60
tonal theory, 189–95
Twinkle, Twinkle Little Star, 189–90
Typewriter Song, 188

U

understanding, not a mental or physical
phenomenon, 54–57
unpicturability, 237
Updike, John, 220–21

V

value, absolute vs. relative, 241–42; expe-
riences with absolute value, 242–46
Variations for Piano, Opus 27, 224–26
Vermeer, Jan, 173–76, 177

W

Webern, Anton, 224–26
Weenix, Jean Baptiste, 162
Wheelock, Arthur, 174–75
wine, 198–203; ordinary ways of describ-
ing, 198–99; metaphorical descriptions
of, 197–200; technical terms concern-
ing, 199–200
Women of Algiers, 186–87
Woman Holding a Balance, 173–76
Woolf, Virginia, 154

Z

Zen Study 6, Cold Mountain Series,
222–24